Data Analytics Applications in Gaming and Entertainment

T0132515

Data Analytics Applications

Series Editor: Jay Liebowitz

PUBLISHED

Actionable Intelligence for Healthcare
by Jay Liebowitz and Amanda Dawson
ISBN: 978-1-4987-6665-4

Analytics and Knowledge Management
by Suliman Hawamdeh and Hsia-Ching Chang
ISBN 978-1-1386-3026-0

Big Data Analytics in Cybersecurity
by Onur Savas and Julia Deng
ISBN: 978-1-4987-7212-9

Big Data and Analytics Applications in Government:
Current Practices and Future Opportunities
by Gregory Richards
ISBN: 978-1-4987-6434-6

Big Data in the Arts and Humanities: Theory and Practice
by Giovanni Schiuma and Daniela Carlucci
ISBN 978-1-4987-6585-5

Data Analytics Applications in Education
by Jan Vanthienen and Kristoff De Witte
ISBN: 978-1-4987-6927-3

Data Analytics Applications in Latin America and Emerging Economies
by Eduardo Rodriguez
ISBN: 978-1-4987-6276-2

Data Analytics for Smart Cities
by Amir Alavi and William G. Buttlar
ISBN 978-1-138-30877-0

Data-Driven Law: Data Analytics and the New Legal Services
by Edward J. Walters
ISBN 978-1-4987-6665-4

Intuition, Trust, and Analytics
by Jay Liebowitz, Joanna Paliszkiewicz, and Jerzy Gołuchowski
ISBN: 978-1-138-71912-5

Research Analytics: Boosting University Productivity and
Competitiveness through Scientometrics
by Francisco J. Cantú-Ortiz
ISBN: 978-1-4987-6126-0

Sport Business Analytics: Using Data to Increase Revenue and Improve
Operational Efficiency
by C. Keith Harrison and Scott Bukstein
ISBN: 978-1-4987-8542-6

https://www.crcpress.com/Data-Analytics-Applications/book-series/CRCDATANAAPP

Data Analytics Applications in Gaming and Entertainment

Edited by
Günter Wallner

CRC Press
Taylor & Francis Group
Boca Raton London New York

CRC Press is an imprint of the
Taylor & Francis Group, an **informa** business

AN AUERBACH BOOK

CRC Press
Taylor & Francis Group
6000 Broken Sound Parkway NW, Suite 300
Boca Raton, FL 33487-2742

First issued in paperback 2021

© 2019 by Taylor & Francis Group, LLC
CRC Press is an imprint of Taylor & Francis Group, an Informa business

No claim to original U.S. Government works

Printed on acid-free paper

ISBN-13: 978-1-138-10443-3 (hbk)
ISBN-13: 978-1-03-209190-7 (pbk)

Library of Congress Cataloging-in-Publication Data

Names: Wallner, Gunter, editor.
Title: Data analytics applications in gaming and entertainment / [edited by] Gunter Wallner.
Description: Boca Raton : Taylor & Francis, a CRC title, part of the Taylor & Francis imprint, a member of the Taylor & Francis Group, the academic division of T&F Informa, plc, 2019. | Series: Data analytics applications | Includes bibliographical references.
Identifiers: LCCN 2019005955 | ISBN 9781138104433 (hardback : acid-free paper) | ISBN 9780429286490 (e)
Subjects: LCSH: Video games industry--Management. | Computer games industry--Management. | Data mining.
Classification: LCC HD9993.E452 D38 2019 | DDC 794.8/16312--dc23
LC record available at https://lccn.loc.gov/2019005955

Visit the Taylor & Francis Web site at
http://www.taylorandfrancis.com

and the CRC Press Web site at
http://www.crcpress.com

A good decision is based on knowledge and not on numbers.

—**Plato**

Contents

Preface

The last decade has witnessed the rise of big data in game development as the increasing proliferation of Internet-enabled gaming devices has made it easier than ever before to collect large amounts of player-related data. At the same time, the emergence of new business models and the diversification of the player base have exposed a broader potential audience, which attaches great importance to being able to tailor game experiences to a wide range of preferences and skill levels. This, in turn, has led to a growing interest in data mining techniques, as they offer new opportunities for deriving actionable insights to inform game design, to ensure customer satisfaction, to maximize revenues, and to drive technical innovation. By now, data mining and analytics have become vital components of game development. The amount of work being done in this area nowadays makes this an ideal time to put together a book on this subject.

This volume seeks to provide a cross section of current data analytics applications in game production. It is intended as an ideal companion for practitioners, academic researchers, and students seeking knowledge on the latest practices in game data mining. The chapters have been chosen in such a way as to cover a wide range of topics and to provide readers with a glimpse at the variety of applications of data mining in gaming. A total of 25 authors from industry and academia have contributed 12 chapters covering topics such as player profiling, approaches for analyzing player communities and their social structures, matchmaking, churn prediction and customer lifetime value estimation, communication of analytical results, and visual approaches to game analytics. I hope this book will spark readers' interest in game analytics, provide them with new perspectives and ideas, and contribute to the advancement of this exciting field.

Günter Wallner

How This Book Is Organized

This book is organized in 12 chapters covering different applications of data mining and analytics within the context of game development and research. In the following, a brief summary of each chapter is given.

Chapter 1: A Brief Overview of Data Mining and Analytics in Games

This chapter provides a brief introduction to data mining and analytics in games. It covers the history of game analytics in a nutshell and discusses the potentials and opportunities as well as limitations and possible risks associated with analytics in gaming. Various application areas, including design, technology, business, and community relations, are briefly described.

Chapter 2: Evaluating Gamer Achievements to Understand Player Behavior

With the rise of digital distribution, publishers and console vendors have created dedicated platforms such as Steam, Xbox Live, or the PlayStation Network, which offer centralized services to purchase games and to interact with other players. In the wake of this, game achievements, directly integrated into the social functions of these platforms, have become widespread practice in digital entertainment. Game achievements thus offer a convenient means to study player behavior across games. In this chapter—taking a multidisciplinary approach combining media, cultural, and game studies—Apperley and Gandolfi discuss how achievements can be used as tools to enable a greater understanding of gaming audiences, and provide pointers on how data mining can support such explorations.

Chapter 3: Building Matchmaking Systems

Matchmaking takes on a key role in modern multiplayer games, as it can severely impact the gaming experience of players. At the same time, building matchmaking systems is incredibly challenging since many, sometimes competing, factors need to be taken into account to ensure good matchmaking. In this chapter, Alex Zook from Blizzard Entertainment provides an overview of the broader challenges involved in building and improving matchmaking systems to offer general guidance on building a basic matchmaking system and to orient readers to the set of open challenges and areas for research. It discusses the core components of a matchmaker and shows how to use data analytics to monitor and refine such systems.

Chapter 4: A Data Science Approach to Exploring Hero Roles in Multiplayer Online Battle Arena Games

In this chapter, taking the multiplayer online battle arena game *Heroes of the Storm* as a use case, Lee and Ramler outline a general methodology for analyzing character roles and team compositions using a data-driven approach. The chapter takes the reader through the process of data collection (including practical code-snippets), preparation, and analysis. Hierarchical clustering is used to identify common roles heroes can take on in a match, while random forest classifiers are trained to predict the earlier identified roles for players from their actual in-game data. The chapter continues by identifying common winning and losing team compositions for the different maps of the game.

Chapter 5: Predicting Customer Lifetime Value in Free-to-Play Games

Game companies nowadays increasingly adopt service-oriented business models, that rely on keeping players engaged with their games over extended time periods. Various activities, such as user acquisition, live game operations, or game design, benefit from information about the choices being made by the players and the choices they are likely to make in the future. This includes predictions about the spending behavior and potential revenue gained from a player, which are of great interest, especially in the context of free-to-play games. In this chapter, Paolo Burelli gives an overview of customer lifetime value modeling across different fields, introduces the challenges specific to free-to-play games, and discusses state-of-the-art solutions with practical examples and references to existing implementations, which should help readers to perform the discussed methods on their own datasets.

Chapter 6: Advanced Data Science Models for Player Behavioral Prediction

The goal of this chapter is to present advanced machine learning models that can be applied to game datasets in order to understand and predict player behavior. Methods from survival analysis, ensemble learning, and deep learning are discussed and explained within the context of two common challenges faced by game studios: churn prediction, that is, forecasting when players are likely to stop playing a game, and customer lifetime value estimation introduced in the previous chapter. The machine learning methods presented in this chapter by Periáñez et al. are computationally efficient, scale well to large datasets, and are general enough to be applied to a variety of games.

Chapter 7: Integrating Social and Textual Analytics into Game Analytics

This is the first of three chapters dealing with social and communicative aspects of player activity. This includes textual artifacts produced by players such as reviews, message board comments, or postings on various social media platforms. These artifacts are a valuable source for providing insight into the player, their play, and the overall player community. This chapter, contributed by Milambiling et al., provides a detailed treatment of social and textual analytics in game analytics, delving into both theoretical and practical aspects. It proposes a framework on how to integrate social and textual analytics into a traditional game analytics pipeline. A case study illustrates on how social media artifacts can help explore retention, engagement, and purchasing behavior.

Chapter 8: Social Network Analysis Applied to Game Communities to Identify Key Social Players

This chapter, co-authored by Canossa and Harteveld, continues the discussion of the social dimensions of play. Communities of players have become fundamental elements for a game's extended lifetime, as the social connections players form can be important motivational drivers for staying engaged. Toward this end, social network analysis provides a convenient way to investigate the social structures of player communities. This chapter explores how social network measures, such as modularity, centrality, and prestige, can help to identify influential players and understand their impact on playtime and the community.

Chapter 9: Methodological and Epistemological Reflections on the Use of Game Analytics toward Understanding the Social Relationships of a Video Game Community

The analysis of player communities is an important but challenging endeavor, as there exists a complex relationship between what a game offers and the ways the community appropriates it. Game analytics offers many possibilities to gain insight into player communities—as the previous chapters have shown—but also has its limitations. In this chapter, Bonenfant et al. discuss the advantages and constraints of social network and sentiment analysis from the viewpoint of communication studies. To illustrate the difficulties faced when dealing with identity as well as communicational and social questions, the chapter presents examples of issues encountered while conducting an exploratory study in cooperation with a major games company.

Chapter 10: An Analyst's Guide to Communication

Proper communication of the insights gained through analytics is essential for taking advantage of them and for driving decision-making. At the same time, however, the importance of communication is also often neglected when discussing data analytics. This chapter, written by Natalie Selin from Paradox Interactive, explores common aspects of communicating analytic results to non-analysts in the gaming industry. After reading this chapter, the reader will come away with an understanding of common communication pitfalls that statisticians, analysts, and data scientists can run into and how to circumvent them. It will also outline some best practices that are used when communicating within an organization.

Chapter 11: A Taxonomy of Visualizations for Gameplay Data

Datasets obtained through games can be very large, highly complex, heterogeneous, dynamic, and noisy. In this regard, visualizations are central to capitalize on the collected data and to facilitate the understanding of complex relationships. In the last decade, many different types of visualizations have been used, adapted for, or specifically created for player behavior analysis. Moreover, visualizations not only support analysis but also ease communication between stakeholders. In this chapter, Simone Kriglstein develops a taxonomy of visualizations, which can be used for analyzing various aspects of gameplay data. It aims to show which types of visualizations are suitable for which types of analysis. It will provide guidance for analysts in choosing the right kind of visualizations for a given task.

Chapter 12: Co-Design of an Interactive Analytics System for Multiplayer Online Battle Arena Game Occurrences

In the final chapter of the book, Li et al. blend visualization with deep learning techniques to create a visual analytics system for automatically identifying and analyzing interesting gameplay segments. The chapter shows how the processing capabilities of computers and the perceptual abilities of humans can be leveraged to assist in the analysis of in-game data. The system was developed in close cooperation with domain experts, and two use cases illustrate how these experts actually used the system.

Acknowledgments

A book like this is always a team effort and would not have been possible without the contributions and support of many people. First, I would like to express my sincere thanks to Jay Liebowitz to whom I'm very grateful for the invitation to edit this book for the *Data Analytics Applications* book series, which he is handling as series editor. Special thanks also go to John Wyzalek, senior acquisitions editor at CRC Press/Taylor & Francis Group, who provided great help and guidance throughout the editing process and who made working on the book a very joyful experience for me. Huge thanks also need to go to Joanne Hakim, Todd Perry, and the whole production team at Lumina Datamatics and CRC Press/Taylor & Francis Group for their great work on the book and their wonderful support. This book would not have been possible without the many good colleagues and friends who helped in reviewing chapter drafts and provided helpful feedback, in particular:

- Brent Harrison — University of Kentucky
- Casper Harteveld — Northeastern University
- Elisa Mekler — University of Basel
- Erik Harpstead — Carnegie Mellon University
- Nathaniel Poor — Underwood Institute
- Pejman Mirza-Babaei — University of Ontario Institute of Technology
- Ross Brown — Queensland University of Technology
- Thomas Debeauvais — Twitch
- Truong Huy D. Nguyen — Fordham University
- Zachary O. Toups — New Mexico State University

Your time and contribution are greatly appreciated. Thanks also go to Tamara Radak for her help in proofreading some chapters. Last but not least, I am deeply indebted to all contributing authors from industry and academia for their contributions, tremendous dedication, and tireless efforts. Thank you! Without you, this book would never have happened.

Editor

Günter Wallner is Assistant Professor at the Eindhoven University of Technology and Senior Scientist at the University of Applied Arts Vienna. He holds a doctorate degree in natural sciences from the University of Applied Arts Vienna and a diploma degree in computer science from the Vienna University of Technology. His research interests lie at the intersection of games user research, data analytics, and information visualization. His work particularly centers on understanding player behavior in games and on researching methods to explore and communicate the collected data to derive actionable insights for game design and development. As a leading expert in game-data visualization, he is developing novel visualizations to support the analysis of the increasingly large-scale player behavioral datasets. Günter is an active member of the games research community, has published more than 60 peer-reviewed articles, and has received various awards and recognitions for his work on games.

Contributors

Thomas Apperley
School of Education
Deakin University
Melbourne, Victoria, Australia

Maude Bonenfant
Université du Québec à Montréal
Montreal, Quebec, Canada

Paolo Burelli
IT University of Copenhagen
and
Tactile Games
Copenhagen, Denmark

Alessandro Canossa
Massive Entertainment—A Ubisoft
    Studio
Malmö, Sweden

Pei Pei Chen
Yokozuna Data
Tokyo, Japan

Patrick Deslauriers
Université du Québec à Montréal
Montreal, Quebec, Canada

Ana Fernández del Río
Yokozuna Data
Tokyo, Japan

Enrico Gandolfi
Research Center for Educational
    Technology
Kent State University
Kent, Ohio

Anna Guitart
Yokozuna Data
Tokyo, Japan

Casper Harteveld
Northeastern University
Boston, Massachusetts

Issam Heddad
Université du Québec à Montréal
Montreal, Quebec, Canada

Michael Katchabaw
The University of Western Ontario
and
Big Blue Bubble, Inc.
London, Ontario, Canada

Simone Kriglstein
Austrian Institute of Technology
Vienna, Austria

Choong-Soo Lee
St. Lawrence University
Canton, New York

Quan Li
Department of Computer Science
and Engineering
The Hong Kong University of Science
and Technology
Hong Kong

Xiaojuan Ma
Department of Computer Science
and Engineering
The Hong Kong University of Science
and Technology
Hong Kong

Lareina Milambiling
The University of Western Ontario
and
Big Blue Bubble, Inc.
London, Ontario, Canada

África Periáñez
Yokozuna Data
Tokyo, Japan

Huamin Qu
Department of Computer Science
and Engineering
The Hong Kong University of Science
and Technology
Hong Kong

Ivan Ramler
St. Lawrence University
Canton, New York

Natalie Selin
Paradox Interactive
Stockholm, Sweden

Damir Slogar
Big Blue Bubble, Inc.
London, Ontario, Canada

Günter Wallner
Eindhoven University of Technology
University of Applied Arts Vienna
Vienna, Austria

Ziming Wu
Department of Computer Science
and Engineering
The Hong Kong University of Science
and Technology
Hong Kong

Alex Zook
Blizzard Entertainment
Irvine, California

Chapter 1

A Brief Overview of Data Mining and Analytics in Games

Günter Wallner

Contents

1.1 Introduction

The twenty-first century has been repeatedly proclaimed to be the century of data. The increasing processing capabilities of computers and the proliferation of Internet-enabled devices have made it easier than ever to gather more and more data about every aspect of our daily lives. The massive amount of data produced every day, however, also needs to be transformed into actual information and knowledge to be of real value and to be of actual use for decision-making. This requires adequate techniques and tools that help uncover hidden and valuable information or patterns within the collected data. Otherwise, the large volumes of data are just that—data bare any deeper meaning. This is the goal of data mining (Kantardzic, 2011). While data mining has been and is receiving considerable attention to be able to cope with the ever-increasing data volumes, the term started to appear in the late 1980s, early 1990s (Coenen, 2011; Dong & Pei, 2007). Data mining is not a single technique but rather a conglomerate of methods, techniques, and algorithms, usually applied in an iterative or explorative process.

The twenty-first century is, however, not only considered to be the age of data mining but has also been coined the ludic century by game designer Eric Zimmerman (2015)—an age that is characterized by play. It may thus only be fitting that during the last decade or so, data mining has found its way into game production and has become a crucial part of game development and maintenance. This has led to the emergence of the new field of "game analytics"—broadly speaking, the application of analytics to game development and research (Drachen, El-Nasr, & Canossa, 2013). It is "the practice of analyzing recorded game information to facilitate future design decisions" (Medler, 2009, p. 188). Game analytics uses data mining techniques to discover patterns and to extract information from game-related data, especially player behavioral data. As it is often the case with new fields, the establishment of game analytics can hardly be tied to a specific point in time or be ascribed to a single factor. Instead, the emergence of game data mining and analytics may rather be attributed to a coincidence of several developments.

The first steps into the direction of game data mining have presumably been made at the turn of the century when online games such as *EverQuest* (Sony Online Entertainment, 1999) slowly started to track data about gameplay (cf. Weber, 2018). A couple of years later, in 2003, one of the first articles on how to improve game design through data mining was published (Kennerly, 2003). Although specifically focused on massive multiplayer online games such as the aforementioned *EverQuest*, many of the described techniques also applied to other types of games. Again, a couple of years later, first articles in popular media appeared with a *Wired* article (Thompson, 2007) on how Microsoft relied on scientific methods to inform games user research being one of the earlier examples. However, it was not until about 2010 when data mining and analytics really started to gain momentum (Weber, 2018). In 2008, Microsoft Game Studios published one of the first research articles (Kim et al., 2008) on how tracking user behavior in games can contribute greatly to the design of video games. As of 2009, Medler (2009) attested that it is hard to find a digital game that does not allow recording of gameplay in some way or the other but also noted that analyzing the recorded information to inform design is still in its infancy. A year later, Zoeller (2010) presented the telemetry suite that BioWare was using for analyzing tracked behavioral data of players, and Schoenblum (2010) presented the data collection backend developed at Epic Games. From then on, things happened very quickly, and by now game analytics has become prevalent across the industry and a major aspect of games research. It is an area that has seen substantial growth in the last 10 years and is still evolving rapidly.

This growing interest in data mining and analytics has been spurred by several developments and technical advances. First, the wide adoption of Internet-enabled gaming devices allows developers nowadays to remotely and unobtrusively track the behavior of a large numbers of players. Before that, playtesting usually happened by bringing customers in-house and observing them in a laboratory-style setting while they are playing the game. Consequently, this happened at a much smaller scale, and the invited players may not have been representative of the whole player population of the game. However, as games have become a mainstream phenomenon and are being played by an increasingly diverse audience, it has become a matter of particular interest to create games that appeal to a wide range of players. In this sense, data mining can be a valuable tool for acquiring representative data. The possibilities offered by the Internet and modern mobile devices, as well as advances in web technology, have also paved the way for new types of games, such as massively multiplayer online games or social network games played on social media platforms such as Facebook which, in turn, attract new audiences. These games are played by hundreds to thousands of players simultaneously and who may even interact with each other. This complexity makes such games challenging to develop, requiring extensive testing with a large player base to properly balance the game, to ensure a satisfying player experience, and to resolve and avoid technical issues. Remote data collection offers a natural and convenient way to gather such large-scale and long-term datasets. Moreover, production budgets of video games have risen considerably in the past years, with budgets of tens to hundreds of millions of dollars not being uncommon anymore. For example, *Grand Theft Auto V* (Rockstar North, 2013) had an estimated development budget of $137.5 million (Sinclair, 2013), and development costs for *Gran Turismo 5* (Polyphony Digital, 2010) were reported to be $60 million (Remo, 2009). Even if these are extreme examples, and not all budgets are this high, the required investments pose a great financial risk for developers in case a game fails. Through gathering actual in-game data, developers have a means to meet audience expectations and, in turn, achieve financial success. The ever-increasing production budgets also caused developers to find ways to extend the lifespan of games and to search for new business models to alleviate the associated risks. Among these are subscription-based services, downloadable content, micro-transactions (purchasing of virtual goods for a very small amount of money), or free-to-play games (games that are basically free to play with monetization happening through micro-transactions). Some developers have started to view games-as-a-service rather than as a one-time purchase. A recent report from DFC Intelligence (Cole, 2018) suggests that the growth of EA and Activision, two of the biggest publishers in the industry, can to a large extent be attributed to this service model. In such a model, revenue is also generated after the initial release using subscriptions or, for instance, by providing new content—spread over a longer period of time—in order to uphold audience interest. Retention of players is essential for such business models, and data mining and analytics offers a valuable approach to monitor and study player engagement. All these developments have been fueled by advances in data storage and processing capabilities (Coenen, 2011), which allow analysts to efficiently process the large volumes of data as they appear in game development today.

1.2 Applications

Consequently, data mining and analytics has been applied to a variety of purposes within game production and research. Four broad and common application areas are briefly discussed in the following.

1.2.1 Data Analytics to Improve Design and Player Experience

Game development is a highly creative process that optimally needs to undergo continuous and critical evaluation to ensure that the final game is engaging and offers a satisfying player experience. This is the primary goal of games user research (GUR), which aims to "help game designers reach their design goals by applying scientific and UX [User Experience] design principles, and by understanding players" (IGDA GRUX, 2018). As data mining, GUR is not a single technique but rather a collection of qualitative and quantitative methods, such as playtesting (Fullerton, Swain, & Hoffman, 2004; Mirza-Babaei, Moosajee, & Drenikow, 2016), biometrics (Nacke, 2015), interviews (Bromley, 2018), and surveys (Brühlmann & Mekler, 2018). Over the years, analytics has become a valuable addition and by now constitutes an essential component of GUR (cf. El-Nasr, Desurvire, Aghabeigi, & Drachen, 2013). Analytics offers many benefits for complementing existing methodologies as telemetry data promises a large-scale and objective view on player behavior (i.e., the data is not biased by players' subjective opinions), which would be difficult, or even impossible, to obtain through other methods. Unsurprisingly, data analytics has thus found broad application in GUR so far, reaching from developing behavioral profiles of player activity (Drachen, Thurau, Sifa, & Bauckhage, 2013) over the study of virtual economies (Castronova et al., 2009; Morrison & Fontenla, 2013) to all aspects of balancing, such as extracting reoccurring behavioral patterns to detect dominant strategies (Bosc, Kaytoue, Raïssi, & Boulicaut, 2013; Wallner, 2015). Apart from that, there is also a large body of work focusing on spatial and spatio-temporal aspects of gameplay (Drachen et al., 2014; Kang, Kim, Park, & Kim, 2013; Wallner & Kriglstein, 2012), which is of particular importance as movement forms one of the most important mechanics in nearly all games. Analytics may also be used in combination with qualitative and observational GUR methods (Desurvire & El-Nasr, 2013) in order to provide context to each other, although triangulating the different data sources is not straightforward (Mirza-Babaei, Wallner, McAllister, & Nacke, 2014).

1.2.2 Data Analytics to Inform Business Decisions

As discussed previously, the game industry is actively seeking alternative business models to the traditional pay-once format to reach new costumers. These models, such as free-to-play or subscription-based services, rely on keeping customers engaged over extended time periods and on providing attractive spending opportunities to generate revenue. At the same time, the number of games being released each year, and thus the number of games competing for customers, steadily increases. For instance, as of December 17, 2018, the statistics site SteamSpy counts 4,696 games being released on the digital distribution platform Steam[1] in 2016, while already 7,047 games were released in 2017 and 8,882 in 2018 (Galyonkin, 2017). Inevitably, it has become more challenging to acquire new customers and to stand out from the plethora of games already on the market. With the business becoming fiercer, analytics-based solutions provide ample opportunities to support business decisions. Analytics can provide insights into player retention and churn, such as how long players keep playing or where they are quitting (Bauckhage et al., 2012; Hadiji et al., 2014; Xie, Devlin, Kudenko, & Cowling, 2015). It can help answer questions concerning conversion rates, that is, what makes a player of free-to-play games convert into a paying customer (Fields & Cotton, 2011; Hanner & Zarnekow, 2015) and about the purchasing behavior of players, for example, for which in-game content players are willing to pay and why (Hamari et al., 2017; Lehdonvirta, 2009). In addition, analytics is vital for the prediction of customer lifetime value (the total amount of revenue earned from a player) (Chen, Guitart, del Río, & Periáñez, 2018; Sifa et al., 2015) and for customer acquisition, for instance, to help plan marketing campaigns (Williams, 2015a). Moreover, players also exert influence on each other, which should not be underestimated, as a game's community can contribute greatly to the success or failure of a game. In this sense, analytics can help to build stronger communities (see Section 1.2.4) and to improve community management (Williams, 2015b). These and other related possibilities are testaments of the value and potential of data analytics for business intelligence in game development.

1.2.3 Data Analytics to Innovate and Optimize Game Technology

Data mining has become a cornerstone in the development and advancement of game technology. Indirectly, this application area may also yield better player experiences as discussed previously, but the main focus here should be on how data can help build technology. Among others, behavioral data forms an integral aspect for many artificial intelligence (AI) algorithms, which take advantage of the massive amounts of domain knowledge contained within game-log data. Examples in this space include works on opponent modeling for AI bots, such as

---

[1] http://store.steampowered.com/ (Accessed: December 2018).

the ones by Weber and Mateas (2009) who applied machine learning techniques to large collections of replay data in order to learn strategies and by Synnaeve and Bessiere (2011) who presented a Bayesian model focused on predicting the opening strategy of opponents—with the model parameters being learned as above from a set of labeled replays. Others, in turn, used tracked player data to drive content creation and to adapt games to the player. Player models, that is, models that encompass the player's traits and behaviors, are a core component of these works and can greatly benefit from being data-driven (Hooshyar, Yousefi, & Lim, 2018). For instance, Pedersen, Togelius, and Yannakakis (2010) relied on tracked user data for level generation in a platform game, whereas Missura and Gärtner (2009) as well as Zook and Riedl (2012) proposed dynamic difficulty adjustment algorithms based on collected player data. Data mining can also be used to build technology for supporting playtesting. Recent and seminal work by Stahlke and Mirza-Babaei (2018) explored how AI can assist in the automatic playtesting of games to reduce time and costs associated with user testing. While this work primarily relied on geometry-based navigation[2] to mimic human behavior, it can be envisioned that by incorporating historic player data such approaches will become even more useful in the future, as they will be able to more accurately imitate user behavior.

1.2.4 Data Analytics to Empower Players and Foster Community Building

While this area is probably not the first to come to mind, and may also be less present when discussing data analytics in games, it nevertheless constitutes an important and growing field of application. This is, on the one hand, reflected in the number of games that offer visualizations that allow players to inspect their recorded gameplay data (Bowman, Elmqvist, & Jankun-Kelly, 2012; Medler, 2011). Indeed, players have been identified as an important target audience for gameplay visualizations (Bowman et al., 2012; Wallner & Kriglstein, 2013). Hazzard (2014) identified two main purposes of such visualizations: representations to convey the in-game status and visualizations for training. While the former has traditionally focused on the active player, these visualizations have—in light of the increasing popularity of esports and of game streaming platforms such as Twitch—also become more and more common for observers. Training visualizations are less common within games itself but rather exist external to games. Their development has been spurred by game developers providing access to the collected data through public application programming interfaces, as it is the case, for example, for *League of Legends* (Riot Games, 2018) and *Destiny* (Bungie, 2018). Other games, such as *Starcraft* (Blizzard Entertainment, 1998) or *World of Tanks* (Wargaming, 2010), record the gameplay in so-called replay files, which can then be shared and analyzed. This has led to proactive efforts on behalf of the player community, which is eagerly utilizing these data sources to build

---

[2] See Algfoor, Sunar, and Kolivand (2015) for an overview of navigation modeling in games.

data-driven websites and tools. In that sense, the data serves as a driver for community building and prolonged involvement with a game.

1.2.5 Summary

The previously discussed application areas are not to be viewed as distinct and independent from each other. For instance, improving game design can impact player retention while new technologies can contribute to better game experiences. Nor should they be regarded as a complete account of applications of game data mining. Rather, they should serve as examples for the immense possibilities game analytics offer.

1.3 Limitations

While data mining and analytics have taken on an important role in game development, creating new and exciting opportunities and offering new benefits, it should not be seen as a panacea for all problems. For example, one of the primary strengths of telemetry data—being objective and unbiased, that is, not being influenced by subjective perception and reporting (Drachen & Canossa, 2009a; Kennerly, 2003; Wallner, 2013)—is also a kind of limitation, as it does not provide reliable data about "why" players behaved the way they did (Kim et al., 2008; Lynn, 2012). Moreover, analytics is not always a straightforward a trivial process, thus making critical reflection and careful interpretation of the data a necessity to avoid pitfalls and to derive meaningful results. These matters may range from issues with the data itself such as low data quality and unrepresentative data to problems associated with data interpretation such as cherry picking results that best support a certain hypothesis or being susceptible to confirmation bias, that is, seeking information that supports a pre-existing hypothesis (e.g., Thomson, Lebiere, & Bennati, 2014). Data analytics requires expertise and experience to accurately model player behavior (e.g., Powell, 2016) and to draw the right conclusions.

With the shift toward quantitative data collection, and particularly with the advent of free-to-play games (cf. Takahashi, 2017), the notion of data-driven game design—where decisions are largely based upon the collected data (King, Churchill, & Tan, 2017)—has emerged. In an effort to alleviate risks potentially caused by making choices based on intuition, developers may increasingly resort to more objective metrics. This has raised critical voices that an overreliance on quantitative analytics bears the risk of replacing individual creativity by a, what Whitson (2012) coined, "design by numbers." Or to put it even more drastically, there is a fear that the art of game design is progressively marginalized and instead replaced by scientific techniques. Others, in turn, have raised concerns that games may become more homogenized in order to appeal to a large audience (e.g., psychotrip, 2016; Whitson, 2012). These are reasonable doubts if data becomes the sole basis for decision-making. Game developers, however, repeatedly highlight the importance of analytics being only a resource to empower designers but not to replace them by analytics (Carr, 2015; Koskenvoima & Mäntymäki, 2015; Mansell, 2015). Instead, data mining and analytics should be regarded as a powerful toolset to inform decisions. In a data-informed design, data is one but not the only input on which decisions are made (King et al., 2017).

1.4 Visual Analytics

As already hinted at previously, two frequently named challenges (e.g., Koskenvoima & Mäntymäki, 2015; Powell, 2016) associated with game data mining are: (1) that it is complex and requires sufficient expertise and skill, and (2) that communicating the results so that they are easily understood and acted upon is not always straightforward but at the same time essential. These two are, however, not specific to game analytics but rather apply to data analytics in general. Information visualization has been recognized (e.g., Keim, 2002) as a powerful tool to assist with the analysis process and can help with analysis, both confirmative and explorative, and presentation (Keim, Mansmann, Schneidewind, & Ziegler, 2006). The aim of confirmatory analysis is to—as the name already implies—confirm or (or falsify) an a priori formed hypothesis. Exploratory data analysis (EDA, Tukey, 1977), in contrast, does not seek to answer specific pre-existing hypotheses but rather to discover patterns, trends, or anomalies. EDA can be very useful in developing an initial understanding of the data, to form or refine hypotheses, and to identify new directions for the analysis. As games are complex systems, which can give rise to emergent behavior hard to anticipate beforehand, EDA takes on a critical role in game analytics (Wallner & Kriglstein, 2015).

Information visualization is beneficial for both approaches, as it takes advantage of the cognitive and perceptual abilities of humans (Fekete, van Wijk, Stasko, & North, 2008). Indeed, many argue (e.g., Keim, 2002; Shneiderman, 2002) that the analysis process is most effective if automatic analysis techniques are combined with interactive visualizations allowing for more efficient reasoning and decision-making. This integration of the processing and analytical capabilities of computers and humans' perceptual abilities is an integral part of "Visual Analytics" (cf. Keim et al., 2008). The benefits of both, information visualization and visual analytics, have been recognized early on among game analysts (Kim et al., 2008; Zoeller, 2010) and form nowadays an indispensable part of game data mining and analytics (Wallner & Kriglstein, 2013). This includes the use and adaption of existing visualization techniques such as heatmaps and node-link diagrams (e.g., Andersen, Liu, Apter, Boucher-Genesse, & Popović, 2010; Drachen & Canossa, 2009b; Thompson, 2007; Wallner, 2013) for gameplay analysis. One of the earliest examples of gameplay visualization is the work of Hoobler, Humphreys, and Agrawala (2004) on visualizing player behavioral patterns in competitive team games.

Since then, many visualization tools and algorithms dedicated to gameplay analysis have been developed. Examples include DataCracker (Medler, John, & Lane, 2011), a visual game analytics tool build at Electronic Arts; Ubisoft's DNA suite (Dankoff, 2014), which offers various visualization and data exploration capabilities; G-Player (Canossa, Nguyen, & El-Nasr, 2016), a visualization system focused on spatio-temporal data; and PLATO (Wallner & Kriglstein, 2014), which integrates several visualization techniques and analytics methods such as clustering and subgraph matching.

While the target audience of the aforementioned examples are first and foremost developers, visualizations must not be restricted to developers but can also be specifically targeted toward players (Bowman et al., 2012; Wallner & Kriglstein, 2013). For instance, Wallner (2018) proposed an algorithm that automatically creates "battle maps" from recorded combat data to give players a means to retrospectively reflect on their performance. In a similar vein, Kuan, Wang, and Chuang (2017) described a visualization system for data from real-time strategy games to help players learn new strategies. Indeed, with more and more games also providing public access to the collected data, the player community has started to use this data to create visualizations on their own (e.g., Belicza, 2014; Temmerman, 2017).

1.5 Conclusions

To conclude, data mining and analytics have paved the way for new innovations in game development and for the evaluation of player behavior. As shortly outlined in this chapter, game analytics has already found many applications including design, technology, business, and community relations, but it can be anticipated that the role of analytics will continue to increase in the future. With the twenty-first century being considered both the "ludic century" and the era of big data, it is only fitting that we are currently witnessing the fusion of big data and games.

References

Algfoor, Z. A., Sunar, M. S., & Kolivand, H. (2015). A comprehensive study on path finding techniques for robotics and video games. *International Journal of Computer Games Technology*, 7.

Andersen, E., Liu, Y. E., Apter, E., Boucher-Genesse, F., & Popović, Z. (2010). Gameplay analysis through state projection. In *Proceedings of the 5th International Conference on the Foundations of Digital Games* (pp. 1–8). ACM.

Bauckhage, C., Kersting, K., Sifa, R., Thurau, C., Drachen, A., & Canossa, A. (2012). How players lose interest in playing a game: An empirical study based on distributions of total playing times. In *IEEE Conference on Computational Intelligence and Games* (pp. 139–146). IEEE.

Belicza, A. (2014). *Scelight*. Retrieved from https://sites.google.com/site/scelight/.

Blizzard Entertainment. (1998). *StarCraft: Brood War* [PC game]. Irvine, CA: Blizzard Entertainment.

Bosc, G., Kaytoue, M., Raïssi, C., & Boulicaut, J. F. (2013). Strategic patterns discovery in RTS-games for e-sport with sequential pattern mining. In *MLSA@ PKDD/ ECML* (pp. 11–20).

Bowman, B., Elmqvist, N., & Jankun-Kelly, T. J. (2012). Toward visualization for games: Theory, design space, and patterns. *IEEE Transactions on Visualization and Computer Graphics, 18*(11), 1956–1968.

Bromley, S. (2018). Interviewing players. In A. Drachen, P. Mirza-Babaei, & L. Nacke (Eds.), *Games User Research* (pp. 163–174). Oxford, UK: Oxford University Press.

Brühlmann, F., & Mekler, E. (2018). Surveys in games user research. In A. Drachen, P. Mirza-Babaei, & L. Nacke (Eds.), *Games User Research* (pp. 141–162). Oxford, UK: Oxford University Press.

Bungie (2018). *The Bungie. Net API*. Retrieved from https://github.com/Bungie-net/api.

Canossa, A., Nguyen, T. H. D., & El-Nasr, M. S. (2016). G-Player: Exploratory visual analytics for accessible knowledge discovery. In *Proceedings of the First International Joint Conference of DiGRA and FDG*.

Carr, H. (2015). *Game design: From data driven to data informed.* Presentation at the 2015 Game Developers Conference Europe. Retrieved from https://www.gdcvault.com/ play/1022796/Game-Design-From-Data-Driven.

Castronova, E., Williams, D., Shen, C., Ratan, R., Xiong, L., Huang, Y., & Keegan, B. (2009). As real as real? Macroeconomic behavior in a large-scale virtual world. *New Media & Society, 11*(5), 685–707.

Chen, P. P., Guitart, A., del Río, A. F., & Periáñez, Á. (2018). *Customer lifetime value in video games using deep learning and parametric models.* Retrieved from https://arxiv. org/abs/1811.12799.

Coenen, F. (2011). Data mining: Past, present and future. *The Knowledge Engineering Review, 26*(1), 25–29.

Cole, D. (2018). *Electronic arts and activision blizzard focus on games as a service.* Retrieved from http://www.dfcint.com/dossier/electronic-arts-and-activision-blizzard-focus-on-games-as-a-service/.

Dankoff, J. (2014). *Game telemetry with DNA tracking on Assassin's creed.* Retrieved from https://www.gamasutra.com/blogs/JonathanDankoff/20140320/213624/Game_ Telemetry_with_DNA_Tracking_on_Assassins_Creed.php.

Desurvire, H., & El-Nasr, M. S. (2013). Methods for game user research: Studying player behavior to enhance game design. *IEEE Computer Graphics and Applications, 33*(4), 82–87.

Dong, G., & Pei, J. (2007). *Sequence Data Mining* (Vol. 33). Springer Science & Business Media.

Drachen, A., & Canossa, A. (2009a). Towards gameplay analysis via gameplay metrics. In *Proceedings of the 13th International MindTrek Conference* (pp. 202–209). ACM.

Drachen, A., & Canossa, A. (2009b). Analyzing spatial user behavior in computer games using geographic information systems. In *Proceedings of the 13th International MindTrek Conference* (pp. 182-189). ACM.

Drachen, A., El-Nasr, M. S., & Canossa, A. (2013). Game analytics–the basics. In *Game Analytics* (pp. 13–40). London, UK: Springer.

Drachen, A., Thurau, C., Sifa, R., & Bauckhage, C. (2013). A comparison of methods for player clustering via behavioral telemetry. In *Proceedings of the 8th International Conference on the Foundations of Digital Games* (pp. 245–252). ACM.

Drachen, A., Yancey, M., Maguire, J., Chu, D., Wang, I. Y., Mahlmann, T., ... Klabajan, D. (2014). Skill-based differences in spatio-temporal team behaviour in Defence of the Ancients 2 (DotA 2). In *IEEE Games Media Entertainment* (pp. 1–8). IEEE.

El-Nasr, M. S., Desurvire, H., Aghabeigi, B., & Drachen, A. (2013). Game analytics for game user research, Part 1: A workshop review and case study. *IEEE Computer Graphics and Applications, 33*(2), 6–11.

Fekete, J. D., van Wijk, J. J., Stasko, J. T., & North, C. (2008). The value of information visualization. In *Information Visualization* (pp. 1–18). Berlin, Germany: Springer.

Fields, T., & Cotton, B. (2011). *Social Game Design: Monetization Methods and Mechanics.* Boca Raton, FL: CRC Press.

Fullerton, T., Swain, C., & Hoffman, S. (2004). *Game Design Workshop: Designing, Prototyping, & Playtesting Games.* Boca Raton, FL: CRC Press.

Galyonkin, S. (2017). *Monthly summaries.* Retrieved from https://steamspy.com/year/

Hadiji, F., Sifa, R., Drachen, A., Thurau, C., Kersting, K., & Bauckhage, C. (2014). Predicting player churn in the wild. In *IEEE Conference on Computational Intelligence and Games* (pp. 1–8). IEEE.

Hamari, J., Alha, K., Järvelä, S., Kivikangas, J. M., Koivisto, J., & Paavilainen, J. (2017). Why do players buy in-game content? An empirical study on concrete purchase motivations. *Computers in Human Behavior, 68*, 538–546.

Hanner, N., & Zarnekow, R. (2015). Purchasing behavior in free to play games: Concepts and empirical validation. In *Proceedings of the 48th Hawaii International Conference on System Sciences* (pp. 3326–3335). IEEE.

Hazzard, E. (2014). *Data visualization in games.* Retrieved from http://vasir.net/blog/game-development/data-visualization-in-games.

Hoobler, N., Humphreys, G., & Agrawala, M. (2004). Visualizing competitive behaviors in multi-user virtual environments. In *Proceedings of the Conference on Visualization'04* (pp. 163–170). IEEE.

Hooshyar, D., Yousefi, M., & Lim, H. (2018). Data-driven approaches to game player modeling: A systematic literature review. *ACM Computing Surveys, 50*(6), 90.

IGDA GRUX. (2018). *What is GUR/UX?* Retrieved from http://grux.org/what-is-gurux/.

Kang, S. J., Kim, Y. B., Park, T., & Kim, C. H. (2013). Automatic player behavior analysis system using trajectory data in a massive multiplayer online game. *Multimedia Tools and Applications, 66*(3), 383–404.

Kantardzic, M. (2011). *Data Mining: Concepts, Models, Methods, and Algorithms.* Hoboken, NJ: John Wiley & Sons.

Keim, D., Andrienko, G., Fekete, J. D., Görg, C., Kohlhammer, J., & Melançon, G. (2008). Visual analytics: Definition, process, and challenges. In *Information Visualization* (pp. 154–175). Berlin, Germany: Springer.

Keim, D. A. (2002). Information visualization and visual data mining. *IEEE Transactions on Visualization & Computer Graphics, 8*(1), 1–8.

Keim, D. A., Mansmann, F., Schneidewind, J., & Ziegler, H. (2006). Challenges in visual data analysis. In *Tenth International Conference on Information Visualization* (pp. 9–16). IEEE.

Kennerly, D. (2003). *Better game design through data mining.* Retrieved from https://www.gamasutra.com/view/feature/131225/better_game_design_through_data_.php.

Kim, J. H., Gunn, D. V., Schuh, E., Phillips, B., Pagulayan, R. J., & Wixon, D. (2008). Tracking real-time user experience (TRUE): A comprehensive instrumentation solution for complex systems. In *Proceedings of the SIGCHI Conference on Human Factors in Computing Systems* (pp. 443–452). ACM.

King, R., Churchill, E. F., & Tan, C. (2017). *Designing with Data: Improving the User Experience with A/B Testing.* O'Reilly Media.

Koskenvoima, A., & Mäntymäki, M. (2015). Why do small and medium-size freemium game developers use game analytics? In M. Janssen et al. (Eds.), *Open and Big Data Management and Innovation* (pp. 326–337). Cham, Switzerland: Springer.

Kuan, Y. T., Wang, Y. S., & Chuang, J. H. (2017). Visualizing real-time strategy games: The example of StarCraft II. In *IEEE Conference on Visual Analytics Science and Technology.* IEEE.

Lehdonvirta, V. (2009). Virtual item sales as a revenue model: Identifying attributes that drive purchase decisions. *Electronic Commerce Research, 9*(1–2), 97–113.

Lynn, J. (2012). Data metrics and user experience testing. In *CHI 2012 Workshop on Game User Research.* Retrieved from http://gur.hcigames.com/wp-content/uploads/2015/02/Data-Metrics-and-User-Experience-Testing.pdf.

Mansell, P. (2015). *Analytics in action: Data in a creative culture.* Presentation at the 2015 Game Developers Conference Europe. Retrieved from https://www.gdcvault.com/play/1022776/Analytics-in-Action-Data-in.

Medler, B. (2009). Generations of game analytics, achievements and high scores. Eludamos. *Journal for Computer Game Culture, 3*(2), 177–194.

Medler, B. (2011). Player dossiers: Analyzing gameplay data as a reward. *Game Studies, 11*(1).

Medler, B., John, M., & Lane, J. (2011). Data cracker: Developing a visual game analytic tool for analyzing online gameplay. In *Proceedings of the SIGCHI Conference on Human Factors in Computing Systems* (pp. 2365–2374). ACM.

Mirza-Babaei, P., Moosajee, N., & Drenikow, B. (2016). Playtesting for indie studios. In *Proceedings of the 20th International Academic Mindtrek Conference* (pp. 366–374). ACM.

Mirza-Babaei, P., Wallner, G., McAllister, G., & Nacke, L. E. (2014). Unified visualization of quantitative and qualitative playtesting data. In *CHI'14 Extended Abstracts on Human Factors in Computing Systems* (pp. 1363–1368). ACM.

Missura, O., & Gärtner, T. (2009). Player modeling for intelligent difficulty adjustment. In *International Conference on Discovery Science* (pp. 197–211). Berlin, Germany: Springer.

Morrison, M., & Fontenla, M. (2013). Price convergence in an online virtual world. *Empirical Economics, 44*(3), 1053–1064.

Nacke, L. (2015). Games user research and physiological game evaluation. In R. Bernhaupt (Ed.), *Game User Experience Evaluation* (pp. 63–86). Cham, Switzerland: Springer.

Pedersen, C., Togelius, J., & Yannakakis, G. N. (2010). Modeling player experience for content creation. *IEEE Transactions on Computational Intelligence and AI in Games, 2*(1), 54–67.

Polyphony Digital. (2010). *Gran Turismo 5* [Video game]. San Mateo, CA: Sony Computer Entertainment.

Powell, R. (2016). Positive and negative effects of game analytics in the game design process: A grounded theory study (Master thesis), Uppsala University.

Psychotrip. (2016). *"The Ubisoft Formula": Repetition and stagnation in video games.* Retrieved from https://comicsverse.com/ubisoft-formula/.

Remo, C. (2009). *Yamauchi: Gran Turismo 5's development cost hit $60 million.* Retrieved from http://www.gamasutra.com/view/news/116910/Yamauchi_Gran_Turismo_5s_Development_Cost_Hit_60_Million.php.

Riot Games. (2018). *Riot developer portal*. Retrieved from https://developer.riotgames.com/.

Rockstar North. (2013). *Grand Theft Auto V* [Video game]. New York, NY: Rockstar Games.

Schoenblum, D. (2010). *Zero to millions: Building an XLSP for Gears of War 2*. Presentation at the 2010 Game Developer Conference. Retrieved from https://www.gdcvault.com/play/1012329/Zero-to-Millions-Building-an.

Shneiderman, B. (2002). Inventing discovery tools: Combining information visualization with data mining. *Information Visualization, 1*(1), 5–12.

Sifa, R., Hadiji, F., Runge, J., Drachen, A., Kersting, K., & Bauckhage, C. (2015). Predicting purchase decisions in mobile free-to-play games. In *Proceedings of the Conference on Artificial Intelligence and Interactive Digital Entertainment* (pp. 79–85). AAAI.

Sinclair, B. (2013). *GTA V dev costs over $137 million, says analyst*. Retrieved from https://www.gamesindustry.biz/articles/2013-02-01-gta-v-dev-costs-over-USD137-million-says-analyst

Sony Online Entertainment. (1999). *EverQuest* [PC game]. San Diego, CA: Sony Online Entertainment.

Stahlke, S. N., & Mirza-Babaei, P. (2018). Usertesting without the user: Opportunities and challenges of an AI-Driven approach in games user research. *Computers in Entertainment, 16*(2), 9.

Synnaeve, G., & Bessiere, P. (2011). A Bayesian model for opening prediction in RTS games with application to StarCraft. In *IEEE Conference on Computational Intelligence and Games* (pp. 281–288). IEEE.

Takahashi, D. (2017). *Data-driven versus intuition-driven game design*. Retrieved from https://venturebeat.com/2017/02/19/data-driven-versus-intuition-driven-game-design/

Temmerman, J. (2017). *World of Tanks replay parser*. Retrieved from https://github.com/evido/wotreplay-parser.

Thompson, C. (2007). *Halo 3: How Microsoft labs invented a new science of play*. Retrieved from https://www.wired.com/2007/08/ff-halo-2/.

Thomson, R., Lebiere, C., & Bennati, S. (2014). Human, model and machine: A complementary approach to big data. In *Proceedings of the 2014 Workshop on Human Centered Big Data Research* (p. 27). ACM.

Tukey, J. W. (1977). *Exploratory Data Analysis*. Reading, PA: Addison-Wesley.

Wallner, G. (2013). Play-Graph: A methodology and visualization approach for the analysis of gameplay data. *In Proceedings of the 8th International Conference on the Foundations of Digital Games* (pp. 253–260).

Wallner, G. (2015). Sequential analysis of player behavior. In *Proceedings of the 2015 Annual Symposium on Computer-Human Interaction in Play* (pp. 349–358). ACM.

Wallner, G. (2018). Automatic generation of battle maps from replay data. *Information Visualization, 17*(3), 239–256.

Wallner, G., & Kriglstein, S. (2012). A spatiotemporal visualization approach for the analysis of gameplay data. In *Proceedings of the SIGCHI Conference on Human Factors in Computing Systems* (pp. 1115–1124). ACM.

Wallner, G., & Kriglstein, S. (2013). Visualization-based analysis of gameplay data–A review of literature. *Entertainment Computing, 4*(3), 143–155.

Wallner, G., & Kriglstein, S. (2014). PLATO: A visual analytics system for gameplay data. *Computers & Graphics, 38*, 341–356.

Wallner, G., & Kriglstein, S. (2015). An introduction to gameplay data visualization. In P. Lankoski & S. Björk (Eds.), *Game Research Methods* (pp. 231–250). ETC Press.

Wargaming. (2010). *World of Tanks* [PC game]. Minsk, Belarus: Wargaming.

Weber, B. (2018). *A history of game analytics platforms*. Retrieved from https://www.gamasutra.com/blogs/BenWeber/20180409/316273/A_History_of_Game_Analytics_Platforms.php

Weber, B. G., & Mateas, M. (2009). A data mining approach to strategy prediction. In *IEEE Symposium on Computational Intelligence and Games* (pp. 140–147). IEEE.

Whitson, J. R. (2012). Game design by numbers: Instrumental play and the quantitative shift in the digital game industry, (Doctoral dissertation), Carleton University.

Williams, D. (2015a). *User acquisition and attribution: The basics (Part 1)*. Retrieved from https://www.gamasutra.com/blogs/DmitriWilliams/20150304/237833/User_Acquisition_and_Attribution_The_Basics_Part_1.php

Williams, D. (2015b). *The tenets of community management series: Part 1 of 3*. Retrieved from https://www.gamasutra.com/blogs/DmitriWilliams/20150528/244497/The_Tenets_of_Community_Management_Series_Part_1_of_3.php

Xie, H., Devlin, S., Kudenko, D., & Cowling, P. (2015). Predicting player disengagement and first purchase with event-frequency based data representation. In *IEEE Conference on Computational Intelligence and Games* (pp. 230–237). IEEE.

Zimmerman, E. (2015). Manifesto for a ludic century. In S. P. Walz & S. Deterding (Eds.), *The Gameful World: Approaches, Issues, Applications* (pp. 19–22). Cambridge, MA: MIT Press.

Zoeller, G. (2010). *Development telemetry in video games projects*. Presentation at the 2010 Game Developer Conference. Retrieved from https://www.gdcvault.com/play/1012227/Development-Telemetry-in-Video-Games

Zook, A., & Riedl, M. O. (2012). A temporal data-driven player model for dynamic difficulty adjustment. In *Proceedings of the Conference on Artificial Intelligence and Interactive Digital Entertainment* (pp. 93–98). AAAI.

Chapter 2

Evaluating Gamer Achievements to Understand Player Behavior

Thomas Apperley and Enrico Gandolfi

Contents

2.1 Introduction

The use of achievements in digital games has become an industry standard on major networked gaming platforms, such as PlayStation Network, X-Box Live, and Steam. Achievements—or sometimes also called trophies or awards depending on platform—that is, rewards collected after reaching specific in-game goals or performing peculiar actions, are integrated into the wider social functions of these platforms, such as displaying them on a player's public profile or otherwise integrating them into social media, suggesting that they have become a crucial part of the user experience, design, and promotion of digital games (Ash, 2015; Moore, 2011). Previous studies have identified how achievements can impact performance and be adopted in gamification processes (Deterding et al., 2011; Jakubowski, 2014). Some scholars also suggest that they work as ideal extrinsic motivators (Deci & Ryan, 1985) by capturing and rewarding in-game milestones. However, there is still a need to investigate and evaluate them as tools that enable a greater understanding of gaming audiences. In this chapter, we will demonstrate how achievements can be used to develop a wide overview of how a particular game is played, that captures a cultural dimension of play through the tracking and mapping of players' trends and habits. Consequently, we argue that these tools do more than offer strategies for increasing player engagement through extrinsic motivation. They can also inform how scholars and game designers understand the ludic experience by providing insight on intrinsic motivation. Achievements also illustrate how developers understand the relationship between the audience and their own products, from the structuring of main challenges and milestones to "Easter eggs" and secondary objectives.

There is a small, but growing, body of scholarly work that examines the impact of game achievements on gaming audiences. A study by Cruz et al. (2017) found that they can improve engagement, involvement, and motivation; however, they also argued that to be effective in these improvements they have to be clear and meaningful. Cruz et al. (2017) argue that this requires that the achievements engage with and reflect the intrinsic play processes of the players rather than imposing extrinsic measures. Mekler et al. (2017) suggest that the intrinsic approach is especially effective when performance metrics need to be improved. Other research is more ambivalent toward achievements. Medler (2011) notices that they reshape how players narrate and report on their experience of play. Creating new ways of measuring and tracking performance achievements also establishes strategies for surveillance and self-surveillance, as they become sort of self-tracking devices that quantify gameplay (Ash, 2015). This dimension of achievements is also highlighted by Jakobsson (2011), who describes this system as a hidden massively multiplayer online game in which players are both active performers (in terms of achievement research and selection) and passive consumers trapped within a deterministic structure.

This chapter explores game achievement data on Steam to better understand what they can tell us about the experience of play with references to their implications for data mining. We do believe that achievement structures may inform and guide these analyses, providing a well-defined outline or a reference criterion of comparison. The approach deployed will be multidisciplinary, from media studies to cultural studies and game studies. The key concept of the encoding/decoding model (Hall, 1973) will support analysis through a comparative lens (according to standards and expectations), which is supported by game design tools (e.g., Adams & Dormans, 2012; Canossa & Drachen, 2009; Elias et al., 2012) to examine gaming features and dynamics at stake. The resulting focus establishes two key questions:

- How do developers use achievements to categorize their products?
- How do players respond to the structures that this categorization creates?

The targeted game is *NieR: Automata* (PlatinumGames, 2017), an action role-playing game with a science-fiction theme. The game was selected because it has a uniquely reflexive use of in-game achievements, which sheds light on achievements more generally. The single achievements and related data were collected and interpreted systematically (Saldaña, 2016) according to formal characteristics and contexts of consumption and production (e.g., design personas versus final users). We have used this information to develop a flexible framework for:

- Examining the phenomenon of game achievements; and
- Using game achievements to understand player behaviors.

What we have found in this study may have useful implications for data mining applications related to gaming. For instance, clustering techniques may be applied to frame different game-paths (or player traces) through achievements that may appear unrelated at first glance (e.g., by following an agglomerative approach where achievements in common become factors of closeness). Otherwise, classification techniques can exploit achievements as main classifiers/models for grouping game data, especially if there are preassigned labels (e.g., see our classification in the next pages). The aim is to provide a research-driven framework for interpreting the impact of game achievements, which will be useful for game designers while underscoring the necessity for further humanities and social science scholarship on achievements that explores the social implications of such software architecture.

2.2 Research Design

According to these premises, the key research challenge is to develop a framework for the analyses of game rewards (achievements, trophies, medals, etc.) as a routine industry-standard feature and in their its relationship with players' habits and experience, without forgetting the connections between the architecture of the award system and other formal elements of games. We will also briefly consider how this approach could contribute to a research design that includes software-based data mining techniques.

As explained previously, the scholarly consensus on game achievements is that they have both internal and external functions. In other words, achievements concern the game (as a multifaceted text) and the context in which it is played and consumed.

Context in particular could be construed quite widely. In this study, we are concerned with the context of the platform. Therefore, when we speak of context, we are referring to the wider social media environment in which the achievements circulate in. We believe context is particularly important, as it emphasizes how game rewards do not just operate within games but that they are also integrated into the social media environments of Steam (and other platforms like PlayStation Network, Xbox Live, or even Facebook). Through this integration, awards and achievements have also become a technique for connecting people within the platform environment.

It should be noted that this chapter shows three main limitations. First, it deals with one case study and one media platform; further examples and environments need to be addressed for staging comparisons and further developing this area of research. Second, the labeling was directed by applying a heuristic evaluation, which can be characterized by subjective biases and opinions; however, several tags were framed by the gameplay itself (e.g., the main plot, completing tasks that are not necessary). Third, its orientation is mainly theoretical, and empirical evidence is required to stress its assumptions and highlights. Nevertheless, we do believe that we will provide stimuli and insights to adopt, problematize, and expand it in future researches. In essence, we are applying an exploratory approach—an analytic strategy without strong hypothesis and in which just selecting the core parameters is a crucial process (Canossa, 2013).

The preliminary overview of *NeiR: Automata* suggests that there are four main internal functions that game achievements perform (see Figure 2.1). Achievements may be procedure driven, performance driven, mastery driven, or ludic driven. These are often connected to the aesthetic, narrative, and performance of the game; thus, they reflect players' experiences of the game. These functions emerged after a twofold analysis (Saldaña, 2016) in which:

1. Steam achievements from *NieR: Automata* were described in great detail in terms of focus (what the achievement is about), accessibility (level of challenge), and motivation (the reason behind the achievement).
2. The main categories were developed for framing leading criteria of differentiation (see below). Although each *NieR: Automata*'s achievement was assigned to only one specific category, it may happen that a game reward fulfills multiple factors. Moreover, developers and players can have divergent viewpoints about the nature of an achievement.

This systematic approach, which draws its premises from Grounded Theory (Glaser, 1992) approaches, tries to go beyond proposals like rewards of glory, rewards of sustenance, rewards of access, and rewards of facility (Hallford & Hallford, 2001; Salen & Zimmerman, 2004; Gazzard, 2011) that may be particularly challenging to operationalize in data mining applications. Moreover, in-game achievements quantitatively record player activity, rather than reflecting the experience of the individual.

Internal Functions

| Procedure | Performance | Mastery | Ludic |

External Functions

| Hegemony | Negotiation | Différance |

Figure 2.1   Overview of internal and external functions achievements fulfilled. (Icon sources: The icons used in Figure 2.1 were taken from flaticon.com. Full icon credits listed at the end of the References section on p. 32.)

Procedure driven: These achievements trace the path that players must follow to complete the game. They reward players for reaching milestones in the main narrative or the execution of mandatory tasks (e.g., tutorial, main story), satisfying the need to connect ludic actions and outcomes. They mark what the designers intend to be the "normal" experience within the ludic system. They address the standard (Salen & Zimmerman, 2004) or ideal player, who is observant and loyal to procedural directives that are given them through the ludic affordances of the game.

Performance driven: These achievements certify performances that go beyond the minimum that is required to complete the game. They attest to a certain level of dedication to the game, which might reflect a long commitment to relatively easy tasks that have resulted in the accumulation of currency, items, scores, points, or more specific heuristics. Other performance-driven achievements mark a "skilled" performance, that the achievement mark is relatively difficult or complex and requires a reasonable level of practiced skill to perform. Such achievements engage the "dedicated players" who want to master the game in all its complexity (Salen & Zimmerman, 2004). This type of achievement often provides motivational stimuli for such players, and when provided publicly (although achievement lists are usually well-known due to developers' insights and community efforts, which make them available after a few days) create additional directives for player behavior.

Mastery driven: These achievements attest the players' diligence and thoroughness in exploring the possibilities of the game. They mark out the minor aspects and secret paths beyond what is required to complete the game, ranging from additional equipment to new areas, side quests, and plot lines. They are often designed for the more competitive gamers (Brathwaite & Schreiber, 2009), who constantly put themselves to the test and map their performance against others. It also appeals to a "completionist" (Cruz et al., 2017) or curatorial (Apperley, 2015) approach, which is found among some fans of games.

Ludic driven: These achievements mark out the in-game tasks, actions, and behaviors that apparently are neither compatible nor coherent with gameplay. They may trigger meta, critical, and utopian implications, which at their most subversive, problematize the product itself. They can aim to trigger serious— therefore, informative—fun; otherwise, they limit themselves to foster a frivolous escapism (Lazzaro, 2004). For instance, *Dead or Alive 4* (Team Ninja, 2005) includes an achievement for losing 20 consecutive matches in a row. Otherwise, the initial trophy in *Dark Souls II* (FromSoftware, 2014) is won by dying for the first time—a strong statement of the brand identity of Hidetaka Miyazaki's notoriously difficult *Dark Souls* series.

Regarding the external functions (see Figure 2.1), our preliminary research with *NeiR: Automata* suggests that game achievements can stage three different relations with the broader environment:

■ **Hegemony**: Achievements that exploit hegemonic and already established conventions. For instance, players can expect a sequence of increasingly rare awards of ascending status (e.g., bronze, silver, gold) throughout their progress in the game.
■ **Negotiation**: Achievements that refine and negotiate expected patterns. For instance, we note that some achievements promote performance of particular secondary tasks within the game, or serve to strengthen social interactions.
■ **Différance**: These achievements overturn typical expectations and conventions. The term was suggested by Jacques Derrida (1973/1967) for describing identity through opposition—in our case, an achievement that is relevant (and legitimated) because it struggles with well-established criteria. For instance, achievements that require the players to lose, die (as is found in FromSoftware's *Dark Souls II*), or otherwise underperform. Such an effect is notable in two ways. First, it connects with Roger Caillois's (1973) concept of "dissymmetry," which depicts cultural processes that are able to overturn our expectations and standards. Second, it illustrates the imbrication of the achievement in the logic of digital games as a formal convention that is open to "subversion."

These distinctions have been inspired by Stuart Hall's (1973) encoding/decoding model, which outlined three positions resulting from the encounter between an object to interpret and the interpreter itself (i.e., acceptance, negotiation, opposition). Hall argues against the idea of a text having one particular dominant meaning; all texts are given meaning by a process of "decoding" that allows individuals to make a negotiated or oppositional interpretation of the text. Thus, in this model, the sender or encoder of a message does not determine meaning. Rather, the members of the audience interpret the meaning through an individual or collective "interaction" with the text in the process of decoding.

In our reinterpretation of the model for use with gaming achievements, the three orientations of hegemony, negotiation, and *différance* each negotiate two reference domains. First, the game "text" itself as a genre, that is a more or less well-defined family of formal textual patterns; and second, the digital games industry as a "sector" with an array of standards and consolidated guidelines. The model does not speak to the effectiveness of these outcomes but rather the positioning and approach of the individual gamer to the gaming achievement. For example, players may take a negotiated or oppositional position on gaming content that they consider particularly ideologically loaded, rather than rejecting a game outright. This is a key strength and utility of Hall's encoding/decoding paradigm, as it provides the basis for a framework that can conceptualize how players respond to uneven or hegemonic power dynamics that are encoded in texts because it acknowledges the potential flexibility of the player to decode meanings outside of a hegemonic framework (Apperley, 2010; Shaw, 2017). Key examples of problematic content in games that diverse groups of players must constantly negotiate meaning are in past portrayals of race (Squire, 2008; Nakamura, 2009), gender (Kafai et al., 2008), and sexuality (Consalvo & Dutton, 2006; Shaw, 2013). By which we acknowledge that some hegemonic solutions are "effective" in terms of engagement, whereas some *différance*-oriented insights may engender blurry gaming experiences.

This twofold framework is applied to the case study selected and stressed and problematized for future data mining applications. Our inquiry relies on a textual analysis approach—a semiotic strategy that depicts cultural objects as multi-faced phenomena and deploys multiple tools to uncover their message (Floch, 1995; McGuigan, 2009). More specifically, we considered both ludic representation and gameplay as bearers of meaning (Mäyrä, 2008). While the former spans the static and sensorial content embedded in the game (from aesthetics to narration), the latter regards the interactive parameters informing the gameplay, from rules to heuristics. In the analysis, representation was articulated in setting (e.g., the world narrative), story (plot and characters), design (e.g., art, interface), and aesthetics (e.g., graphics, sound) (Schell, 2008), while gameplay spanned mechanics (the game rules), practices (actions and tactics applied by players), heuristics (best strategies to rule the game), players' autonomy (i.e., probability space, customization), and difficulty (accessibility, feedback, and challenge) (Adams & Dormans, 2012; Elias et al., 2012; Fullerton, 2008).

Methodologically, the achievements from *NieR: Automata* have been collected with related statistics on Steam and categorized according to aforementioned traits and the four functions with a two-round process—detailed selection than narrowed in less core categories (Saldaña, 2016). In the meantime, the game was explored to develop an advanced awareness of the rewards. However, our lens also embraces the contextual dimension (e.g., audience habits, reference policies) of the video game, which cannot be easily separated from the text (Consalvo, 2007; Gandolfi, 2017; Kowert & Quandt, 2015). Therefore, we have sketched comparisons with the social, cultural, and technical surrounding, targeting

Steam, one of the "media platforms" (Apperley & Parikka, 2018, Gillespie, 2010) involved with game achievements, and gathered the overall outcome in terms of the framework of *différance*, negotiation, and hegemony we developed. With the media platform, we adopt the definition suggested by Gillespie (2010, pp. 349–350), according to which media can work as a computational (i.e., *"an infrastructure that supports the design and use of particular applications"*), figurative (i.e., *"a metaphysical [platform] ... for opportunity, action, and insight"*), and political (i.e., a tool for political goals and debates) platform. In essence, Steam becomes a place of action where the relationship between players and trophies is informed, shaped, and structured.

2.2.1 NieR: Automata

NieR: Automata, developed by PlatinumGames and published by Square Enix, was released in 2017 for PlayStation 4 and Microsoft Windows. It is an action role-playing game set in a dystopic future; players are offered the choice between two combat androids (the female 2B and the male 9S) to use as avatars. The gameplay is based on strategic combat against a machine army in an almost open world setting. It is possible to upgrade the avatar and to undertake different paths within the game that allow players to experience the main plot from multiple points of view. *NieR: Automata* was widely acclaimed by critics (metascore on metacritic: 88% for PlayStation 4, 84% for PC—as of September 20, 2018) and players alike with over 3 million copies sold at the time of writing (Khan, 2018). The in-game achievement system presents both standard elements, for example, the achievement "A new battle begins," which encourages the replay of the game by requiring the story to be repeated, and innovative elements, such as the in-game trader the Resistance Camp that allows players to subvert the whole reward systems, by selling them for in-game currency. These elements motivated us to select it as a reference case study, as it both follows a highly conventional pattern of achievement design, while also subverting those patterns.

2.2.2 Steam

The platform chosen to explore *NieR: Automata* was Steam, which is the leading PC gaming media hub in digital entertainment with over 100 million active accounts. Developed by Valve Corporation and released in 2003, it provides several features, from digital purchase and social networking to editing tools and in-game achievements. It is worthy to note that adding the trophy system on Steam is neither mandatory (e.g., games like *RimWorld* do not have it) nor related to specific scores and weights like trophies and achievements on other leading gaming platforms like PlayStation Network and Xbox Live. This means that the players who play specific titles just for increasing their gamescore and then use them for getting peculiar outcomes, described by Jakobsson (2011) as "achievement hunters," are narrowed.

This often means that the players' attention to the achievement becomes less instrumental and more focused on the game experience. However, Steam players do get to choose which achievements they display on the front page of their Steam Profile, so there is still an element of achievement hunting among some players, although what is desirable in this context is not quantifiable in a score and is contextually valued within the individual players Steam network (Moore, 2011).

2.3 Results

Table 2.1 lists all 47 of *NieR: Automata*'s rewards with type and percentage of players who have achieved them on Steam, while Table 2.2 provides a summarizing overview. The assignment of type was directed through the twofold process explained in Section 2.2.

Almost half (22) of *NieR: Automata*'s achievements reward the narrative progression of the player by marking key milestones. For example, players receive the achievement "It's a Healthy Baby Boy!" when they make it through the Desert Region, which is required if the player is following the storyline of the game. Another three achievements ("The Circle of Death," "First Errand," "Fighting's Not My Thing") record actions that are (almost) mandatory for finishing the game. It should be noticed that the game experience is articulated in four different rounds, in the first three of these rounds the same game events are repeated from different perspectives and then new plot steps are depicted. In the fourth round, the player gains considerably more flexibility of access to storylines and trophies. This is also found in games like *Grand Theft Auto IV* (Rockstar North, 2008)—and its sequels *The Lost and the Damned* (Rockstar North, 2010a) and *The Ballad of Gay Tony* (Rockstar North, 2010b)—where plotlines are explored from multiple perspectives in scenes that are reworked across the series. The deliberately designed replayability is a now a common feature in contemporary digital entertainment, one example being the "New Game Plus" feature used by FromSoftware in its popular and critically acclaimed *Dark Souls* (FromSoftware, 2011) series (Bedford, 2014). *NeiR: Automata* similarly provides narrative and agential reasons to go beyond the initial ending, which are signaled in the achievement system. It is interesting to notice the differing proportions of players who stopped after they had completed the narrative of the game for the first time. While "One Battle Ends," which is awarded upon the first completion, was received by 42.0% of Steam players, "A New Battle," which is unlocked when completing the story for a second time from a different perspective, was only achieved by 29.5% of Steam players.

Skill-based achievements are considerably less predominant, with only five entries. For instance, "Ruler of the Skies" is acquired when the player defeats 255 enemies while controlling a flight unit. "The Power of Hate" requires players to destroy 50 machines in the "Berserk Mode" in order to be unlocked. While "Naughty Children" requires the defeat of a trader called Emil, who will become hostile if the player performs the optional side quest "Emil's Memories."

TABLE 2.1 List of *NieR: Automata*'s Achievements

Name	Type	% of All Steam Players
Resuscitated Body	Procedure	76.2
Vestiges of prosperity	Procedure	71.1
First Errand	Procedure	68.7
It's a Healthy Baby Boy!	Procedure	64.4
We await your next visit	Procedure	60.2
The Circle of Death	Procedure	55.8
Creation and insurrection	Procedure	53.9
The mechanical kingdom	Procedure	48.0
Ruler of the Skies	Performance	47.3
Ruler of the deep	Procedure	45.4
Those who love humans	Procedure	44.0
Iron soul	Procedure	42.9
One Battle Ends	Procedure	42.0
Fighting's Not My Thing	Procedure	41.0
Desire without emotion	Mastery	40.4
Come Take a Look!	Mastery	40.3
A new battle begins	Procedure	29.5
Treacherous blade	Procedure	28.6
Final wish	Procedure	28.6
Farewell, Pascal	Procedure	26.8
Chip collector	Mastery	26.5
Justice	Procedure	25.9
Crime and punishment	Procedure	25.8
Tools of the Trade	Mastery	25.4
Beautiful world	Procedure	25.3

(*Continued*)

TABLE 2.1 (*Continued*)   List of *NieR: Automata's* Achievements

Name	Type	% of All Steam Players
Wait! Don't Kill Me!	Ludic	25.2
Cherish our resources	Mastery	23.4
Leaving for the new world	Procedure	21.7
Pod hunter	Mastery	19.8
The minds that emerged	Procedure	19.5
Harvest king	Mastery	19.4
A scanner's power	Performance	17.9
Destruction is my job	Mastery	17.0
Animal rider	Mastery	16.7
Lunar tear	Mastery	14.0
The Mercenary	Mastery	13.7
What Are You Doing?	Ludic	13.0
Machines vs. machines	Performance	8.5
A Round by the Pond	Mastery	7.3
Naughty Children	Performance	6.6
Information Master	Mastery	6.5
The Power of Hate	Performance	6.2
Not That I Mind…	Ludic	5.8
Inorganic Blade	Mastery	5.5
Weapons maniac	Mastery	5.3
Supreme support weapons	Mastery	5.0
Transcendent Being	Mastery	4.5

TABLE 2.2   Summary of Achievement Types in *NieR: Automata*

Achievement Type	Number
Ludic	3
Mastery	17
Performance	5
Procedural	22

The mastery category, on the other hand, is much more predominant with 17 trophies, which span the collection of specific dystopian resources, such as bodies, unit data, and chips (e.g., "Information Master" and "A Round by the Pond"), the completion of optional side quests and endings (e.g., "The Mercenary" and "Transcendent Being"), upgrading equipment (e.g., "Tools of the Trade" and "Inorganic Blade"), and various secondary actions, such as "Come Take a Look!" which is received when the player talks to Emil the trader for the first time. In both the skilled and mastery categories, the percentages of players unlocking the achieving presents a remarkable variety from 47.3% to 4.5%. The qualities of an achievement that create this variation probably relate to the difficulty and commitment that it requires. This is one area that clearly needs further research.

Finally, the ludic (subversive) achievements are the least populated group. For example, "Wait! Don't Kill Me!" is unlocked by (presumably accidentally) killing 10 friendly machines, although the presence of the achievement itself creates doubt over whether this will be genuinely accidental for many players. Achievement hunters, who have a "completionist" attitude toward trophies, may kill a friendly machine deliberately in order to collect the achievement. For other players, this would create a moral quandary, as killing a friendly machine goes against one's ethics, or one that they have adopted, which is based on the character of their avatar, the robot 2B. Another achievement "What Are You Doing?" plays with the potential scopic pleasure that players may find in the provocatively dressed 2B. This achievement is unlocked when the players have (inadvertently or deliberately) placed and held the game camera to look up 2B's skirt 10 times. This achievement has a complex relationship to the fan culture of digital games in general, as it celebrates an objectification of women and creates a gamified motivation for players to conduct such an activity. On Steam, 13% of the players had unlocked this achievement, which suggests it is not something that people are likely to unlock by accident. The achievement thus encourages the integration of 2B into the wider sexual subcultures of digital gaming where characters and avatars from games are used by fans, or fan-related commercial producers, to make pornographic artwork, machinima, and films. Yoko Taro, the creator of *NieR: Automata*, has previously announced that he would like to make a pornographic film using the characters from the game (Ashcraft, 2017).

It is worthy to note that all the achievements aside the narrative ones can be purchased with in-game currency in the digital "trophy shop" (accessible after completing the game for the third time in both the PC and PlayStation game versions). Such a shortcut means that the whole reward experience can be mystified. At the same time, we are dealing with an *embrayage* (Floch, 1995): a formal strategy in which hidden mechanisms are revealed and exposed within the text itself. *NieR: Automata*'s trophy shop becomes an embedded game platform itself ruled by purely economic drivers; it reminds us how the medium is increasingly characterized by a service-oriented focus, from downloadable content to subscriptions, in which anything can be purchased. This tendency is glaring in two of the subversive rewards—"Not That I Mind…" and "What Are You Doing?"—which emphasize and celebrate the voyeuristic dimension of the game. This meta-perspective highlights the ambiguity of achievements as it strengthens both the games distinct transparency and its heteronormative and potentially exclusionary understanding of gamer identity. "What Are You Doing?" clearly seeks to encode an "edgy" *différance* toward the genre, by using it to publicly declare the usually unstated, and often critiqued, mainstream acceptance in the games industry of a nominal notion of the female avatar also being an object that provides a heteronormative masculine visual pleasure (Carr, 2002; Kennedy, 2002). However, this is in itself not a critique of the industry; it is rather an encoded alignment with what has been noted by many scholars and critics as the prevalent heterosexual and masculine orientation of the industry (Salter & Blodgett, 2012). *NieR: Automata* also has potential for queer readings, which would fall into categories of negotiation or *différance*.

2.4 Discussion

While the mastery and skill achievements follow the hegemonic industry standards with an emphasis on completion and performance, the procedural and ludic ones show elements of originality. In *NieR: Automata* the procedure group expresses a desire to gamify the tendency to make games replayable. They add new narratives, rewards, and patterns to later replays of the game, which also have consequences on the other types of trophies because they set the stage for different rounds of ludic engagement. Rather than a repetition, they push for a new immersion with novel elements and dynamics (i.e., the different rounds structuring the game and its endings). The Steam players of *NeiR: Automata* have responded to this development in mixed ways; while almost half of them reached the first final scene, only 29.5% completed the game for a second time. The ludic/subversive category was used to frame the game in relation to industry trends impacting the whole games industry, a self-reflecting and ostensibly bold move. It is notable that a reasonably large percentage of players (13% in the case of "What Are You Doing?") achieved them despite that they were secondary and non-instrumental.

Of course, *NieR: Automata* reflects a specific taste within the gaming industry, in terms of subject, content, and ludic style. The developers clearly understand their target audience in terms of this interest and taste, but the achievements on Steam reflect a very aspirational understanding of the commitment of the players, as the loyalty expected to unlock many of the achievements was too demanding for a great majority of players. However, the relative rarity and difficulty of achievements may have a relationship with their status and role in the social sharing of achievements within the platform. Such a statement highlights the fact that external function outcomes should not be taken for granted. Innovation may be both awkward and engaging, while standards can be repetitive as well as familiar.

2.5 Conclusions

The fact that Steam does not provide specific weights for its achievements allows us to explore this phenomenon in a more game-related way. This point of view can also be compared with other analyses involving behavioral profiles and performance statistics (e.g., Rattinger et al., 2016; Sifa et al., 2015) and spatio-temporal variables (Wallner & Kriglstein, 2012) in order to find correlations, matches, and divergences. Moreover, comparisons may be staged between the multiple features (e.g., reviews, user generated content, videos, online discussions) that characterize Steam as a multi-angle media platform (Gandolfi, 2017) and different game achievement systems to frame platform peculiarities in supporting specific game styles rather than others.

To advance this line of research, we suggest the development of an advanced framework, supported by data mining interventions. As mentioned previously, the initial categories we have generated and explored in this chapter can inform classification and clustering techniques in which the developers outline what it is about procedure, performance, mastery, and ludic. This overview can then be compared and refined with the actual results. Otherwise, clusters of specific achievement paths can emerge using trophies (and their relations and order) as markers. Alternatively, for more audience and user-focused research it would be appropriate to interrogate the labels themselves, by gathering qualitative data on what is necessary (or subversive, and so on) to experience from the user perspective. Furthermore, data from social media (e.g., Reddit channels, Steam discussions) could be used to create effective empirical triangulations. Another approach would be to develop a diachronic player-model, described as a play persona (Canossa & Drachen, 2009), which is based on designers' expectations and game analytics. In these regards, methods like association rule learning can make a difference in finding patterns (and achievement personas) among the gaming audiences.

For instance, targeted players (how developers envision the final user during the productive process) may be contradicted by achievement statistics (and especially single-user paths)—mastering players may be expected to get also the ludic milestones, but maybe they are not so interested in undertaking paths that go beyond the formal meaning of the game. In the end, game rewards are one of the core metrics for understanding how gaming audiences experience a ludic product in quantitative terms. It may be seen as a summative benchmark facilitated by media platforms that asks us to reflect on how achievements fit into motivation, interpretation, and media experience between intrinsic and extrinsic drivers.

References

Adams, E., & Dormans, J. (2012). *Game Mechanics: Advanced Game Design*. San Francisco, CA: New Riders Publishing.

Apperley, T. (2010). What game studies can teach us about videogames in the English and Literacy classroom. *Australian Journal of Language and Literacy,33*(1), 12–23.

Apperley, T. (2015). Glitch sorting: Minecraft, curation and the post-digital. In D. M. Berry & M. Dieter (Eds.), *Postdigital Aesthetics: Art, Computation, and Design* (pp. 232–244). Basingstoke, UK: Palgrave MacMillan.

Apperley, T., & Parikka, J. (2018). Platform studies' epistemic threshold. *Games and Culture, 13*(4), 349–369.

Ash, J. (2015). *The Interface Envelope: Gaming, Technology, Power*. London, UK: Bloomsbury.

Ashcraft, B. (2017). *Too late Yoko Taro, they're already making a Nier porno*. Retrieved from https://www.kotaku.com.au/2017/10/too-late-yoko-taro-theyre-already-making-a-nier-porno/

Bedford, J. (2014). *Dark Souls 2: New Game Plus, preparation, differences, boss drops*. Retrieved from https://www.eurogamer.net/articles/2014-04-08-dark-souls-2-walkthrough-and-guide?page=62

Brathwaite, B., & Schreiber, I. (2009). *Challenges for Game Designers*. Newton Center, MA: Charles River Media.

Caillois, R. (1973). *La Dissymétrie*. Paris, France: Gallimard.

Canossa, A. (2013). Meaning in gameplay: Filtering variables, defining metrics, extracting features and creating models for gameplay analysis. In M. Seif El-Nasr, A. Drachen, & A. Canossa (Eds.), *Game Analytics: Maximizing the Value of Player Data* (pp. 255–283). London, UK: Springer-Verlag.

Canossa, A., & Drachen, A. (2009). Patterns of play: Play personas in user-centred game development. In B. Atkins, T. Krzywinska, & H. Kennedy (Eds.), *Proceedings of the DiGRA 2009* (pp. 1–10). Tampere, Finland: DiGRA.

Carr, D. (2002). Playing with Lara in virtual space. In G. King & T. Krzywinska (Eds.), *ScreenPlay: Cinema/Videogames/Interfaces* (pp. 171–180). London, UK: Wallflower Press.

Consalvo, M. (2007). *Cheating: Gaining Advantage in Videogames*. Cambridge, MA: MIT Press.

Consalvo, M., & Dutton, N. (2006). Game analysis: Developing a methodological toolkit for the qualitative study of games. *Game Studies: An International Journal of Computer Game Research, 6*(1), Retrieved from http://gamestudies.org/0601/articles/consalvo_dutton

Cruz, C., Hanus, M. D., & Fox, J. (2017). The need to achieve: Players' perceptions and uses of extrinsic meta-game reward systems for video game consoles. *Computers in Human Behavior, 71*, 516–524.

Deci, E. L., & Ryan, R. M. (1985). The general causality orientations scale: Self-determination in personality. *Journal of Research in Personality, 19,* 109–134.

Derrida, J. (1973/1967). *Speech and Phenomena, and Other Essays on Husserl's Theory of Signs.* (D. B. Allison & L. Lawlor, Trans.). Evanston, IL: Northwestern University Press.

Deterding, S., Dixon, D., Khaled, R., & Nacke, L. (2011). From game design elements to gamefulness: Defining gamification. In *Proceedings of the 15th International Academic MindTrek Conference: Envisioning Future Media Environments* (pp. 9–15). New York, NY: ACM.

Elias, G. S., Garfield, R., & Gutschera, R. K. (2012). *Characteristics of Games.* Cambridge, MA: MIT Press.

Floch, J. M. (1995). *Identité's visuelles.* Paris, France: Puf.

FromSoftware. (2011). *Dark Souls.* Tokyo: Bandai Namco Games [PlayStation 3 game].

FromSoftware. (2014). *Dark Souls II.* Tokyo: Bandai Namco Games [PlayStation 4 game].

Fullerton, T. (2008). *Game Design Workshop.* Boca Raton, FL: CRC Press.

Gandolfi, E. (2017). Playing the post 9/11 on game service platforms: Premediation in The Division via Twitch.tv and Steam. *Convergence.* Advance online publication.

Gazzard, A. (2011). Unlocking the gameworld: The rewards of space and time in video-games. *Game Studies: The International Journal of Computer Game Research, 11*(1). Retrieved from http://gamestudies.org/1101/articles/gazzard_alison

Gillespie, T. (2010). The politics of 'platforms.' *New Media & Society, 12*(3), 347–364.

Glaser, B. (1992). *Basics of Grounded Theory Analysis.* Mill Valley, CA: Sociology Press.

Hall, S. (1973). *Encoding and Decoding in the Television Discourse.* Birmingham, UK: Centre for Cultural Studies.

Hallford, N., & Hallford, J. (2001). *Swords and Circuitry: A Designer's Guide to Computer Role Playing Games.* Roseville, CA: Prime Publishing.

Jakobsson, M. (2011). The Achievement Machine: Understanding Xbox 360 achievements in gaming practices. *Game Studies: An International Journal of Computer Game Research,11*(1). Retrieved from http://gamestudies.org/1101/articles/jakobsson

Jakubowski, M. (2014). Gamification in Business and Education: Project of Gamified Course for University Students. In *Developments in Business Simulation and Experiential Learning: Proceedings of the Annual ABSEL Conference, 41,* 339–342.

Kafai, Y. B., Heeter, C., Denner, J., & Sun, J.Y. (Eds.). (2008). *Beyond Barbie and MortalKombat: New Perspectives on Gender and Gaming.* Cambridge, MA: MIT Press.

Kennedy, H. (2002). Lara Croft: Feminist icon or cyberbimbo? On the limits of textual analysis. *Game Studies: An International Journal of Computer Game Research,2*(2). Retrieved from http://www.gamestudies.org/0202/kennedy/

Khan, I. (2018). *Nier Automata crosses three million units sold.* Retrieved from https://www.gameinformer.com/2018/06/06/nier-automata-crosses-three-million-units-sold

Kowert, R., & Quandt, T. (Eds.). (2015). *The Video Game Debate: Unravelling the Physical, Social, and Psychological Effects of Video Games.* London, UK: Routledge.

Lazzaro, N. (2004). *Why We Play Games: Four Keys to More Emotion in Player Experiences.* Presentation at the 2004 Game Developer Conference. Retrieved from https://www.gdcvault.com/play/1022908/Why-We-Play-Games-The

Ludeon Studios (2013). *RimWorld.* Montréal: Ludeon Studios [PC game].

Mäyrä, F. (2008). *An Introduction to Game Studies.* London, UK: Sage.

McGuigan, J. (2009). *Cultural Analysis*. London, UK: Sage.

Medler, B. (2011). Player dossiers: Analyzing gameplay data as a reward. *Game Studies, 11*(1). Retrieved from http://gamestudies.org/1101/articles/medler

Mekler, D., Brühlmann, F., Tuch, A. N., & Opwis, K. (2017). Towards understanding the effects of individual gamification elements on intrinsic motivation and performance. *Computers in Human Behavior, 71*, 525–534.

Moore, C. (2011). Hats of affect: A study of affect, achievements and hats in Team Fortress 2. *Game Studies: The International Journal of Computer Game Research, 11*(1). Retrieved from http://gamestudies.org/1101/articles/moore

Nakamura, L. (2009). Don't hate the player, hate the game: The racialization of labor in World of Warcraft. *Critical Studies in Media Communication, 26*(2), 128–144.

PlatinumGames. (2017). *NeiR: Automata*. Tokyo: Square Enix [PlayStation 4].

Rattinger, A., Wallner, G., Drachen, A., Pirker, J., & Sifa, R. (2016). Integrating and inspecting combined behavioral profiling and social network models in Destiny. In G. Wallner, S. Kriglstein, H. Hlavacs, R. Malaka, A. Lugmayr, & H. S. Yang (Eds.), *Entertainment Computing: ICEC 2016. Lecture Notes in Computer Science* (pp. 77–89). Berlin, Germany: Springer.

Rockstar North. (2008). *Grand Theft Auto 4*. New York, NY: Rockstar Games [PlayStation 3 game].

Rockstar North. (2010a). *Grand Theft Auto 4: The Lost and the Damned*. New York, NY: Rockstar Games [PlayStation 3 game].

Rockstar North. (2010b). *Grand Theft Auto 4: The Ballard of Gay Tony*. New York, NY: Rockstar Games [PlayStation 3 game].

Saldaña, J. (2016). *The Coding Manual for Qualitative Researchers* (3rd ed.). London, UK: Sage.

Salen, K. & Zimmerman, E. (2004). *Rules of Play: Game Design Fundamentals*. Cambridge, MA: MIT Press.

Salter, A. & Blodgett, B. (2012). Hypermasculinity & dickwolves: The contentious role of women in the new gaming public. *Journal of Broadcasting & Electronic Media, 56*(3), 401–416.

Schell, J. (2008). *The Art of Game Design: A Book of Lenses*. Boca Raton, FL: CRC Press.

Shaw, A. (2013). The lost queer potential of Fable. *Culture Digitally*. Retrieved from http://culturedigitally.org/2013/10/the-lost-queer-potential-of-fable/

Shaw, A. (2017). Encoding and decoding affordances: Stuart Hall and interactive media technologies. *Media, Culture & Society, 39*(4), 592–602.

Sifa, R., Drachen, A., & Bauckhage, C. (2015). Large-scale cross-game player behavior analysis on Steam. In *Proceedings of the Eleventh Artificial Intelligence and Interactive Digital Entertainment (AIIDE 2015)* (pp. 198–204). Palo Alto, CA: AAAI Press.

Squire, K. (2008). Open-ended video games: A model for developing learning in the interactive age. In K. Salen (Ed.), *The Ecology of Games: Connecting Youth, Games and Learning* (pp. 167–198). Cambridge, MA: MIT Press.

Team Ninja. (2005). *Dead or Alive 4*. Tokyo: Tecmo [Xbox 360 game].

Wallner, G., & Kriglstein, S. (2012). A spatiotemporal visualization approach for the analysis of gameplay data. In *Proceeding CHI'12 Proceedings of the SIGCHI Conference on Human Factors in Computing Systems* (pp. 1115–1124). New York, NY: ACM.

Icon Sources for Figure 2.1

Procedure:

Icon made by Freepik from www.flaticon.com is licensed by CC 3.0 BY
https://www.flaticon.com/premium-icon/workflow_487349

Performance:

Icon made by SimpleIcon from www.flaticon.com is licensed by CC 3.0 BY
https://www.flaticon.com/free-icon/seo-performance-marketing-graphic_33381

Ludic:

Icon made by Icomoon from www.flaticon.com is licensed by CC 3.0 BY
https://www.flaticon.com/free-icon/pacman_24547#term=pacman

Mastery:

Icon made by Freepik from www.flaticon.com is licensed by CC 3.0 BY
https://www.flaticon.com/free-icon/settings_584574

Hegemony:

Icon made by Freepik from www.flaticon.com is licensed by CC 3.0 BY
https://www.flaticon.com/free-icon/crown_91202

Negotiation:

Icon made by Freepik from www.flaticon.com is licensed by CC 3.0 BY
https://www.flaticon.com/free-icon/handshake_66607

Différance:

Icon made by Freepik from www.flaticon.com is licensed by CC 3.0 BY
https://www.flaticon.com/free-icon/process-arrows_1584

Chapter 3

Building Matchmaking Systems

Alex Zook

Contents

3.1 Introduction

Multiplayer games (unsurprisingly) revolve around playing with other people. Matchmaking systems solve the problem of players having a hard time finding others to play with in multiplayer online games. It is often impractical to find the people to play a match of a game together—matchmaking systems provide the glue for these gameplay experiences to happen. Matchmakers provide players with easy access to others to play with and generally offer some control over the players included in a session of play. While any player may not be able to find players of similar skill or interests in a player's game of choice, a matchmaking system can readily partner that player with a full group to start a session of play.

Competitive games in particular heavily rely on matchmaking. Competitors in games like *Starcraft*, *Dota 2*, *Battlefield*, or *Hearthstone* take on other players in solo or group competitions to see which player or team has the greatest skill. Definitions of a "match" vary—here we call any session of play with the same group of players involved a match and limit our discussion to competitive play with a winner.

Matchmaking systems evolved to fulfill players' needs to find diverse partners in matches. In the pre-Internet era, players needed to gather local playmates for a multiplayer game. When games moved online, players adopted online lobbies to manually find and assemble matches. Matchmakers emerged to provide players with quick and easy access to others to play with, while offering a better matching to desired playmates for a match. While a player may not be able to find people of similar skills or interests in their network of acquaintances, a matchmaking system can readily partner that player up to build a full group to start a session of play.

Matchmakers, however, are complex and multiply constrained systems that can be daunting to design and maintain. Players provide constraints in terms of the amount of time they are willing to wait for a match, the type(s) of game content they want to play, and the type(s) of teammates or opponents they seek. Designers come with their own goals for the matchmaker: providing fair matches, minimizing the latency in matches, or exposing players to a diverse pool of playmates. Matchmakers must also respond to player behavior: fluctuations in when (and how many) players want to play, players gaming the system to appear better or worse than they are, and shifts in the player population as players become increasingly skilled or exhibit new play strategies.

In this chapter, we introduce the core components of a matchmaker and describe how to use data analytics to monitor and refine matchmaker design. We examine a number of common design goals for matchmaking, showing how data-driven systems can enable designer control while also optimizing for player desires from matchmaking.

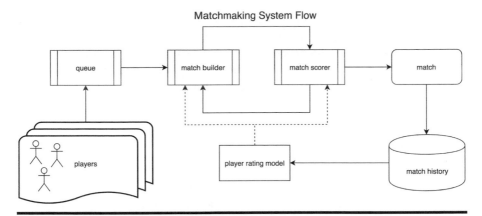

Figure 3.1 Matchmaking system flow and architecture. Players enter the queue, which feeds them into a (potentially iterative) process of building and scoring potential matches, where matches use (in part) a player rating. After a match occurs, the match history for all players as well as the player ratings are updated.

For the purpose of discussion, we subdivide matchmakers into four core components, though in practice these components often heavily overlap (see Figure 3.1):

■ **Queue**: Queues track players seeking to enter matches. Analytics identify how well queues are performing and can highlight cases where queues degrade (e.g., at times of day with few players).
■ **Match builder**: Match builders assemble players from the queue for a match while enforcing constraints on the composition of players in a match (e.g., balancing player roles in role-based games like *Dota 2* or Team Fortress 2). Analytics inform decisions on which match constraints to use and how to relax these constraints as players wait longer in queues.
■ **Match scorer**: Match scorers assign a quality value to matches and decide whether to start a match, rearrange the players in the match, or reject a possible match. Analytics informs how to estimate the quality of the match.
■ **Player rating model**: Player rating models provide an estimate of player skill, based on a player's match history. Example systems include Elo, Glicko-2, and TrueSkill (see Section 3.6). Analytics assesses how well a rating system identifies individual performance and whether the rating is functioning properly for the entire population.

When discussing each component, we will first introduce the design of the component (what problems it solves and how it works) and then common ways of analyzing how well the component is functioning. In the next section, we first introduce

Heroes of the Storm as a running example for discussing matchmaking systems. Throughout the chapter we will reference other games for comparison in terms of design goals, game contexts, and implementation choices. As mentioned earlier, this chapter discusses competitive games, though the concepts introduced can often be directly translated to cooperative matchmaking.

3.2 Running Example

To ground our discussion of matchmaking, we will use Blizzard Entertainment's *Heroes of the Storm* (Blizzard Entertainment, 2015) as a running example. *Heroes of the Storm* (*HotS* for short) is a multiplayer online battle arena (MOBA) game where two opposing teams of five players compete in a match. Players choose among a set of characters divided into four classes to compose a team with a set of synergistic skills. Players can play a match in one of several core game modes: quick match, unranked draft, or ranked draft. All modes enable players to queue for a match in a party, where a party is a player-created group of up to five players. In quick match, players choose their characters before beginning a match, and the matchmaker assembles two opposing teams of players using these preselected characters. Unranked draft mode has players first enter a match, and then select their characters in a format where teams take turns picking or banning characters for the available roster to sequentially construct the teams. Ranked draft modes have players climbing a ladder that ranks players based on their match history, with two ranked modes separating between different sizes of player parties that enter the queue for matches.[1]

HotS is designed as a team-based, competitive game with matchmaking emphasizing player skill (Valenta, 2014). Other games with similar structure and design goals include MOBAs like *League of Legends* and *Dota 2* as well as first-person shooters like *Counterstrike* or *Overwatch*. As a contrasting case, *Call of Duty: Black Ops 2* emphasizes single-player accomplishment and speed, leading to a design that builds matches based on party ping[2] and latency, rather than skill (Petitte, 2012). In the following sections, we assume some form of skill-based matchmaking. Among the matchmaking system components discussed, the only element not needed in games without skill-based matchmaking is the player rating model; queues, match building, and match scoring are all core components to matchmaking systems in general. For a game like *Call of Duty* where skill is not used in matchmaking, the system can

---

[1] The party size constraints for these two modes have changed over time. At the time of writing, one mode supports only single players while the other supports player parties of size two or three. Four-player parties are not possible, as this would demand parties of one in the same queue to create a full five-player team.

[2] Ping refers to the network latency between a player's client and the game server.

omit the player rating model and use the remaining components to create matches. Alternatively, player ping (or other metrics) can be used in place of a skill rating, with matches made to balance expected ping.

3.3 Queues

In this section, we discuss queue systems and analytics to monitor queues. Most design changes to other parts of the matchmaking system will impact how players are removed from, remain in, or get returned to queues, causing queue design to be a core component of moving players from starting up a game to entering a match.

3.3.1 Design

Queues are the entry point for players into the matchmaking system, maintaining a list of parties[3] seeking matches and moving them into matches. Games often have multiple queues: in *HotS* each game mode has a separate queue of players. Queues track parties by priority, sending the highest priority party(ies) to the match builder to create a match.

Queue design focuses on how to track and subdivide parties into appropriate groups for matchmaking. Creating multiple queues serves two primary goals: a design goal of ensuring similar parties play with one another and an engineering goal of matchmaking scalability. Matchmaking generally aims to give players "good" matches. For a competitive game, "good" generally translates to "fair," implying players should be fairly similar to have an even playing field. Queues can split parties into pools of similar players to facilitate this goal by separating out relevant subgroups in the population. For example, *Hearthstone* (Brode, 2016) maintains a queue for new players in the casual game mode to give players a more fairly matched pool of opponents. *League of Legends* (Riot Games, 2018) has (at times) also implemented a "Prisoner's Island" queue for players deemed to be toxic, to prevent these players from entering matches with the general population and to act as a punishment for toxic behavior. In general, queues give designers a tool to break the population into target groups that need special treatment.

From a technical standpoint, queues are important when there are large populations of players to matchmake. From a computational perspective, assigning players to matches is a bipartite graph matching algorithm—the Hopcroft–Karp algorithm yields

---

[3] Throughout matchmaking, the core unit of interest is the player party, which consists of one or more players that should be treated as an atomic unit for matchmaking. Depending on game modes or design choices, players may only be able to queue as a party that fills the exact size needed for a team. Forcing players to play as teams allows the matchmaker and related systems to treat these teams as atomic units, rather than modeling player differences when composing teams. The primary limitation of forcing parties to be teams stems from imposing the need on players to have a consistent group of teammates to play with. This can be a substantial barrier to entry for players in games with large team sizes.

a solution on the order of the total number of parties and matches raised to the power of 2.5 (Hopcroft & Karp, 1973) or 2.3 with some optimizations (Mucha & Sankowski, 2004). This makes it infeasible to exhaustively consider all combinations of party assignments to matches. Queues improve matchmaking scalability by subdividing the party population into smaller subpopulations that can be matchmade in parallel.

3.3.2 Analytics

Queue analysis is primarily concerned with understanding how long players need to wait in queues and pinpointing whether specific groups are suffering unusually long queue times. Queue time analysis is straightforward: gather data on when parties enter, exit, or cancel queues and evaluate the typical time spent in queues.[4] Tracking the average time players wait in a given queue over the time of day can show when and where queue times become long. Evaluating the distribution of queue times can reveal whether certain players are experiencing long queues and open further investigations of what causes those players to have long queue times. Common causes for long queue times include being in a party with a size that is underpopulated in the queues or being a high-skilled player, where there are few other players to be matchmade with. Below we will see how queue time analysis is a component to evaluating other parts of matchmaking, like the trade-off between time in the queue and match quality.

3.4 Match Builder

In this section, we discuss the process of assembling players into a match and using analytics to inform any constraints used to shape the types of teams and matches created.

3.4.1 Design

Match builders assemble parties into tentative matches from a queue. Designers use match building to shape which types of players are in a match and how the players on opposing teams are balanced. To accomplish these goals, match builders use rules to define valid match compositions. In *HotS* quick match, players choose their roles before a match starts, and the match builder uses this role information to balance how many players of which roles are on each team (Valenta, 2014, 2015). For example, rules constrain the maximum number of players in each role in a match (e.g., no more than three warriors) or balance the presence of roles on teams (e.g., requiring both teams to have the same number of supports).

---

[4] In practice, however, this analysis can be complicated when players are allowed to enter multiple queues simultaneously or pause queues (holding their position in the queue).

Filtering with composition rules ensures matches have compositions that are known (from analysis) to be fair or meet players' perceptions of fairness. Composition rules can also enable designers to control the strategic landscape of game modes and can drive desired play patterns.

Composition rules may pertain to other features of players or parties: filtering based on how similar player ratings are, whether players have similar ping, or whether players have a record of (recent) toxic behavior. Rules controlling match composition introduce the risk of long queue times by prohibiting matches from being readily formed. To combat how much queue time is increased by match composition rules, the rules can be defined to be relaxed based on how long players have been waiting in the queue (Valenta, 2015). For example, the match builder may require parties in a match to be within a 50 rating (on an Elo scale of roughly [0,3000], where in chess 2000–2200 is an expert and 2500–2700 is a grand master) when first entering the queue and then relax this constraint gradually to a 250 difference after a player has waited in the queue for several minutes. Similarly, constraints on party composition may also be relaxed or removed to facilitate creating matches. Tuning and balancing how relaxation works is an analytics problem, which we turn to next.

3.4.2 Analytics

Match builder analysis focuses on identifying the need for filters on matches and informing how filters can be relaxed to optimize match quality while allowing matches to be made quickly. Empirical evidence for team composition rules can be drawn from the win rates of matches when comparing teams with different compositions. For example, in *HotS* this analysis compares teams with different numbers of players in each of the possible roles, looking to see whether one side generally has an advantage in win rates—such an analysis led to adding a rule that required both teams to have a warrior and rules to limit the number of certain characters in a match (Valenta, 2015, 2016). Roles are only one factor: features like the size of player parties, rating difference between teams, or character choices on teams can all inform how to constrain match assembly. The goal of this analysis is to identify cases that sharply deviate from the norm of match balance, rather than remove any slight imbalance. In the above cases, a 70% win rate may be deemed imbalanced, while a 55% win rate may be acceptable. Minor imbalances are common in competitive games and often fluctuate over time as players explore the strategic landscape of the game—reacting strongly to minor balance changes risks a game feeling unstable or alienating to players if they take a break from playing.

What match constraints are used and how they are relaxed (if at all) can be tuned using comparisons of the win rates and wait times in queues. Figure 3.2 illustrates this approach with a plot of the difference between team ratings in *HotS* and observed win rates for the team with the larger rating. The plot shows that most matches have similar teams (ratings within 0.5 on a [0,3] scale) and are

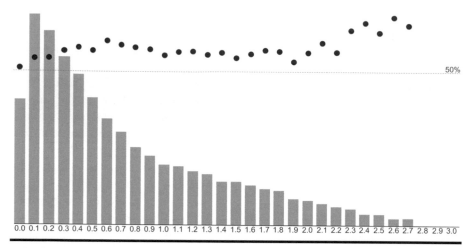

Figure 3.2 **Analyzing matchmaking closeness and effects on win rates. The *x*-axis bins matches into groups based on the rating difference between teams. The bars depict the number of matches, and the points indicate the observed win rates. Most matches have small (<0.5) rating differences and fair win rates (near 50%).**

fair (win rate near 50%). Using this kind of plot, designers can evaluate how system changes alter what matches are made and what effect this has on player experience. For example, a change that allowed wider team rating differences would show more matches with a larger rating difference (the bar plot getting skewed to the right) but may not impact win rates (points remaining at the same places). Conversely, releasing a new hero that requires high skill to play well may increase the win rate of players who have more skill. This would shift up win rates at large rating differences (points moving up) but would have no effect on matchmaker behavior (bars remaining the same).

3.5 Match Scorer

In this section, we discuss how to score the quality of a match and refine the composition of matches to meet design goals.

3.5.1 Design

Match scorers estimate the quality of matches created by the match builder, determining whether to start a match, rebalance teams in a match, or reject a potential match. Match builders are responsible for assembling players into a match, while match scorers fine-tune the match composition, using information on the parties in the match to determine match quality. Match scoring enables design to refine the assignment of players in a match and often involves an iterative loop of swapping parties around in a match to optimize the match quality score. For discussion, we combine the notion of match scoring and the process of optimizing player assignments in a match, though in practice these are generally separate systems.

Scoring functions are designed by assigning scores to features of the opposing teams in a match, with the combined score determining whether a match is good enough to be allowed. For example, *HotS* scored matches using the variance of player ratings in each team, difference in average ratings between teams, time teams spent waiting, latency of team members, and sizes of parties (Zook, 2016). The choice of features used in the scoring function reflects design goals around what to balance matches for. For comparison, *Dota 2* includes behavioral toxicity scores and how many matches players have played when optimizing composition (Valve Corporation, 2017), while *Call of Duty: Black Ops 2* focuses solely on the network performance metrics of ping and latency (Petitte, 2012).

Once a scoring function evaluates a match, there is a decision whether to start the match, rearrange parties among teams, or reject the match. This is an optimization process: searching the space of possible party assignments to teams to get the best score possible. In *HotS*, the initial scoring function was paired with a greedy hill-climbing algorithm to optimize the assignment of parties allocated to a match among the two match teams (Zook, 2016). In the hill-climbing approach, parties are randomly allocated to the two teams, and the match is scored. Parties from that match and other parties that are highest priority in the queue are then randomly swapped into teams in the match, and the new match is evaluated. If the new match increases match quality, it is saved as the new potential match to further improve. The process repeats until a high enough score is reached or a time limit is reached, at which point the match starts. This is one example of a greedy, local process to optimize matches according to match quality, with many alternatives being possible.

3.5.2 Analytics

Analytics is used to define and tune scoring models to be the best possible proxy for match outcomes. For a competitive game, scoring models can be evaluated by comparing the win rates expected from the model with observed win rates among the population. To score a model, one useful metric compares the distribution of predictions against observed match outcomes over the range of predictions. By making the comparison across a range of predictions, it is easy to identify areas where the model is underperforming.

Figure 3.3 shows an example of evaluating match scoring functions in *HotS* by comparing two methods to score matches when building matches using the hill-climbing approach above. The x-axis bins matches into 1% buckets based on the scoring function win prediction. The y-axis indicates the proportion of matches within that bucket where the favored team wins. Each bin includes the proportion of matches that were predicted or observed to have a given win rate. Most matches

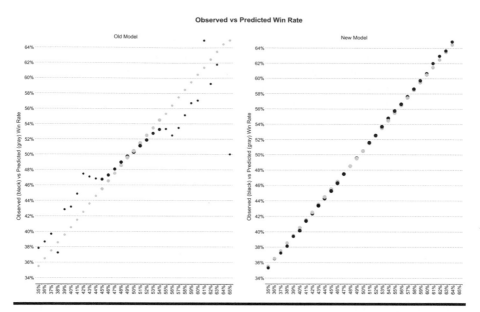

Figure 3.3 Evaluating the *HotS* match scoring function. The plot shows differences between actual and predicted win rates by win rate prediction bucket. Mark sizes are proportional to the number of matches in a given prediction bucket. The left and right panels show comparisons of two model versions: the new model predictions (right) align with actual outcomes more closely, particularly for matches farther from 50% win rates.

were predicted to be around 50% win rates, with the system designed to generally favor matches with expected 45%–55% win rates.

This analysis allows comparison of two models based on predicting the probability of a team winning (see Section 3.5.3). Match predictions spread more widely in the newer model, but with the predicted and actual match win rates being much closer (marks overlapping more). The spread to the wider range reflects the design decision to improve model predictive power in exchange for a slightly wider range of matches. Using this plot, matchmaking system designers can fine-tune the range of allowed matches in terms of predicted win rates (more or less heavily constraining what is allowed in the system) by making changes and checking how the predictions shift.

Note that this plot can be converted to a single [0,1] normalized score by calculating the absolute difference between actual and observed win rates by bin, weighting this value by the number of matches in the bin, summing these values over all the bins, and dividing the value by the total number of matches to normalize to the [0,1] range. This single metric can serve as a useful summary statistic when tracking predictive model performance over time.

3.5.3 Extension: Win Prediction Models

Match scoring models are designed to be a proxy for whether a match is good. In competitive games, this often translates to both teams having a roughly 50% chance to win the match. An alternative to manually defining a match quality scoring model is to train a model based on prior matches to predict the odds of a team winning a given match. Conceptually, this model automates the process of analyzing and tuning match scoring features. Matchmaking can then aim to provide matches with an expected win rate near 50% using these model predictions.

In *HotS*, the initial scoring function was not fully effective at providing good matches and was replaced with a predictive model (Zook, 2016). A logistic regression model was trained to predict match outcomes using recent historical data and features based on team rating differences and rating spread among the teams. This new model provided fairer matches for more players and was adopted as a replacement of the previous utility function, while leaving the hill-climbing match builder untouched. Figure 3.3 shows two iterations of this scoring model as different design constraints were applied and different features were tested.

Compared to manually defined functions, win prediction models offer the benefit of automatically responding to changes in game balance, as the models can be continually retrained and updated to account for shifts in game balance or player strategies. The primary weakness of win prediction models is that they are sensitive to sudden, large changes in game design or balance, such as the introduction of new characters, items, maps, or weapons. Without caution, a model can become outdated when changes occur, resulting in low-quality matches—this mandates the need to have fallback models or initially train a model on testing data before changes go out to the full player population. An additional challenge for predictive models is that their predictions constrain the types of matches that occur, polluting the data that future predictive models are trained on.

3.6 Player Rating Model

In this section, we discuss models to rate player skill for use in the matchmaking systems above and ways to monitor or alter player ratings to facilitate quick and fair matchmaking.

3.6.1 Design

Player rating models create and update a matchmaking rating (MMR) as an estimate of player skill. Rating models use players' match history to predict the outcome of future matches between players, treating the MMR as a hidden variable that summarizes all relevant aspects of player skill in a game. These ratings are, in turn, used by other components of the matchmaking system to ensure matches have evenly skilled players. Skill-based ratings are central to games with skill-based matchmaking—other types of matchmaking may use other metrics to describe players, like ping or toxicity.

A rating system aims to provide an accurate measure of player skill that remains true to changes in player skill over time. This imposes a set of conflicting goals on the rating design: the rating should converge quickly to player skill for new players, the rating should recognize when player skill decays due to inactivity, the rating should be stable over time, and the rating should be predictive of match outcomes. Ratings should also account for individual player performance when players act in teams. As with queues, players typically have a separate rating for each game mode—this allows the rating system to account for differences in playstyles or team sizes in different game modes.

A number of rating systems have been developed, stemming from the early Elo model for chess (Elo, 1978). The Elo system was initially developed to rank chess players in tournaments, providing a rating that could rank all players in the world built on mathematical models of pairwise comparisons. This thinking was later extended in the Glicko (Glickman, 1999) and Glicko-2 (Glickman, 2001) models, which introduced a measure of the accuracy of a rating and the volatility of that rating over time, respectively. The TrueSkill™ and TrueSkill 2 models (Herbrich, Minka, & Graepel, 2007; Minka, Cleven, & Zaykov, 2018) generalized Elo in a Bayesian framework, extending the Elo model to apply to team settings and include a measure of uncertainty in player rating. While TrueSkill is often a natural first choice for team-based games, it is also possible to generalize other models to the team context (Williams, 2013).

3.6.2 Analytics

Analytics can determine whether ratings meet their design goals and can identify whether additional systems need to be in place to address problems with ratings. Rating analysis needs to consider both the individual player/team level as well as the overall population level. At the individual level, the primary question is how ratings relate to win rates. In an ideal case, players at any rating will have a 50% win rate in matches—this indicates that regardless of skill the matchmaking system is finding fair matches for players. Deviations from a fair win rate can indicate areas for further attention, such as players having low win rates in their first matches in a game mode. A slow convergence to target win rates can suggest the need for changes to rating systems or match building to protect new players from more experienced players. Solutions to this problem include creating a separate queue for new players, giving new players a temporary rating handicap when they first play a game or mode, or using player history in other game modes to initialize players to an appropriate rating in a new mode.

The need for population-level analytics stems from the assumptions behind the mathematical models used for ratings. In all the above models, player skills are assumed to fall on a normal distribution (a.k.a. bell curve or Gaussian distribution). The models make updates to player ratings assuming that the full population has this distribution, but in practice this assumption may be violated. Violations stem from the fact that the population is not a closed system (players join and quit the game over time) and that player skill is not stationary (players get better at the game over time and even the entire population may become more skilled at a game as they better learn the game). Analysis can identify whether ratings have the desired distribution and provide targets for changes to improve the distribution. If the rating distribution does not have the desired shape, it is possible to renormalize player ratings to the desired distribution by preserving the relative ordering of player ratings but placing them at values that match a normal distribution.

3.6.3 Extension: Performance-Based Ratings

Elo, Glicko and Glicko-2, and TrueSkill are all models built purely on the outcomes of matches between players.[5] This ensures the models focus on the most important component of matchmaking—how likely a player is to win against another player. Only using match outcomes, however, ignores the rich information on *how* a player won: ignoring whether a player contributed to her team or not and ignoring whether the match was a near defeat or a landslide victory. Performance-based matchmaking models augment match outcome information with additional information on in-game performance, offering the ability to move player ratings more rapidly to their true skill rating.

Performance-based matchmaking uses additional information from in-game activity during a match when updating a player's rating. In *HotS*, this update accounts for the map and character a player plays as well as the current player rating (Blizzard Entertainment, 2017). The matchmaking system can use this information to increase or decrease the amount of rating change when a player wins or loses, in turn causing player ratings to more rapidly converge to the player's true skill. Creating this more detailed updating comes with a risk: players can now more directly manipulate the rating system by changing their performance to match statistics tracked by the rating system, rather than favoring truly better gameplay. As an example, players in *Overwatch* can fire attacks that directly damage their own avatar—if raw damage dealt was used as a performance statistic, this behavior would improve the player rating even though it does nothing to help achieve victory. Avoiding this pitfall requires careful selection of what statistics are tracked to not penalize potentially positive behaviors while still accounting for player contributions to victory.

---

[5] TrueSkill 2 is an extension to TrueSkill™ that includes a component of modeling player performance, including modeling player party size and experience. These elements are factored into the core Bayesian modeling framework, rather than treated as an additional rating modeling problem.

3.7 Conclusions

Matchmaking systems are designed to help players quickly find groups of others to play with and against in an online game. Matchmakers are built around four primary components: queues, match builders, match scorers, and player rating models. Queues track players ready to enter matches and are monitored through analytics on player wait times. Match builders assemble players into potential matches and enforce designer rules on match composition. Match scorers evaluate potential matches against detailed design criteria and refine team assignments to optimize these criteria, often a 50% win rate for competitive games. Analytics examines match builders and scorers in terms of the distribution of match win rates; win rates are often paired with queue times to balance the holistic player experience around entering matches. Player rating models are used in skill-based matchmaking systems to assign a measurement of player skill to use when building matches.

The heavy integration of analytics into every step of matchmaking demonstrates the value of and potential for game analytics to improve player experiences in complex game systems. The extensions of win prediction models and performance-based ratings highlight some of the emerging opportunities to turn from data analysis as a way to inform decisions to using data models as part of game features and services. In the future, we can expect to see matchmaking systems adopt increasingly sophisticated techniques to dynamically alter game systems to meet design goals and player needs.

References

Blizzard Entertainment. (2015). *Heroes of the Storm* [PC game]. Irvine, CA: Blizzard Entertainment.

Blizzard Entertainment. (2017). *Introducing: Performance-based matchmaking*. Retrieved from http://us.battle.net/heroes/en/blog/21179036/introducing-performance-based-matchmaking-11-17-2017

Brode, B. [bbrode]. (2016). @itshafu the newbie pool is for casual constructed. It lasts (I think) 10 games or until you have 2 legendary minions [Tweet]. Retrieved from https://twitter.com/bdbrode/status/719740928089399296

Elo, A. E. (1978). *The Rating of Chessplayers, Past and Present.* New York, NY: Arco Pub.

Glickman, M. E. (1999). Parameter estimation in large dynamic paired comparison experiments. *Journal of the Royal Statistical Society. Series C (Applied Statistics), 48*(3), 377–394.

Glickman, M. E. (2001). Dynamic paired comparison models with stochastic variances. *Journal of Applied Statistics, 28*(6), 673–689.

Herbrich, R., Minka, T., & Graepel, T. (2007). TrueSkill™: A Bayesian skill rating system. In B. Schölkopf, J. Platt, & T. Hofmann (Eds.), *Advances in Neural Information Processing Systems 19* (pp. 569–576). Cambridge, MA: MIT Press.

Hopcroft, J. E., & Karp, R. M. (1973). An $n^{5/2}$ algorithm for maximum matchings in bipartite graphs. *SIAM Journal on Computing, 2*(4), 225–231.

Minka, T., Cleven, R., & Zaykov, Y. (2018). *TrueSkill 2: An Improved Bayesian Skill Rating System* (MSR-TR-2018-8). Microsoft Research.

Mucha, M., & Sankowski, P. (2004). Maximum matchings via Gaussian elimination. In *Proceedings of the Annual IEEE Symposium on Foundations of Computer Science* (pp. 248–255). IEEE.

Petitte, O. (2012). *Call of Duty: Black Ops 2 uses ping and latency 'exclusively' for multiplayer matchmaking.* Retrieved from http://www.pcgamer.com/black-ops-2-matchmaking-ping-latency/

Riot Games. (2018). *Matchmaking guide.* Retrieved from https://support.riotgames.com/hc/en-us/articles/201752954-Matchmaking-Guide

Valenta, N. (2014). *Matchmaking design in Heroes of the Storm.* Retrieved from http://us.battle.net/heroes/en/blog/15145471/matchmaking-design-in-heroes-of-the-storm-8-8-2014

Valenta, N. (2015). *Matchmaking improvements: Phase One.* Retrieved from http://us.battle.net/heroes/en/blog/19991818/

Valenta, N. (2016). *The current state of matchmaking.* Retrieved from http://us.battle.net/heroes/en/blog/20034041/the-current-state-of-matchmaking-2-17-2016

Valve Corporation. (2017). *Dota 2 Update—October 3, 2017.* Retrieved from http://store.steampowered.com/news/33258/

Williams, G. J. (2013). *Abstracting Glicko-2 for team games* (Master's thesis). University of Cincinnati, Cincinnati, OH.

Zook, A. (2016). *A brief history of matchmaking in Heroes of the Storm.* Retrieved from https://archives.nucl.ai/recording/a-brief-history-of-matchmaking-in-heroes-of-the-storm/

Chapter 4

A Data Science Approach to Exploring Hero Roles in Multiplayer Online Battle Arena Games

---

Choong-Soo Lee and Ivan Ramler

Contents

49

4.1 Introduction

Video game genres such as multiplayer online battle arena (MOBA), first-person shooter (FPS), and real-time strategy (RTS) have started an era of electronic sports (esports) that has gained further ground over the past decade. Business Insider reports that esports are expected to bring in revenues of 1.5 billion dollars by 2020 (Dunn, 2017). In addition to players, there are many viewers around the world who tune in to major esports events. *LoL* Esports (Riot Games, 2017) reports that there were 364 million unique viewers over the course of the 2017 Mid-Season Invitation event of *League of Legends* (*LoL*) compared to 103 million and 3 billion viewers for the Super Bowl LII (Otterson, 2018) and the World Cup 2014 (FIFA, 2015), respectively.

MOBA is one of the most popular esports genres, but research related to MOBAs has yet to pick up its pace. A literature review on MOBA games reveals 23 research papers published between 2012 and 2015 (Mora-Cantallops & Sicilia, 2018), most of these papers involving social aspects of MOBAs, such as retention and toxicity. Expanding the search until 2017, we find only a handful of papers (e.g., Kwak, Blackburn, & Han, 2015; Losup, van de Bovenkamp, Shen, Jia, & Kuipers, 2014; Shores, He, Swanenburg, Kraut, & Riedl, 2014; Véron, Marin, & Monnet, 2015) utilizing game analytics. The data in these papers can quickly become outdated, and the papers do not always provide a general methodology on how to approach data collection and analysis. We believe that such a general methodology is crucial to keep up with the constantly changing nature of MOBA games. Game analytics can be beneficial to MOBA developers, as they can learn about the way players approach their games, the presence of imbalances, and potential directions regarding the question of how to improve player experience. MOBA players, on the other hand, can use analytics to learn from successful strategies in order to improve their skills and experience. We assume that many MOBA developers already have internal teams investigating these issues based on the full data available, but unfortunately, neither the analysis nor the data is available to the general public.

For the present analysis, we use *Heroes of the Storm* (*HotS*) (Blizzard Entertainment, 2015) as a case study to present a research methodology. The papers mentioned in the previous paragraph answer many research questions about *LoL* and *Dota 2* but not about *HotS*. Being different from the abovementioned MOBA games, *HotS* poses different requirements with regard to analytics. Like *Dota 2*, *HotS* also records replay files on the players' end for every match played. These replay files have the potential to provide much more information than preselected sets of information from developers.

Blizzard Entertainment developed and released *HotS* in 2015. Players can choose from more than 75 heroes to form a team of 5 to play against another team. Competitive players, including esports athletes, play on one of the available maps[1]

---

[1] As of June 21, 2018, the game includes 15 maps. Details are available at https://heroesofthestorm.com/en-us/battlegrounds/ (Accessed: December 2018).

(which is randomly selected). A map consists of either two or three lanes that lead to each team's base, and each lane has a fort and a keep, both of which are defended by two towers. There are different types of mercenary camps and objectives spread out over the maps. Once captured or fulfilled, they provide an advantage to the respective team. Blizzard Entertainment developed the game but did not offer any official strategies other than classifying the game's champions into five categories: Warrior, Assassin, Support, Specialist, and Multiclass. HOTSLogs (ZAM Network LLC, 2018), a *HotS* fan site, suggests nine roles that heroes can take on: Tank, Bruiser, Healer, Support, Ambusher, Burst Damage, Sustained Damage, Siege, and Utility. However, it is unclear how these roles were constructed, how they contribute to team compositions, and what contributes to successful compositions.

This chapter presents a detailed methodology of collecting and analyzing data of *HotS* matches and their participants. *HotS* differentiates itself from other MOBA games such as *LoL* and *Dota 2* by introducing multiple competitive maps instead of one. We collected and analyzed replay files of over 350,000 matches from a crowd-sourced repository called HotsApi.[2] Our data analysis shows that:

1. Cluster analysis based on endgame statistics (such as kills, deaths, damage dealt, and healing done) of each hero in winning teams results in four hero roles (Damage Dealers, Healers, Tanks, and Pushers);
2. Each hero role has a distinct set of endgame statistics in which they tend to perform better or worse than the average;
3. A dominant team composition based on our hero roles does not exist; and
4. Many heroes can have more than one hero role.

In the remainder of this chapter, we will elaborate on recent related work, our data collection methodology and dataset, cluster analysis for hero role identification, and team composition analysis, and present a summary of our findings.

4.2 Related Work

Research papers included in the MOBA literature review conducted by Mora-Cantallops and Sicilia (2018) pose a wide range of research questions, which are sometimes answered based on datasets. One common shortcoming of many of these papers is a small sample size (even as small as 50 matches). In the review by Mora-Cantallops and Sicilia (2018), only four papers rely on sample sizes greater than a million, and these are limited to either *LoL* or *Dota 2*. This includes the

---

[2] https://hotsapi.net/ (Accessed: December 2018)

work of Shores et al. (2014), who collected over 18 million *LoL* matches including 2.5 million players, but relied on a third-party add-on, which is not available in regions outside of China. It also requires Chinese players to have installed the add-on voluntarily. Kwak, Blackburn, and Han (2015), on the other hand, compiled player reports from the *LoL* tribunal system from 6 million *LoL* matches on 1.5 million potentially toxic players. These reports, however, focused on good and toxic behaviors reported by players rather than in-match data. Véron, Marin, and Monnet (2015) acquired data from over 28 *LoL* million matches using an open source software called lolrtmpsclient,[3] which is unfortunately no longer maintained. Losup et al. (2014) gathered over 2 million *Dota 2* matches from DotAlicious and DotA-League, both of which seem to have stopped their data provision operations.

Outside of the literature review paper and beyond 2015, there are a few research papers that collect and analyze *Dota 2* replay files. Cavadenti, Codocedo, Boulicaut, and Kaytoue (2016) collected over 9,000 replay files to discover strategic patterns deviating from the norm. Schubert, Drachen, and Mahlmann (2016) performed an encounter-based analysis of about 400 replay files to predict win probabilities. Cleghern, Lahiri, Özaltin, and Roberts (2017) analyzed about 500 *Dota 2* replay files to predict how players' health points evolve over time.

In other studies, researchers explored gameplay analytics in *LoL* and *Dota 2*, such as player styles, match outcome predictions, teamwork versus skill level, level of non-verbal communication, and encounter detection. For example, Donaldson (2015) explored binary elements in mechanical and metagame expertise in *LoL*. Ong, Deolalikar, and Peng (2014) performed a cluster analysis on *LoL* match data to identify different player styles and developed a match outcome prediction model based on a dataset of 10,000 matches gathered between 2013 and 2014 (Ong, Deolalikar, & Peng, 2014). Kim, Keegan, Park, and Oh (2016) investigated the effect of team congruency (teamwork) and proficiency (expertise and skills) on team performance in *LoL*, and concluded that team proficiency had a greater impact on the match outcomes than congruency. Leavitt, Keegan, and Clark (2016) showed that the amount of non-verbal communication, such as pings, had a positive impact on *LoL* match outcomes. Schubert, Drachen, and Mahlmann (2016) predicted encounter outcomes based on initial conditions and then proceeded to predict the match outcomes in *Dota 2*. In our own previous work, we analyzed over 10 million *LoL* matches from 2014 to 2015 to classify metagaming roles of players, also known as summoners, from endgame statistics and identified successful team compositions in North America and Europe West regions (Lee & Ramler, 2017).

---

[3] https://github.com/PaulBGD/lolrtmpsclient (Accessed: December 2018)

4.3 Data Collection

In this section, we describe our approach to secure data of interest from *HotS* matches. Our previous work on *LoL* relied on the Riot Games' official application programming interface (API), which provided the data of our interest directly (Lee & Ramler, 2015, 2017). However, Blizzard Entertainment does not provide an official API for data collection for *HotS*. Instead, we rely on a crowdfunded *HotS* replay file repository called HotsApi to download replay files for every match. *HotS* players can volunteer to upload the replay files of their matches to HotsApi using the provided uploader. Even though HotsApi may not host all the *HotS* matches played online, it has hosted over 10 million replay files as of June 21, 2018.

4.3.1 Replay File Collection

HotsApi provides a set of queries to acquire metadata about the replay files it hosts. We focused on Hero League matches in the last season of 2017 (Season 3, June 13 through December 11) prior to the major gameplay changes in 2018. Season 3 of 2017 introduced 14 patches, which include balance changes and 12 hero updates but no gameplay update (which arrived afterward) (Valenta, 2017). None of the hero updates was aimed at changing their roles but rather at updating them to the then current game mechanics. Hero League is the mode in which a player queues individually, and the system finds nine players with a similar skill level for a match.[4] It is a ranked mode where players' rankings move up and down based on the outcome of individual matches. A Hero League match starts with players picking their hero in a draft,[5] while a total of six (previously four) heroes are banned by both teams at the beginning and the middle of the draft. Our assumption is that most players will try to optimize their team composition, strategy, and gameplay to win the match, even though they may not know one another prior to the match.

The HotsApi documentation[6] lists many different ways to acquire information about the matches hosted on the site. The query method we relied on returns metadata for up to 100 replay files available on the HotsApi site at once. We use the following parameters to control what metadata we get from the query: start date (inclusive), end date (exclusive), game type, and minimum ID. The minimum ID is used to control which replays are returned by the query. For storage, we use an SQL database to keep track of replay files that we need to download and of those we already downloaded. The database has one table with three columns: `filename`, `url`, and `status`. `filename` is the name of the replay file, `url` is the URL (uniform resource locator) for the replay file, and `status` indicates whether the file was downloaded (1) or not (0).

---

[4] Chapter 3 discusses matchmaking systems using the example of *HotS*.
[5] https://heroesofthestorm.gamepedia.com/Draft (Accessed: December 2018)
[6] http://hotsapi.net/docs (Accessed: December 2018)

We wrote a query script in Python based on the pseudocode shown in Listing 4.1. The script starts with the end date of Season 3 of 2017 with the minimum ID of 0. For each set of query results, we adjust the minimum ID to be one larger than the largest ID in the set. This allows us to retrieve information on all the replay files available for the date and to avoid duplicates for each query. The query result is a JSON (JavaScript Object Notation) string, which represents a list of dictionaries, each dictionary containing metadata for a replay file. Listing 4.2 shows a JSON string that represents a single dictionary. The dictionary has a set of keys, such as ID and filename, and each key is matched with a value. For a replay with an ID of 2522619 and filename fc3fc17d-0de4-6f68-0a2d-03c969dace5b, the replay file can be downloaded at http://hotsapi.s3-website-eu-west-1.amazonaws.com/fc3fc17d-0de4-6f68-0a2d-03c969dace5b. StormReplay, as indicated by the value of the key url.

We run the query script periodically to capture replay files that have become available between executions or have been uploaded by new users. As information

LISTING 4.1 PSEUDOCODE FOR QUERYING THE HOTSAPI TO RETRIEVE METADATA FOR REPLAY FILES OF INTEREST

```
currentDate = December 11, 2017
while currentDate >= June 12, 2017
        minID = 0
        nextDate = currentDate + 1 day
        while True
                results = hotsapiReplayQuery
                                (startdate = currentDate,
                                 endDate = nextDate,
                                 minimumID = minID,
                                 gameType = HeroLeague)
                if len(results) > 0
                        for each metadata in results
                                if metadata.filename not in
                                database
                                        insert metadata.filename
                                        and metadata.url
                                                with status = 0
                                if metadata. ID > minID:
                                        minID = metadata. ID
                                midID = minID + 1
                else
                        break
        currentDate = currentDate - 1 day
```

Icon source: Icon made from www.flaticon.com. Full icon credit listed at the end of the References section on p. 78.

**LISTING 4.2 A LIST OF ONE SAMPLE METADATA
RETURNED BY THE HOTSAPI REPLAYS QUERY**

```
[
  {
    "id": 2522619,
    "filename": "fc3fc17d-0de4-6f68-0a2d-03c969dace5b,"
    "size": 2048184,
    "game_type": "HeroLeague,"
    "game_date": "2017-09-18 00:08:59,"
    "game_length": 1134,
    "game_map": "Dragon Shire,"
    "game_version": "2.27.4.57286,"
    "region": 2,
    "fingerprint":
    "fc3fc17d-0de4-6f68-0a2d-03c969dace5b,"
    "url": "http://hotsapi.s3-website-eu-west-1.
    amazonaws.com/fc3fc17d-0de4-6f68-0a2d-03c969dace5b.
    StormReplay,"
    "processed": true,
    "created_at": "2017-09-17 12:04:34,"
    "updated_at": "2017-10-08 19:10:17"
  }
]
```

*Icon source: Icon made from www.flaticon.com. Full icon
credit listed at the end of the References section on p. 78.*

on available and relevant replay files is accumulated in the database, we use a separate Python script (outlined in Listing 4.3) to download the replay files themselves. Because HotsApi is crowdsourced, the HotsApi developers do not have the resources to make their replay files available for free. Instead, these replay files are available for download using a requester pay model, where the downloader pays according to the sizes of the replay files at $0.10/GB as of September 28, 2018. A typical *HotS* replay file has about 1.6 megabytes; therefore, for example, 300,000 replay files (about 480 GB) will cost about $48. Because the replay files are not available for free, using the URL directly will result in an error, indicating that the requester is expected to pay for the download. boto3[7] is a Python module written to facilitate the use of Amazon Web Services (AWS) such as S3, where the *HotS* replay files are hosted. boto3 requires a configuration of `aws_access_key_id` and `aws_secret_access_key`, which can be set up using an Amazon S3 account. Once the configuration is complete, we use the `get_object` method, whose parameters include `Bucket`, `Key`, and `RequestPayer` for our purposes. The `Bucket` parameter can be

---

[7] https://github.com/boto/boto3 (Accessed: December 2018)

LISTING 4.3 PSEUDOCODE FOR DOWNLOADING REPLAY FILES LISTED IN THE SQL DATABASE

```
results = sqlquery(all filenames with status = 0)
for each filename in results:
        download(filename) with boto3 module
        set status of filename to 1 in the database
```

Icon source: Icon made from www.flaticon.com. Full icon credit listed at the end of the References section on p. 78.

identified from the host part of the URL. In our example from Listing 4.2, the host is `hotsapi.s3-website-eu-west-1.amazonaws.com`, and the `Bucket` parameter can be the first part of the host, which is `hotsapi` in our example. The `Key` parameter is the last part of the URL, in our example: `fc3fc17d-0de4-6f68-0a2d-03c969dace5b.StormReplay`. The `RequestPayer` parameter should be set to requester to indicate that the requester is paying for the download.

4.3.2 Replay File Analysis

Although Blizzard Entertainment does not offer access to its repository of *HotS* data, there is an official Python module called heroprotocol[8] to parse *HotS* replay files. *HotS* replay files are MPQ[9] archives, and the heroprotocol module decodes and provides information in the JSON format discussed in Section 4.3.1. The attributes in Table 4.1 are recorded for every player per replay file into a comma separated file (CSV) for later analysis.

For our purposes, it was necessary to write a dedicated program (using the heroprotocol module) because of the variety of information we wanted to compile into a single CSV file. First, we retrieved the version and time of the replay file from the header information to verify that it is from Season 3 of 2017. Second, replay files also include a list of events of type `trackerEvent`, which describe a wide range of events that happen throughout the match. For our purposes, we relied on `NNet.Replay.Tracker.SScoreResultEvent` events to query the match duration and `Net.Replay.Tracker.SStatGameEvent` events to retrieve further variables such as `hero`, `winner`, and `team` (cf. Table 4.1). There were 14 maps in rotation for Season 3 of 2017. Table 4.2 shows all the maps and their corresponding map codes.

---

[8] https://github.com/Blizzard/heroprotocol (Accessed: December 2018)
[9] MPQ is a proprietary archiving file format used by Blizzard Entertainment.

Table 4.1   Attributes Extracted from *HotS* Replay Files

Attribute	Abbreviation	Description
Filename	–	Name of the replay file
Version	–	Client build number on which the match was played
Time	–	Date and time of the match in UTC
Duration	–	Length of the match
mapCode	–	Code of the map on which the match was played
Hero	–	Name of the hero picked by a player
Team	–	Team ID (0 or 1)
Winner	–	Whether the player is in the winning team or not (1 or 0)
SoloKills	Solo	Number of killing blows executed by a player
Assists	Asts	Number of kills that a player participated in
Takedowns	Tkdw	Sum of SoloKills and Assists
Deaths	–	Number of deaths of a player
Experience Contribution	ExpC	Amount of experience a player contributed to the team
Healing	Heal	Amount of healing a player performed on the team
SelfHealing	SlfH	Amount of healing a player performed on his/her hero
HeroDamage	HrDm	Amount of damage a player inflicted on enemy players
MinionDamage	MnDm	Amount of damage a player inflicted on minions
StructureDamage	StDm	Amount of damage a player inflicted on structures
SiegeDamage	SgDm	Sum of MinionDamage and StructureDamage

(*Continued*)

Table 4.1 (*Continued*) Attributes Extracted from *HotS* Replay Files

Attribute	Abbreviation	Description
MercCampCaptures	MrCC	Number of times a player captured a mercenary camp
WatchTowerCaptures	–	Number of times a player captured a watch tower
TimeCCdEnemyHeroes	TCCE	Length of time a player crowd controlled enemy players
TimeSpentDead	–	Length of time a player was dead

Table 4.2 Maps and Their Map Codes

Map	Map Code	Map	Map Code
Battlefield of Eternity	BattlefieldOfEternity	Haunted Mines	HauntedMines
Blackhearts Bay	BlackheartsBay	Infernal Shrines	Shrines
Braxis Holdout	BraxisHoldout	Sky Temple	ControlPoints
Cursed Hollow	CursedHollow	Tomb of the Spider Queen	Crypts
Dragon Shire	DragonShire	Towers of Doom	TowersOfDoom
Garden of Terror	HauntedWoods	Volskaya Foundry	Volskaya
Hanamura	Hanamura	Warhead Junction	WarheadJunction

As of January 12, 2018, we gathered 349,283 replay files with 370,263 unique players from four regions. Table 4.3 shows a summary by maps. Only 3.56% of matches took place on Volskaya Foundry. This, however, is not particularly surprising, as Volskaya Foundry was only added to the game on September 26, 2017. In addition, only 3.97% of the matches were played on Hanamura, but since Hanamura was only in rotation for about four months from April 25, 2017, until August 8, 2017, this percentage is not surprising either.

Table 4.3 Summary of Collected Hero League Replay Files

Map	Matches	Unique Players
Battlefield of Eternity	28,853	120,533
Blackhearts Bay	22,045	100,823
Braxis Holdout	27,794	117,053
Cursed Hollow	38,632	141,626
Dragon Shire	38,857	142,323
Garden of Terror	18,195	85,130
Hanamura	13,864	68,837
Haunted Mines	16,536	81,105
Infernal Shrines	28,017	117,794
Sky Temple	27,347	116,336
Tomb of the Spider Queen	32,046	128,068
Towers of Doom	25,393	106,856
Volskaya Foundry	12,421	65,303
Warhead Junction	19,283	89,234
Total	**349,283**	**370,263**

4.4 Data Analysis

In this section, we outline an approach to identifying roles for gameplay in *HotS*. Given the ever-changing landscape of *HotS* (and esports more broadly), our general philosophy is to use common statistical and machine learning methods that can be easily adapted to new data or to data that slightly changes format. Moreover, the proposed approach should be relatively easy to apply to other games that have a similar structure in terms of gameplay and data availability.

4.4.1 Clustering Performance Attributes

Cluster analysis is an unsupervised machine learning method commonly used in exploratory analyses to group "similar" items (and separate dissimilar ones) within a dataset based on certain numeric attributes. Since the aim of this study is to show-case a method for learning about hero roles in *HotS* based on the available endgame statistics, cluster analysis is a natural first step in identifying the main playstyles of characters and participants in the game.

Prior to clustering these attributes, the data needs to be prepared. First, we separate the participants by map. Since in-game goals can change from map to map, we only allow clusters to be formed within each map. Then, if roles are similar across maps, results are merged together to ease interpretation.

Next, we only consider participants from winning teams. While not perfect, the rationale behind this is to focus on teams that were successful and reduce some potential noise that could occur from teams that play poorly (especially from teams that play poorly on purpose).

Subsequently, for each map, we construct a training set of randomly selected 25,000 participants (from 5,000 teams) to reduce computation time. Since we are only looking for the prominent roles and team compositions, a subset of the data should be sufficient in identifying these features. If we were instead interested in detecting rare events, abnormalities, or mapping changes across time, we would be better served by using the entire data (or at least a substantially larger sample).

Finally, we scale the performance data (using the attributes with abbreviations listed in Table 4.1) used for clustering in two ways: first, we scale each participant's data by the duration of the match (to equally weight both short and long matches[10]) and second, we transform each of the performance attributes (across all participants) to have zero mean and unit variance.[11] This last step is done to ensure that performance attributes on vastly different numerical scales (e.g., `SoloKills` versus `HeroDamage`) are given equal weighting in distance-based clustering algorithms.

There are numerous popular clustering algorithms that can be used to identify the main groups within datasets like these. For example, many of the varieties of *k*-means (e.g., MacQueen, 1967; Pal, Bezdek, & Hathaway, 1996; Maitra & Ramler, 2010), hierarchical clustering algorithms (see Johnson [1967] for an overview), Gaussian mixture modeling (Banfield & Raftery, 1993), and density-based clustering (Ester, Kriegel, Sander, & Xu, 1996) could all be suitable choices for partitioning data like these. We elect to use hierarchical clustering with Ward's minimum variance linkage (Ward, 1963) based on cosine similarity.

Hierarchical clustering has the advantage that, in addition to being able to partition the data into a fixed number of groups, it is relatively easy to visualize the results[12] (through a heatmap and/or dendrogram). A hard partitioning can ease the interpreting of clusters (in this case across maps) while the full heatmap/dendrogram can show cluster structures—including the variables that play a prominent role in defining the features of a cluster as well as any subclusters that may exist within the main partitioning. More specifically, for data such as these,

---

[10] See also Chapter 12.

[11] This is commonly referred to as *standardizing, z-normalization,* or *computing z-scores* for each variable.

[12] Data visualization will be discussed in depth in Chapter 11.

hierarchical clustering makes it possible to observe subgroup structures within the main groups (potentially corresponding to subcategories within the main roles) and better see how some maps may slightly deviate from the majority.

There are also numerous choices for the linkage criterion (with Ward, complete, average, and centroid being popular choices). Ward's method, which seeks to merge clusters that minimize the increase in the total within-cluster variance, is appropriate for the goals of this analysis, as it generally produces compact clusters. We also use cosine similarity as the distance metric, as it allows us to measure similarity based on the correlations between participants instead of the absolute difference in their endgame performance statistics. Finally, to assist in determining the number of clusters for a hard partitioning of the data, we apply a variation of the Elbow method (Thorndike, 1953) that compares the relative change in the total within-cluster sum of squares of k versus $k+1$ groups.

After applying the above methodology to the *HotS* data, most maps showed a clear tendency toward four main groups. The exceptions to this were Battlefield of Eternity (either three or possibly five groups), Dragon Shire (three or four groups), and Sky Temple (three or four groups). Figure 4.1 illustrates the hierarchical clustering results for four selected maps (Blackhearts Bay, Battlefield of Eternity, Infernal Shrines, and Volskaya Foundry). Color on the heatmap displays the z-scores for each performance attribute, with green indicating above-average scores and purple below-average. Shading is used to indicate the magnitude of the score. Similar plots for the other 10 maps are available in Appendix A.

Blackhearts Bay (Figure 4.1a) shows four distinct clusters (denoted by the colored sidebar to the left of the heatmap). The first group (gray) tends to display higher than average scores in `SelfHealing` (abbreviated as `SlfH` in the plot; see also Table 4.1) and either high scores in `Assists` (Asts) and `Takedowns` (Tkdw) or in Mercenary Camp Captures (MrCC). They tend to score at or below average in most of the other categories. The second group (blue) is the only cluster in which `Healing` (Heal) is prominent, and most damage-related statistics are well below average. Many of these players also have high `Assists` and `Takedowns`. The third group (orange) scored highest in `SoloKills` (Solo) and `HeroDamage` dealt (HrDm). They also tend to score high in `Takedowns` and have a subgroup that administers crowd control effects (TCCE) or captures mercenary camps (MrCC). The last group (red) mainly consists of players ending with high scores in `Minion`, `Siege`, and `StructureDamage` (MnDm, SgDm, and StDm respectively). They contribute more to `ExperienceContribution` (ExpC) and have the lowest scores in `MercCampCaptures` (MrCC), `Assists` (Asts), and `Takedowns` (Tkdw).

Figure 4.1b and Figure 4.1c display Volskaya Foundry and Infernal Shrines. They essentially show the same four clusters as Blackhearts Bay (sidebar colors are used to link similarly composed clusters across maps). While both Volskaya Foundry and Infernal Shrines have fairly similar cluster structures, there are a few differences. In Infernal Shrines, the (red) cluster consisting of those with high

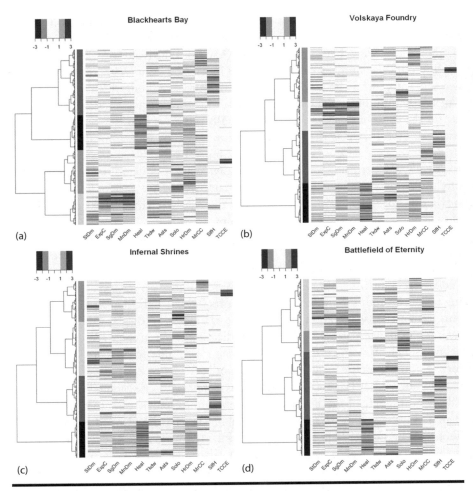

(a)   (b)   (c)   (d)

Figure 4.1 (See color insert.) Clustered heatmaps of 25,000 participants from winning teams on the (a) Blackhearts Bay, (b) Volskaya Foundry, (c) Infernal Shrines, and (d) Battlefield of Eternity maps (see Table 4.1 on pp. 57–58 for an explanation of the abbreviations). The colored sidebars indicate similarly structured clusters across maps.

StructureDamage has a subgroup that also has fairly large amounts of Hero Damage and SoloKills. This subgroup is seen as part of the orange cluster in Volskaya Foundry that is more prominently characterized by high Solo Kills and HeroDamage. The main difference between these subgroups is that in Infernal Shrines, they also tend to have high minion and siegedamage statistics while lacking those values in Volskaya Foundry. While Volskaya Foundry and Infernal Shrines have only one objective point activated at a time, the mechanisms to secure the objective differ. In Infernal Shrines, the first team to defeat 40 min-ions[13] at a certain map location wins the objective, while in Volskaya Foundry, the team who captures a certain map location from the other team for a certain period of time wins. The difference of having neutral minions at the objective points in Infernal Shrines is reflected in the difference of `Minion` and `SiegeDamage` in the subgroups.

Battlefield of Eternity (Figure 4.1d) shows a slight deviation from this clear four-cluster trend with only three clusters being the preferred choice when using the `elbowmethod`. When partitioned into four groups, there is still a clear "Healer group" (blue) as well as a `SelfHealing/MercCampCaptures` group (gray). However, the other two groups (red and orange) are less distinct than in other maps. There is still a clear (but small) cluster of players with very high `SoloKills` and `HeroDamage`, but the part of the group that is mainly defined by high `Structure`, `Siege`, and `Minion  Damage` (red) also contains a portion with high `HeroDamage`. In Battlefield of Eternity, players must defeat the enemy team's immortal faster than the other team to secure the objective. Heroes capable of inflicting extra damage to non-heroes contribute more to winning the objective. While there is a small group of players who focus more on `HeroDamage`, there is a larger group of players who focus on capturing the objective instead.

Given this tendency toward four groups in most maps, we elect to partition all maps into four groups for consistency. As a next step toward identifying roles for heroes, we calculate the means of each of the performance attributes (based on the z-scores) for each of the four derived clusters in each map and then cluster these results again to compare group means across maps. When these 56 group means are partitioned into four clusters, exactly one set of group means from each map shows up in each of the four clusters. This implies that we are able to clearly identify four main roles across all maps with a similar set of noteworthy performance attributes. This result is indicated in Figure 4.1 through the use of the matching sidebar colors across maps.

In order to make it easier to identify roles, we next plot the rank of the mean performance attributes (already clustered previously) averaged across all 14 maps. Figure 4.2 displays these results, with higher rankings (darker green) indicating higher values for the corresponding performance metric. Further, we develop the following labels for each group:

■ **Damage Dealers** are those with high `Hero  Damage` and `Solo  Kills` and moderately high `Assists` and `Takedowns` (corresponding to the orange sidebars in Figure 4.1).

---

[13] Minions are units that are spawned periodically and which players can kill to gain experience. See https://heroesofthestorm.gamepedia.com/Minion (Accessed: December 2018).

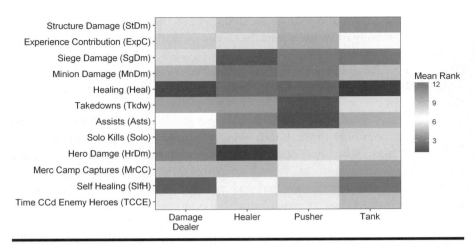

Figure 4.2 (See color insert.) Heatmap of the performance attribute metrics (by mean rank across maps) for each of the four identified groups. High ranks (green) indicate higher attribute scores while low ranks (purple) indicate lower attribute scores.

- **Healers** are those with high values in Healing only (blue sidebars in Figure 4.1).
- **Pushers** are those with high scores in Structure, Minion, and Siege Damage along with high Experience Contribution and very low Takedowns and Assists (red sidebars in Figure 4.1).
- **Tanks** are those with very high Self Healing scores along with high Time Crowd Controlling (CC) Enemy Heroes, Mercenary Camp Captures, or Assists/Takedown scores (gray sidebars in Figure 4.1).

4.4.2 Identifying Hero Roles

Having identified the four main hero roles of players in *HotS* (Damage Dealer, Healer, Pusher, and Tank), our next goal is to predict the role for all participants in the dataset. For that matter, we train a random forest classifier (Breiman, 2001), reusing the data from the cluster analysis (again, keeping maps separated) with the identified role as the response variable. Table 4.4 displays the overall and the role-dependent out-of-bag (OOB) error rates (James, Witten, Hastie, & Tibshirani, 2013) for each map (as well as the average across all maps) where errors are counted as the random forest not predicting the same role that was identified by the cluster analysis. Overall error rates are relatively low (ranging from 6.2% to 9.0% with an average of 7.96%), with Healers having extremely low error rates on nearly all maps (between 1.2% and 2.2%). Tanks have errors rates of roughly 6%–9%, Damage Dealers between 8% and 15%, and Pushers between 8% and 12% across most maps.

Table 4.4 Random Forest Model's Out-of-Bag Error Rates by Map and Role

Map	Overall	Damage Dealer	Healer	Pusher	Tank
Battlefield of Eternity	8.0	21.5	1.7	8.9	6.6
Blackhearts Bay	7.9	10.8	1.7	11.4	7.6
Braxis Holdout	7.9	10.8	1.3	17.4	6.1
Sky Temple	6.2	22.1	1.9	4.0	6.8
Tomb of the Spider Queen	8.7	16.0	2.2	9.5	7.7
Cursed Hollow	7.8	8.6	2.2	12.3	7.8
Dragon Shire	8.3	14.8	1.6	8.6	8.1
Hanamura	8.3	12.4	1.5	11.2	7.6
Haunted Mines	6.6	5.6	2.1	16.2	6.0
Garden of Terror	8.9	10.2	2.0	11.9	9.3
Infernal Shrines	7.1	12.3	1.3	8.4	5.5
Towers of Doom	8.4	14.5	1.7	8.8	8.6
Volskaya Foundry	8.4	10.8	1.9	12.5	8.4
Warhead Junction	9.0	14.0	2.2	10.1	9.1
Average	**7.96**	**13.16**	**1.8**	**10.80**	**7.50**

There are a few maps in which one of these four roles has higher error rates. Most notably, in both Battlefield of Eternity and Sky Temple, the error rates for Damage Dealers are in the low 20% range. At this point, we should recall that in Battlefield of Eternity, the cluster identified as Pusher (due to high minion and siege damage) had a subgroup with high hero damage scores. This subgroup caused the higher error rate for Damage Dealers within this map. Sky Temple has a similar cluster structure (including the subgroup), which also explains its higher error rate.

Finally, it should be noted that although these are considered as errors by the random forest model, the role predicted by the random forest model may in fact represent them better than the role defined by the cluster analysis.

Having identified broadly defined roles and trained an adequate random forest classifier, we use the random forest model to predict the roles for all participants in the data. We use the entire dataset for two reasons:

1. Making predictions from the model is not too computationally intensive, and
2. When cross-tabulating classifications with 70+ heroes, we ensure sufficient sample sizes for even the less popular heroes.

Next, we investigate the most popular team compositions (by predicted role) and identify the primary and secondary roles for all heroes released prior to the end of Season 3 (i.e., Hanzo and any heroes released later are not included in this analysis).

4.4.3 Team Compositions

Figure 4.3 breaks down the most common winning and losing team compositions for each map. We define a winning composition as any that has a win rate of greater than 50% (and losing as ≤50%). Shading is used to indicate the number of teammates in each role (with white signifying zero members and the darkest color indicating two and three members, respectively). The first number next to each map name corresponds to the percentage of teams with that row's team composition, and the second number indicates the winning percentage for that row's composition.

In general, no team composition is significantly preferred in any map, with the most common winning and losing compositions being 26.7% (Blackhearts Bay) and 28.0% (Sky Temple), respectively.

The most common winning and losing compositions share the characteristic of having exactly one Healer and at least one Tank across maps. The most common winning compositions on Braxis Holdout, Cursed Hollow, and Haunted Mines are missing a Pusher. The map objectives on these maps spawn powerful minions that help push a lane, reducing the `Minion`, `Structure`, and `SiegeDamage` of the players.

The most common losing compositions tend to lack Damage Dealers and to have more Pushers. This may be due to the fact that the players on the losing team are pushed back on lanes, and they are only able to farm minions passively during the games. The most common winning compositions are in line with the unique characteristics of the maps. Two Tanks are present in maps that are huge and/or whose solo lane is more important. There is no Pusher in maps where the map objectives offer an effective push in a lane. We observe two Damage Dealers on maps that are smaller and/or where team fights are more common.

4.4.4 Classifying Individual Heroes

Since heroes have the potential to be classified into multiple roles (as roles were developed independently of the actual hero being used), a rough set of guidelines was used to define primary and secondary roles for each hero. Heroes with

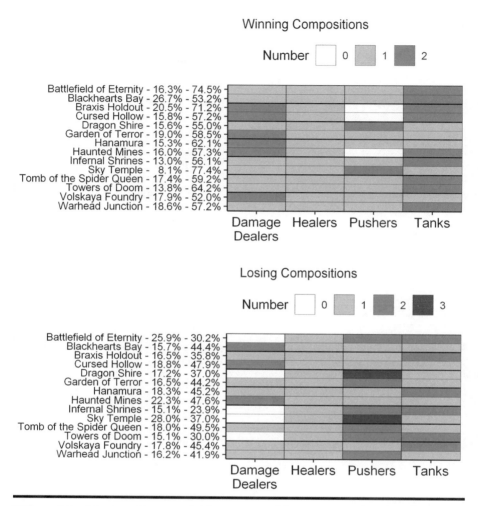

Figure 4.3 **Most common winning composition (top) and losing composition (bottom) for each map. The first number next to each map name indicates the percent of teams with that composition, and the second number is the win rate for the composition.**

primary roles were only those in which at least 70% of matches (across all maps) were played in a specific role, and the second most common role was less than 20%. If both a primary and secondary role were identified, the primary role was between 55% and 70% while the secondary role was (essentially) the only other prominent role (appearing in roughly 20%–40% of the matches). Hybrid style heroes were those in which no role showed up in the majority of matches, and all hybrid roles were seen at least 20% of the time. Table 4.5 lists these groupings.

While Table 4.5 classifies heroes across all maps, the proportion of matches observed in each role was not always consistent across them. For example, the three heroes

Table 4.5   Hero Classifications by Role

Primary Role	Secondary Role	Heroes
Damage Dealer	–	Nova, Veleera
Damage Dealer	Pusher	Alarak, Cassia, Chromie, Genji, Malthael, Tracer, Tychus
Damage Dealer	Healer	Tyrande
Damage Dealer	Tank	Zeratul
Healer	–	Alexstraza, Ana, Auriel, Brightwing, Kharazim, Li, Lt. Morales, Lucio, Malfurion, Rehgar, Stukov, Uther
Hybrid (DD–Pusher)	–	Li-Ming, Lunara, Valla
Hybrid (DD–Pusher–Tank)	–	Diablo, Jaina, Samuro, The Butcher, Zuljin
Hybrid (DD–Tank)	–	Varian
Hybrid (DD–Healer)	–	Medivh
Hybrid (Pusher–Tank)	–	Rexxar
Pusher	Damage Dealer	D.Va, Falstad, Gall, Greymane, Junkrat, Kael'thas, Kel'Thuzad, Raynor, Sgt. Hammer
Pusher	Tank	Guldan,
Pusher	–	Abathur, Azmodan, Gazlowe, Murky, Nazeebo, Probius, Ragnaros, Sylvanas, The Lost Vikings, Xul, Zagara
Tank	Damage dealer	Stitches
Tank	Pusher	Dehaka
Tank	–	Anub'arak, Artanis, Arthas, Chen, Cho, E.T.C., Garrosh, Illidan, Johanna, Kerrigan, Leoric, Muradin, Sonya, Tassadar, Thrall, Tyrael, Zarya

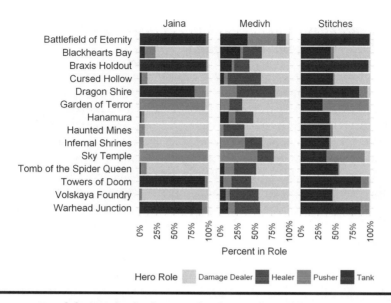

Figure 4.4 Breakdown of roles by map for three selected heroes.

displayed in Figure 4.4 (Jaina, Medivh, and Stitches) show how roles can differ by map depending on the hero. Jaina fulfills one dominant role in all the maps. She is a Pusher in Garden of Terror, but mostly either a Damage Dealer or a Tank in others. While a Tank is not a typical role for a mage such as Jaina, she applies a slowdown effect on targets with her basic attacks and abilities. She is classified more often as a Tank on maps where poking damage at enemy heroes near the map objectives is a common strategy. Stitches is a Tank on most maps, but sometimes steps up as a Damage Dealer or a Pusher. This is probably due to the choice of his heroic talent, which either provides crowd control (Gorge) or area effect damage (Putrid Bile). While Jaina and Stitches tend toward one or two roles, Medivh's role is not as clear. This speaks to the diversity of builds and playstyles that players can achieve with Medivh. While he is not a conventional Healer, his basic ability (Force of Will) can provide a significant amount of effective healing if used at appropriate times, since it heals the target for a certain percentage of the damage it absorbed. Both of his heroic abilities provide a form of crowd control, and Force of Will can also help Medivh to heal himself. Players who deploy Medivh at the front line may have been classified as Tanks. Medivh also shows up as a Damage Dealer, because the same ability can also provide an area effect damage around its target (an ally player) in addition to his talent choice that increases the basic ability damage once the quest is complete. Medivh also has a unique mount mechanic, which allows him to transform into a raven and fly across the map. This enables him to move from one lane to another faster than other heroes, and he can gather experience while in the air. Moreover, if he chooses a talent allowing him to kill minions in one shot, it helps him to increase his minion damage significantly. This can contribute to him being classified as a Pusher.

4.4.5 Comparison to Classifications of Blizzard Entertainment and Popular Fan Sites

Blizzard provides descriptive but static classifications for each of their heroes—Assassin, Specialist, Support, Warrior, and Multiclass. For many players (especially newer and/or inexperienced individuals), this is likely the main way they differentiate between the types of heroes. Figure 4.5 displays the relationship between the classifications provided by Blizzard and the role classifications for heroes using our data-driven method in percentages. Blizzard's Assassins tend to be split evenly between Damage Dealer and Pusher roles (with a few Tanks scoring high), Specialists tend to be pure Pushers, Supports is Blizzard's name for Healers, and Warriors tend to be the Tanks on the team. As of the end of Season 3, Varian was the only Multiclass hero (as defined by Blizzard). Perhaps not surprisingly, he was defined as a Damage Dealer/Tank hybrid in our classifications.

The popular fan site HOTSLogs (ZAM Network LLC, 2018) provides nine static classifications of heroes. While it is not clear how the site reaches its classifications, we can use our own classifications to uncover associations between their classes and our identified roles. Figure 4.6 shows the percentage of matches in which each hero appears in our four roles, broken down by the nine HOTSLogs classes. Many of their classes match very closely with our classifications (their Bruiser & Tank = our Tank, Healer = Healer, Siege = Pusher, Ambusher tends

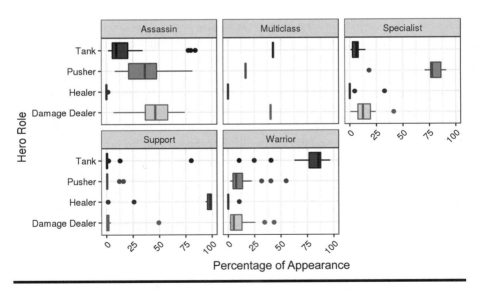

Figure 4.5 Comparison of the percentage of appearance of heroes in each of the four identified roles broken down by the Blizzard assigned hero role.

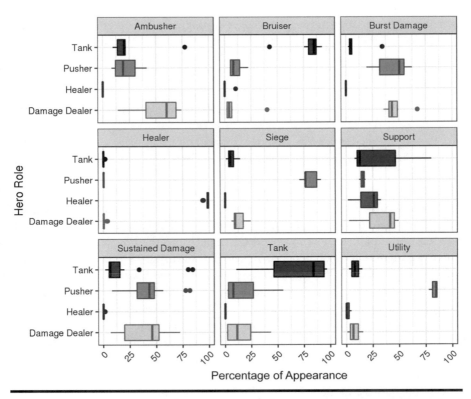

Figure 4.6 Comparison of the percentage of appearance of heroes in each of the four identified roles broken down by the static roles defined by the fan site HOTSLogs.

to be Damage Dealer, and Utility = Pusher), while some of the others seem to be split amongst our Damage Dealer and Pushers (their Burst Damage and Sustained Damage classes are all combinations of our Pushers and Damage Dealers), and the Support tends to be split across all four of our categories (mainly between Tank and Damage Dealers).

4.5 Conclusions

This study contributes to the emerging field of esports analytics by outlining replicable methods for analyzing character roles and team compositions using a data-driven approach. Our approach to data collection can provide insights for collecting similar data through APIs of other games. The statistical and machine learning algorithms used in this study are common enough that they can be implemented in many other statistical software packages or programming languages and provide a clear process for analyzing data such as these. Generally speaking, our approach is to:

1. Collect and extract information from replay files,
2. Apply cluster analysis and random forests to endgame statistics on each map to identify hero roles, and
3. Analyze roles to achieve a better understanding of team compositions, the flexibility of individual heroes, and how these roles connect to roles developed by others.

More specifically, we collected *HotS* replay files from a crowdsourced repository called HotsApi. Because replay files are not available for free at Amazon Web Services, we explained how to download them using the boto3 Python module. Then, we analyzed about 350,000 replay files by using heroprotocol to extract information about over 1.7 million players and their endgame statistics.

Our analysis provides a few data-driven insights into *HotS* based on these endgame performance statistics. To identify the hero roles, we used cluster analysis on a random sample of 25,000 participants (using all 5 members from 5,000 randomly sampled winning teams) for each map. With a few exceptions, each map showed a clear tendency toward four distinct clusters (three maps indicated that three clusters would also be reasonable). Given the similarity across maps, we identified four hero roles: Damage Dealers, Healers, Pushers, and Tanks. We then used a random forest model to classify all 1.7 million participants into one of the four identified roles. Then, we compared our classifications for each hero to the static, predetermined labels provided by both Blizzard and the popular fan site HOTSLogs. We also calculated the percentage of the time that each hero was played in each role and assigned primary and secondary roles for each of the 74 heroes for which we had data. Our analysis reveals that heroes are capable of filling different roles depending on maps and team composition. Players can learn which hero roles are viable in each map and try to understand what their role can be for the team.

We also identified the most common winning and losing team compositions for each map, noticing that no single composition occurred in the majority of matches. There is a variety of compositions that are advantageous or disadvantageous depending on individual maps, although the most common compositions—winning and losing— do consist of at least one Tank and exactly one Healer. We speculate that the diversity of talents for heroes, unique characteristics of maps, and different viable strategies render the variety we observe in our analysis possible. Players can keep an open mind during the draft to see how their hero choice can influence the synergy of their team as well as the enemy team to formulate the optimum strategy to win the game.

Our analysis relied on endgame statistics only, but future studies may use additional information such as players' ranks, draft, talent choices, positions, and interaction throughout matches to identify strategies. In particular, talents enhance a hero's abilities or add new abilities in more ways than just offensive and defensive hero statistics. Analyzing how the selection of talents for a hero impacts their role on a team may help make better-informed decisions when forming teams. Additionally, player movements and actions can help us enhance *HotS* hero role classification. However, in order to retrieve more information based on movements and events, we would need to build a tool that can playback replay files without relying on the game client.

While many popular fan sites focus on filtering data based solely on static choices (e.g., heroes and maps), machine learning and data science methods can dynamically identify similarities amongst heroes and maps. Our approach provides a starting point for gaining a deeper understanding of the game. That being said, due to its numerous hero choices and maps, the complexity of *HotS* provides a rich set of data for further analysis and exploration.

Appendix

4A.1 Additional Figures

Figure 4A.1 shows the clustered heatmaps for the remaining 10 maps not displayed in Figure 4.1.

4A.2 Remarks about Implementing Machine Learning Algorithms in R

There are numerous packages and functions available in R (or other software) to implement the machine learning algorithms that were used in this analysis. In particular, this study made use of the following:

■ Hierarchical clustering was performed using the `hcluster` function of the amap package (Lucas, 2014).
■ Heatmaps with dendrograms were generated using the gplots package (Warnes et al., 2016).
■ Random forests were implemented through the randomForest (Liaw and Winener, 2002) package and parallelized using the foreach (Revolution Analytics and Weston, 2015) and doMC (Revolution Analytics and Weston, 2017) packages.

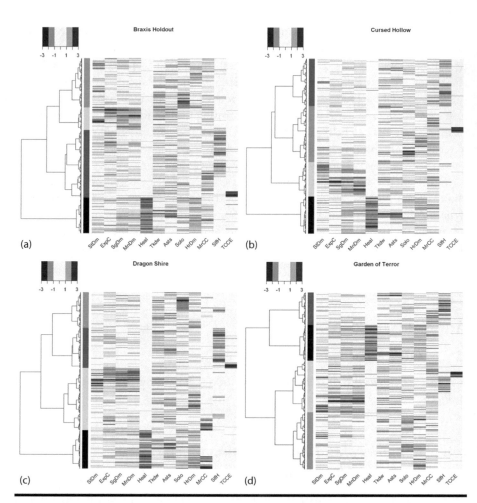

Figure 4A.1 (See color insert.) Clustered heatmaps of 25,000 participants from winning teams on the (a) Braxis Holdout, (b) Cursed Hollow, (c) Dragon Shire, and (d) Garden of Terror maps (see Table 4.1 on pp. 57–58 for an explanation of the abbreviations). The colored sidebars indicate similarly structured clusters across maps. **(Continued)**

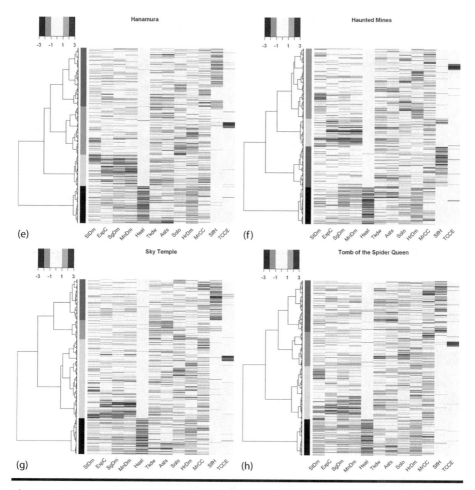

Figure 4A.1 (See color insert.) (Continued) Clustered heatmaps of 25,000 participants from winning teams on the (e) Hanamura, (f) Haunted Mines, (g) Sky Temple, and (h) Tomb of the Spider Queen maps (see Table 4.1 on pp. 57–58 for an explanation of the abbreviations). The colored sidebars indicate similarly structured clusters across maps. *(Continued)*

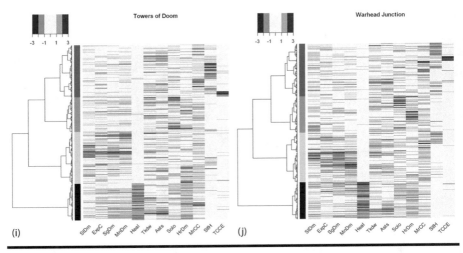

Figure 4A.1 (See color insert.) (Continued) Clustered heatmaps of 25,000 participants from winning teams on the (i) Towers of Doom and (j) Warhead Junction maps (see Table 4.1 on pp. 57–58 for an explanation of the abbreviations). The colored sidebars indicate similarly structured clusters across maps.

References

Banfield, J. D., & Raftery, A. E. (1993). Model-based Gaussian and non-Gaussian clustering. *Biometrics*, 49(3), 803–821.

Blizzard Entertainment. (2015). *Heroes of the Storm* [PC game]. Irvine, CA: Blizzard Entertainment.

Breiman, L. (2001). Random forests. *Machine Learning*, 45(1), 5–32.

Cavadenti, O., Codocedo, V., Boulicaut, J. F., & Kaytoue, M. (2016). What did I do wrong in my MOBA Game? Mining patterns discriminating deviant behaviours. In *2016 IEEE International Conference on Data Science and Advanced Analytics* (pp. 662–671). IEEE.

Cleghern, Z., Lahiri, S., Özaltin, O., & Roberts, D. L. (2017). Predicting future states in DotA 2 using value-split models of time series attribute data. In *Proceedings of the International Conference on the Foundations of Digital Games* (pp. 5:1–5:10). ACM.

Donaldson, S. (2015). Mechanics and metagame. *Games and Culture*, 12(5), 426–444.

Dunn, J. (2017). *Competitive video gaming will be a $1.5 billion industry by 2020, researchers say*. Retrieved from http://www.businessinsider.com/esports-popularity-revenue-forecast-chart-2017-3

Ester, M., Kriegel, H. P., Sander, J., & Xu, X. (1996). A density-based algorithm for discovering clusters in large spatial databases with noise. In *Proceedings of the 2nd International Conference on Knowledge Discovery and Data Mining* (pp. 226–231).

FIFA. (2015). *2014 FIFA World Cup™ reached 3.2 billion viewers, one billion watched final*. Retrieved from https://www.fifa.com/worldcup/news/2014-fifa-world-cuptm-reached-3-2-billion-viewers-one-billion-watched--2745519

James, G., Witten, D., Hastie, T., & Tibshirani, R. (2013). *An Introduction to Statistical Learning*. New York: Springer. pp. 316–321.

Johnson, S. C. (1967). Hierarchical clustering schemes. *Psychometrika* 32(2), 241–254.

Kim, J., Keegan, B. C., Park, S., & Oh, A. (2016). The proficiency-congruency dilemma: Virtual team design and performance in multiplayer online games. In *Proceedings of the 2016 CHI Conference on Human Factors in Computing Systems* (pp. 4351–4365). ACM.

Kwak, H., Blackburn, J., & Han, S. (2015). Exploring cyberbullying and other toxic behavior in team competition online games. In *Proceedings of the 33rd Annual ACM Conference on Human Factors in Computing Systems* (pp. 3739–3748). ACM.

Leavitt, A., Keegan, B. C., & Clark, J. (2016). Ping to win?: Non-verbal communication and team performance in competitive online multiplayer games. In *Proceedings of the 2016 CHI Conference on Human Factors in Computing Systems* (pp. 4337–4350). ACM.

Lee, C. S., & Ramler, I. (2015). Rise of the bots: Bot prevalence and its impact on match outcomes in League of Legends. In *Proceeding of the 2015 International Workshop on Network and Systems Support for Games* (pp. 1–6). IEEE.

Lee, C. S., & Ramler, I. (2017). Identifying and evaluating successful non-meta strategies in League of Legends. In *Proceedings of the International Conference on the Foundations of Digital Games* (pp. 1:1–1:6). ACM.

Liaw, A., & Wiener, M. (2002). Classification and regression by randomForest. *R News* 2(3), 18–22.

Losup, A., van de Bovenkamp, R., Shen, S., Jia, A. L., & Kuipers, F. (2014). Analyzing implicit social networks in multiplayer online games. *IEEE Internet Computing*, 18(3), 36–44.

Lucas, A. (2014). *amap: Another Multidimensional Analysis Package. R package version 0.8-14*. Retrieved from https://CRAN.R-project.org/package=amap

MacQueen, J. (1967). Some methods for classification and analysis of multivariate observations. In *Proceedings of the Fifth Berkeley Symposium on Mathematical Statistics and Probability* (pp. 281–297).

Maitra, R., & Ramler, I. (2010). A *k*-mean-directions algorithm for fast clustering of data on the sphere. *Journal of Computational and Graphical Statistics*, 19(2), 377–396.

Mora-Cantallops, M., & Sicilia, M. Á. (2018). MOBA games: A literature review. *Entertainment Computing*, 26, 128–138.

Ong, H., Deolalikar, S., & Peng, M. V. (2014). Player behavior and optimal team composition in online multiplayer games. Retrieved from https://arxiv.org/pdf/1503.02230.pdf

Otterson, J. (2018). *TV Ratings: Super Bowl LII slips 7% from 2017 to 103.4 million viewers*. Retrieved from https://variety.com/2018/tv/news/super-bowl-lii-ratings-1202687239/

Pal, N. R., Bezdek, J. C., & Hathaway, R. J. (1996). Sequential competitive learning and the Fuzzy c-means clustering algorithms. *Neural Networks*, 9(5), 787–796.

Revolution Analytics & Weston, S. (2015). *foreach: Provides Foreach Looping Construct for R. R package version 1.4.3*. Retrieved from https://CRAN.R-project.org/package=foreach

Revolution Analytics & Weston, S. (2017). *doMC: Foreach parallel adaptor for 'parallel'. R package version 1.3.5*. Retrieved from https://CRAN.R-project.org/package=doMC

Riot Games. (2017). *2017 events by the numbers*. Retrieved from https://www.lolesports.com/en_US/articles/2017-events-by-the-numbers

Schubert, M., Drachen, A., & Mahlmann, T. (2016). Esports analytics through encounter detection. In *Proceedings of the MIT Sloan Sports Analytics Conference*. MIT Sloan.

Shores, K. B., He, Y., Swanenburg, K. L., Kraut, R., & Riedl, J. (2014). The identification of deviance and its impact on retention in a multiplayer game. In *Proceedings of the 17th ACM conference on Computer Supported Cooperative work & Social Computing* (pp. 1356–1365). ACM.

Thorndike, R. L. (1953). Who belongs in the family? *Psychometrika*, 18(4), 267–276.

Valenta, N. (2017). *2018 Gameplay update: A more meaningful early game*. Retrieved from https://heroesofthestorm.com/en-us/blog/21295033/2018-gameplay-update-a-more-meaningful-early-game-12-5-2017/

Véron, M., Marin, O., & Monnet, S. (2015). Matchmaking in multi-player on-line games: Studying user traces to improve the user experience. In *Proceeding of the 2014 Network and Operating System Support on Digital Audio and Video Workshop* (pp. 7:7–7:12). ACM.

Ward Jr, J. H. (1963). Hierarchical grouping to optimize an objective function. *Journal of the American Statistical Association*, 58(301), 236–244.

Warnes, G. R., Bolker, B., Bonebakker, L., Gentleman, R., Liaw, W. H. A., Lumley, T., ... & Venables, B. (2016). *gplots: Various R programming tools for plotting data. R package version 3.0.1*. Retrieved from https://CRAN.R-project.org/package=gplots

ZAM Network LLC. (2018). *HOTSLogs*. Retrieved from: https://www.hotslogs.com/

Icon Source

listing.png:

Icon made by Kiranshastry from www.flaticon.com is licensed by CC 3.0 BY
https://www.flaticon.com/free-icon/file_1316229

Chapter 5

Predicting Customer Lifetime Value in Free-to-Play Games

Paolo Burelli

Contents

5.1 Introduction

As game companies increasingly embrace a service-oriented business model, the need for predictive models of player behavior becomes more pressing. Multiple activities, such as user acquisition, live game operations, or game design, need to be supported with information about the choices made by the players and the choices they could make in the future. This is especially true in the context of free-to-play games, where the absence of a pay wall and the erratic nature of the players' playing and spending behavior makes predictions about the revenue and allocation of budget and resources extremely challenging. In this chapter, we present an overview of customer lifetime value (CLV) modeling across different fields. We will introduce the challenges specific to free-to-play games across different platforms and genres, and we will discuss the state-of-the-art solutions with practical examples and references to existing implementations.

Customer lifetime value refers broadly to the revenue that a company can attribute to one or more customers over the length of their relationship with the company (Pfeifer, Haskins, & Conroy, 2005). The process of predicting the lifetime value consists of producing one or more monetary values that correspond to the sum of all the different types of revenues that a specific customer, or a specific cohort, will generate in the future. The purposes of such a prediction are manifold. For example, having an early estimation of a customer's potential value allows more accurate budgeting for future investments. Moreover, monitoring the residual potential revenue from an established customer could permit preemptive actions in case of a decreased engagement.

Predicting CLV is a complex challenge, and to this date, there is no single established practice. Furthermore, due to its wide potential impact in different business aspects, the problem is being researched in different communities using a plethora of different techniques, varying from parametric statistical models to deep learning[1] (Gupta et al., 2006; Sifa, Runge, Bauckhage, & Klapper, 2018). One of the initial primary drivers of research in CLV was direct marketing (Berger & Nasr, 1998) with a focus on its use in marketing decision problems, such as acquisition or the acquisition/retention cost trade-off (Blattberg & Deighton, 1996). Research expanded progressively to other fields of marketing and customer relationship management, especially thanks to the pervasiveness of digital technology and the possibility to have more accurate tracking of the customer relationship (Jain & Singh, 2002).

The increased quality and quantity of customer data did not only enlarge the areas of application of CLV-related principles but also allowed it to progressively develop and improve models for CLV prediction. Initial analytical models were developed based on assumptions about constant and uniform characteristics of the user behavior (e.g., transaction frequency, margin of profit). Over time, models have evolved to take into account uncertainty and variations of user

---

[1] Deep learning techniques are covered as part of Chapter 6.

behavior (Schmittlein, Morrison, & Colombo, 1987) and to be able to draw information from a wide spectrum of variables (Sifa et al., 2015).

Models have traditionally been based on transactional data, meaning that the variables describing the user behavior are based on different characteristics of the customers' transactions with the company, for example, recency, frequency, and monetary value—also known as the RFM model of Schmittlein et al. (1987). However, with the advent of e-commerce and similar technologies, the available information regarding customer behavior became increasingly richer since it started to become possible to track not only the purchases but also which objects were observed, how often would the customer visit the store, and many other non-strictly transactional details.

One of the application areas with probably the richest amount of user data are video games. However, until recently, due to its distribution and revenue models, the need for CLV prediction was relatively minor. Traditionally, computer games distribution has relied on a premium pricing model in which a game is developed, released, and sold once for a certain price. Following this pricing scheme, the monetization of the customer happens before the player starts playing the game, and its post-purchase behavior does not affect the CLV directly (Baden-Fuller & Haefliger, 2013).

Two main aspects radically changed the relationship between the game developers and the players/customers: digital distribution platforms and the free-to-play business model. Digital distribution platforms, such as Steam[2] or the Apple App Store[3], along with game developers' own online services, allow tracking of user behavior beyond a single game, making it more meaningful and necessary to predict the CLV across multiple games, either being purchased at the same store or being linked to the same online account.

Free-to-play (or sometimes also called freemium) games follow a different revenue model than the traditional one. These games are freely available, at no cost, to the players and the revenue comes from in-game advertisement and the sale of in-game items. These two revenue streams, contrarily to the classic game revenue model, begin only after the players/customers have been acquired and vary dramatically between players. This kind of relationship between the company and the players resembles in part the relationship between a store and its customer. For example, monetary transactions happen at irregular intervals, the transaction value is not constant, and there is no explicit customer churn event.

However, in contrast to physical or online stores, the users are not only customers but also players, and the data available about their behavior includes a wide range of features that goes beyond transactions or goods browsing, such as player progression within the game or players' skill levels. Within the field of game analytics, the analysis of these features plays a major role in evaluating the quality and the

---

[2] https://store.steampowered.com (Accessed: December 2018)
[3] https://www.apple.com/lae/ios/app-store (Accessed: December 2018)

potential success of a game (Drachen, El-Nasr, & Canossa, 2013). Furthermore, the behavior has been linked with major business-related metrics such as retention (Periáñez, Saas, Guitart, & Magne, 2016) or CLV (Sifa et al., 2018).

This abundance of accurate and high-frequency data, covering different aspects of the customer experience make free-to-play games an ideal application area for research in user modeling and prediction of future customer behavior. In turn, the development of such models would have an immediate application in the industry, as they would allow a better optimization of important processes, such as user acquisition and customer relationship management (Alves, Lange, Lenz, & Riedmiller, 2014).

This, as well as the ever-expanding share of the game industry that leverages this business model, highlights CLV prediction as a key challenge in games data science and games research. For these reasons, in this chapter, we will make an attempt to give an overview of the research and applications of CLV modeling including an in-depth analysis of the works that have focused on the free-to-play field. In the next section, we will outline a number of foundational concepts that will serve as a basis for the rest of the chapter. In Section 5.3, we will describe different ways in which CLV can be used inside and outside of the game industry. In Section 5.4, we will give an overview of different models used to predict CLV with a more in-depth focus on models employed in the game industry. In Section 5.5, we will describe a number of software packages that can be used to perform CLV prediction, and finally in Section 5.6, we will outline a number of current and future directions within the field.

5.2 Definitions and Terminology

Pfeifer et al. (2005) point out a central problem present across the different research works on CLV: incoherent terminology. The reasons behind this problem are probably manifold, including the different research communities. In this section, we will, however, attempt to synthesize a number of concepts and terms that are common across the different fields involved and are foundational to the study of CLV prediction in games and beyond.

First of all, it is important to define what CLV is. Pfeifer et al. (2005) summarize it as: "the present value of the future cash flows attributed to the customer relationship" (p. 17). As the authors point out, this definition makes a couple of important assumptions: First, the value is associated to the "cash flow," which means it is not only limited to the inbound flow of revenue generated by a customer but also to the costs attributed to that customer. However, the costs considered in this definition are only the ones directly attributable to a given customer. Second, the term *value* expresses a valuation at the current point in time of some future revenues and costs. This implies some form of discount based on the time in which the future cash flows are predicted.

In their definition, Pfeifer et al. (2005) do not attempt to encompass all possible definitions of CLV within the literature. Instead, they propose one possible explicit definition of CLV that is terminologically correct and coherent. This means that other research works on predicting CLV do not necessarily adhere to the aforementioned definition. Berger and Nasr (1998), for instance, do not consider acquisition costs as part of the lifetime value calculation, considering instead CLV to be the "maximum profitable acquisition cost" as an acquisition cost higher than the CLV would yield no profit (Jain & Singh, 2002). Sifa et al. (2015), on the other hand, do not take into consideration the present value and use no factor to discount the future predicted revenue.

One further aspect of the above definition that is not shared by the different research works is the time frame considered for the calculation. Gupta et al. (2006), in their review, find that a number of researchers employ an arbitrary time horizon for the future prediction (e.g., Reinartz & Kumar, 2000), while others use an infinite horizon (e.g., Fader, Hardie, & Lee, 2005b). While it might appear that employing a fixed time horizon is just a way to simplify the modeling process, both approaches have their own merits. Using an infinite horizon avoids having to make any assumption about the maximum length of the customer relationship with the company. It therefore allows for a more accurate prediction of Pfeifer et al.'s definition of CLV. However, for budgeting or other purposes, it is often important to know the return on investment within a given period of time (e.g., 1 year), making a fixed horizon CLV prediction extremely useful.

Another consideration relative to the temporal aspect of the customer relationship that has to be taken into account when studying CLV prediction is whether the relationship is exclusive or it allows the customer to use other competitors' services. These two different types of relationships are often labeled as either "lost-for-good" or "always-a-share" (Dwyer, 1997). Identifying which type of relationship is being modeled for CLV prediction is extremely important, as it affects the temporal length of the relationship and the definition of "churn" (i.e., when a customer stops using the service).

This is especially true in free-to-play games where there is no visible churn event. In this context, the definition of the user state at any given moment (active or inactive) depends on an ad-hoc formula based on some synthesis of the players' actions (Runge, Gao, Garcin, & Faltings, 2014). Many CLV prediction models include or are built on top of a churn prediction model, and both the formula and the choice of CLV model will depend on whether it is possible for the customer to return after a period of inactivity (Pfeifer & Carraway, 2000) or whether his or her relationship with the company is considered finished (Glady, Baesens, & Croux, 2009).

Finally, it is important to specify that all of the works cited and described in this chapter do not consider the effects of competition with other services on the CLV. As pointed out by Gupta et al. (2006), this is the case for most current modeling approaches because of the lack of data about the competitors.

5.3 Applications of CLV Prediction

While marketing serves as the primary application area of CLV prediction, a number of other activities, such as customer relationship management or live game operations, are increasingly driven by data and different key performance indicators (KPIs) such as CLV. Schmittlein et al. (1987), in one of the earliest works on CLV estimation, motivate their research by stating that:

> the issue is important in at least three settings: monitoring the size and growth rate of a firm's ongoing customer base, evaluating a new product's success based on the pattern of trial and repeat purchases, and targeting a subgroup of customers for advertising and promotions. (p. 1)

They envision that, by knowing which customers are active and what purchases they make, a manager is able to perform more accurate budgeting, a better product evaluation, and target the customers more accurately with reengagement initiatives. Similar to Schmittlein et al. (1987), a number of other research works have tackled the above problems. Table 5.1 gives an overview of the main application areas in which CLV prediction has been employed.

Each application area includes a number of different activities (e.g., special offers or advertisement) united by a similar use of CLV prediction. In the case of budgeting and finance, CLV predictions are used to predict revenue and to plan budgets for the different activities within the company (Schmittlein et al., 1987; Donkers et al., 2003), to find the balance between acquisition and retention investments (Blattberg & Deighton, 1996), or to make a financial estimation of the company (Gupta & Lehmann, 2006). The second activity, product development, is mentioned only by Schmittlein et al. (1987). Nevertheless, CLV is an important KPI in the evaluation of the game quality in free-to-play games, and it can be very useful to drive the game design process, as described later in this section.

5.3.1 Customer Acquisition

Customer acquisition encompasses all activities aimed at getting new customers to start using the service or buying the products offered. As mentioned by Berger and Nasr (1998) and Berger et al. (2003), having an estimation of the CLV can help to more accurately decide on how much money to spend on a given promotional campaign and how much margin for profitability there could be in a new market segment. Dwyer (1997) further develops these concepts by identifying the ceiling of the customer acquisition spend. Having an early indication of whether the costs of acquisition are matched by the CLVs can help decide whether a certain promotional initiative should be continued or stopped (Alves et al., 2014; Sifa et al., 2015, 2018).

Table 5.1   Applications of CLV Prediction in Different Business Activities

Application Area	Article
Budgeting and finance	Schmittlein et al. (1987); Blattberg & Deighton (1996); Donkers, Verhoef, & de Jong (2003); Gupta & Lehmann (2006)
Product development	Schmittlein et al. (1987)
Customer acquisition	Dwyer (1997); Berger & Nasr (1998); Berger, Weinberg, & Hanna (2003); Alves et al. (2014); Sifa et al. (2015, 2018)
Customer retention/ Loyalty	Berger & Nasr (1998); Mulhern (1999); Reinartz & Kumar (2000); Lachowetz, McDonald, Sutton, & Clark (2001); Rosset, Neumann, Eick, Vatnik, & Idan (2002); Rosset, Neumann, Eick, & Vatnik (2003); Malthouse & Blattberg (2005); Shen & Chuang (2009); Cheng, Chiu, Cheng, & Wu (2012); Runge et al. (2014); Sifa et al. (2018)
Customer targeting/ Segmentation	Mulhern (1999); Reinartz & Kumar (2000); Verhoef & Donkers (2001); Venkatesan & Kumar (2004); Hwang, Jung, & Suh (2004); Haenlein, Kaplan, & Beeser (2007); Shen & Chuang (2009); Kumar (2010); Khajvand, Zolfaghar, Ashoori, & Alizadeh (2011)
Other	Aeron, Bhaskar, Sundararajan, Kumar, & Moorthy (2008)

5.3.2 Customer Retention

Customer retention and segmentation initiatives are often intertwined and not completely distinguishable. For the purpose of this chapter, we describe customer retention/loyalty activities as any activity explicitly aimed at prolonging the lifetime of a customer, while with customer targeting/segmentation we identify all activities aimed at identifying different homogeneous groups within the customer base that can be targeted with a custom user experience. Such a customer experience could be aimed at prolonging the customer lifetime. However, for the purpose of this categorization, we define this as a secondary objective.

Lachowetz et al. (2001), in their study on the impact of season ticket holders on the NBA franchise's revenue, argue that a customer should not be evaluated solely on the revenue that he or she generates within a season. At the time of their estimation, an average season ticket holder had a lifetime value of more than 80,000 US dollars. The authors therefore advice the entertainment industry to acknowledge the importance of using CLV and to develop long-term retention strategies for their customers.

Berger and Nasr (1998) discuss how knowing the CLV can help determining the effects of adopting different marketing strategies for retention and acquisition and how to balance the spending between the two activities. The authors further point out that any acquisition strategy might also impact the customers' retention. Therefore, the two activities should not be viewed independently, and both their budgets must be aligned with the predicted CLV. Mulhern (1999) further extends Berger and Nasr's idea about the strategic use of CLV prediction by seeing it as a primary indicator for driving resource allocation in the marketing mix.

Rosset et al. (2002, 2003) extend the idea of using CLV prediction to drive retention activities and expand it by investigating how to estimate the impact of retention efforts on the CLV. They demonstrate the application of their approach in the context of a retention campaign for a group of potential churners. They show how, by having a model able to predict CLV in different configurations of the service, it is possible to compare the current estimated lifetime value of a group of potential churners with different projected lifetime values given a number of different incentives to improve the cohort's retention. This, in turn, allows for a more informed decision on the correct initiative to be taken.

The predictions used for these decisions, as any other prediction of future events, have some degree of uncertainty in the form of prediction error or bias. Taking this uncertainty into account can also be important in decision-making itself. Malthouse and Blattberg (2005) study the impact of uncertainty in the management of customer relationships, helping to understand not only whether engaging with a retention activity can be profitable but also how often it could be.

5.3.3 Customer Segmentation

Most of the research works presented in this section make the assumption that a higher retention (i.e., a longer lifetime for the customers) will have a positive impact on the company's revenue in the form of an increased CLV. However, while this is generally true, Reinartz and Kumar (2000) found that this assumption does not always hold, and different customer segments have different spending patterns, which means that, in a number of cases, prolonging the customer's lifetime would not yield any more revenue. For this reason, they suggest that the company should not necessarily pursue a long-term customer relationship, but it should instead customize the relationship based on predictions of future CLV and retention.

Segmenting the target audience and personalizing marketing activities is an established practice (Dickson & Ginter, 1987). For a long time, the predominant guiding factors used to define the segments and the most appropriate actions have been based on demographics, questionnaires, and interviews (Malhotra, 2007). However, the advent of large-scale data collection and analytics—in many industries—has dramatically changed many of the common practices in marketing research, allowing practitioners to access more detailed information from wider audiences at lowers costs.

Mulhern (1999), for example, proposes CLV as a possible segmentation criterion besides usage volume and brand loyalty. He suggests that one simple segmentation could divide the users in customers worth keeping, as their CLV is profitable, and customers who are not worth the retention cost. Verhoef and Donkers (2001) propose a similar segmentation to design personalized insurance offers.

Venkatesan and Kumar (2004) pose the question whether using predicted CLV for segmentation can yield better results than more established KPIs, such as previous-period customer revenue or past customer value. To compare the effectiveness of the different metrics, they first rank the customers based on each metric and then segment the customers based on the ranking. The results show that segmentation based on CLV is superior to the other segmentation approaches.

Similar strategies to the ones mentioned so far have been applied to a number of different industries, such as telecommunications (Hwang et al., 2004), banking (Haenlein et al., 2007), retailing (Shen & Chuang, 2009; Kumar, 2010), or beauty (Khajvand et al., 2011). In the last few years, a similar trend has emerged in the gaming industry, and especially in the mobile game and free-to-play industry, all the aforementioned marketing practices are established and widely undertaken (Shankar & Balasubramanian, 2009).

5.3.4 Free-to-Play Games

Free-to-play video games are games that can be played without an upfront payment and potentially completely free of charge. Players can, however, purchase some virtual goods within the game and pay to enable certain features. While such games were originally mostly distributed through online social media platforms, the business is currently vastly diffused and spread over many different platforms, such as mobile phones, home consoles, and personal computers (Alha, Koskinen, Paavilainen, Hamari, & Kinnunen, 2014).

Figure 5.1 shows an example of a mobile free-to-play game. As it is possible to see on the leftmost screenshot, the game is freely available on the phone's store; however, the store specifies that the game contains the possibility to perform in-app purchases. The rightmost image shows the in-game store that allows the customer to purchase different packs of in-game currency, which can be used throughout the game to unlock different features. Using an intermediary currency, while a very common practice, is not a defining characteristic of free-to-play games, and some games allow customers to enable in-game features directly using a real currency.

The second main source of revenue in free-to-play games constitutes advertisement. A large portion of free-to-play games display ads to the players in different formats (e.g., videos or interstitials). These ads are provided by external services that act as mediators between the advertiser and the publisher. The game (i.e., the publisher) receives advertisements from the ad provider through an application programming interface (API) and shows them to the player. In return, the ad provider will pay the game developer depending on the number of ads being displayed,

Figure 5.1   Three screenshots from the iOS version of *Bee Brilliant Blast* (From Tactile Games, *Bee Brilliant Blast* [Mobile game], Tactile Games, Copenhagen, Denmark, 2018) depicting, from left to right, the phone's store interface, a typical puzzle level, and the in-game store interface in which the customer can purchase different amounts of in-game currency.

the number of times the ads are clicked, or the number of times the product being advertised is being purchased.

Both aforementioned revenue streams—in-app purchases and advertisements—have a non-contractual nature, as the player can freely choose if and when to make a purchase or click on an advertisement campaign. Furthermore, a conversion rate (i.e., the percentage of players making an in-app purchase) well below 10% is considered normal in the game industry (Nieborg, 2015), making it especially challenging to predict the CLV. At the same time, activities such as customer acquisition and retention rely on accurate CLV predictions for accurate targeting and budgeting.

As of November 2018, there are around 816,000 games available on the Apple App Store[4] only. Given the extremely high number of games competing for the same users, targeting the right customers and accurately measuring their potential impact on the company's revenue is thus particularly important for customer acquisition in the free-to-play games market. A significant part of the customer acquisition efforts in the industry is executed through performance marketing campaigns. In these campaigns, the advertiser competes with other advertisers to show ads to potential new customers, often through some form of auctioning system. Customer lifetime value predictions

---

[4] https://www.pocketgamer.biz/metrics/app-store/categories/ (Accessed: December 2018)

can be used as a benchmark to evaluate the profit margin of these campaigns, as both the potential revenue coming from the new customers and their cost of acquisition vary greatly depending on the segmentation chosen for the campaign, the market context, and the quality of the advertised creative content (Sifa et al., 2018). Even beyond performance marketing, an accurate CLV prediction is very important to be able to budget expensive and higher-risk marketing efforts such as television advertisement.

Moreover, as briefly mentioned above, the free-to-play games market is characterized by very low retention rates—for example, the best Android games have a day 30 retention rate below 5% (Koetsier, 2017)—making any effort to improve such low numbers a priority for most companies. Within this context, CLV prediction can be used, as previously described, to target different segments of users with special offers. However, it is also possible to personalize the game experience at large by adapting, for instance, the flow of the game or by providing custom events. Harrison and Roberts (2014) show an example of such adaptation aimed at improving retention in a digital version of Scrabble.

Given the importance of CLV prediction in the free-to-play and other industries, a number of algorithms have been developed over time. In the next two sections, we will discuss the most significant ones and describe a number of software packages that can be used for CLV prediction.

5.4 Models

Berger and Nasr (1998) were the first researchers that attempted a categorization of CLV prediction models. In this early review of the field, all methods mentioned are aimed at calculating an average CLV for the entirety of the company's customer base or a given cohort. In a latter review, Kumar, Ramani, and Bohling (2004) grouped these approaches under the label "average CLV approach," while Jain and Singh (2002) used the term "basic structural model." In this chapter, we adopt the definition used by Kumar et al. (2004), and we include a number of other practices commonly used in the free-to-play industry that approach CLV prediction in a similar fashion.

The methods for CLV prediction discussed in this chapter can be divided into two further categories: customer history models and machine learning models. The first category contains all methods that attempt to predict either a single customer's or a cohort's lifetime value based on some mathematical projection of the past behavior of the given customer or cohort. The second category includes all techniques that make use of some learning algorithm to build a computational model of the customer behavior, which is then used to make predictions.

5.4.1 Average Models

The aim of the models discussed in this section is to give an estimation of the future discounted cash flow for a group of customers or for the whole user base.

The common aspect of these models is that they make a number of assumptions: they assume a constant (or otherwise known) margin of profit over time, they do not consider the stochastic nature of the purchase behavior of the customers, and they assume that the customer behavior is uniform across the estimated cohort.

The most basic model proposed by Berger and Nasr (1998) assumes that the customer retention rate and the costs of retention are constant over time, and both costs and revenues happen periodically at a constant rate. Within these conditions, the formula for CLV is given by

$$CLV = GC * \sum_{i=0}^{n} \frac{r^i}{(1+d)^i} - M * \sum_{i=0}^{n} \frac{r^{i-1}}{(1+d)^{i-0.5}} \tag{5.1}$$

where GC is the customer's expected gross contribution margin per period, M are the promotion costs per customer per period, n is the prediction horizon expressed in number of periods, r is the retention between one period and the next, and d is the discount rate. Further iterations of this model presented by Berger and Nasr (1998), by Jain and Singh (2002), and by Kumar et al. (2004) allow more sophisticated ways to express non-constant retention rates and margins of profit and to include acquisition costs in the calculation.

In an article about the relationship between the length of service and CLV, Rosset et al. (2003) formulate an extended average model that employs a Kaplan–Meier estimator[5] (Kaplan & Meier, 1958) to calculate the duration of the relationship between the company and the average customer. A similar approach is currently among the basic models used in the free-to-play industry for CLV prediction (Seufert, 2013). After selecting a specific function to express the retention curve of a given cohort, the function is fit on the training data (i.e., past user data used as a reference) and the resulting CLV is calculated as

$$CLV = \sum_{i=0}^{n} ARPDAU * ret(i) \tag{5.2}$$

where ARPDAU stands for average revenue per daily active user, and $ret(i)$ is the value of the chosen retention function on the ith day. This method for CLV prediction, while quite simplistic and not necessarily extremely accurate, has the advantage of being easily readable and being based on established business KPIs such as ARPDAU and retention.

Another example of a simplistic but widely adopted model is described by Runge (2014): Instead of basing the projected revenue on retention and ARPDAU, the method fits a function to approximate the average monetization curve, which

---

[5] The Kaplan–Meier estimator is a nonparametric statistical method commonly used to estimate the survival function of a given cohort.

is then used to project the CLV for a player based the amount of money the player spent on the present day. If we consider $rev(n)$ as the revenue produced by a customer until the nth day of the customer relationship and $mon(n)$ as the average fraction of the revenue that is produced by day n, the formula for CLV prediction is

$$\text{CLV} = \frac{rev(n)}{mon(n)}. \tag{5.3}$$

The major advantage of this model is its simplicity and, similarly to the retention-based model, its readability. However, with such a model, it is not possible to predict the CLV for customers who have not yet produced any revenue; that is, the projection would always result in zero. Moreover, in a context such as free-to-play games, in which the number of paying users is very small, the variability of the behavior between different paying users has a large impact on the prediction. Such variability is, however, completely disregarded by the model.

5.4.2 Customer History Models

The aforementioned methods based on retention and monetization curves are partly based on historical customer data as, in both methods, a function representing the average retention or monetization behavior is fit on some past customer data and then used for prediction. These methods, however, do not allow the use of any particular user's track record to personalize the prediction, hence, the average nature of the methods.

Based on the customer categorization by Jackson (1985) that divides customers into two types—"always-a-share" and "lost-for-good"—Dwyer (1997) argues that an average retention model is not sufficient to model CLV for customers belonging to the "always-a-share" category. For these types of customers, he proposed a migration model based on the customers' recency of purchases.

"Always-a-share" customers differ from "lost-for-good" customers in that the latter have a long-term commitment with the company, and switching to a competitor is costly; therefore, when such a switch happens, it is unlikely that the customer will return. In contrast, "always-a-share" customers can have simultaneous relationships with multiple companies competing for the same product or service. Typical examples of "lost-for-good" customers are bank customers or tenants in a rental property. Whether free-to-play game players can be considered belonging to the first or second category is an open question, as there is no monetary barrier that stops a player from switching to another game. However, to a certain extent, the more time a player invests in a game, the less likely the player will stop playing that game.[6]

---

[6] This is to a certain extent related to the sunk cost fallacy discussed in Chapter 7.

In his customer migration model, Dwyer (1997) uses purchase recency to estimate the customer's probability of performing a purchase in the next period and the potential value of such a purchase. In the training phase—based on past data from all customers—the method builds a model of purchase probabilities and values that depend on the length of the period of inactivity in the form of a table containing a probability for a number of recency ranges. This table is used to predict, depending on each customer's past purchase behavior data, his or her purchases in the next time unit. Dwyer's model allows leveraging of customers' past behavior for a personalized CLV prediction and considers the probabilistic nature of the customers purchase behaviors.

5.4.2.1 Recency, Frequency, and Monetary Value

The main limitation of Dwyer's method is that the probability of a purchase in a given period is based only on the recency of the last purchase, which is not necessarily true for all businesses. Especially in free-to-play games, different types of purchases will differently affect the future purchases. For example, a player purchasing a large package of virtual currency recently might be less likely to make another purchase in the near future, as it will take the player some time to use up all the obtained currency within the game before needing more of it.

The concept of recency used by Dwyer is an established metric in direct marketing and has alongside purchase frequency and average purchase monetary value—commonly known together as RFM—long been used in the field to predict customer behavior (Gupta et al., 2006). Hughes (2000) describes a method for customer quality estimation based on these three variables: the customer base of the company is sorted along these three variables each split into five quantiles, creating therefore $5 * 5 * 5$ groups. These groups are then used to score the different customers and target them with specific offers.

Inspired by Hughes's work, Shih and Liu (2003) proposed a method based on RFM and CLV clustering to rank the customers according to their profitability. As a first step, the method relies on expert evaluations to identify the relative importance of the recency, frequency, and monetary variables using analytical hierarchical processing. The customers are than clustered based on the RFM space, and the resulting clusters are ranked through a simple weighted sum of the three normalized variables.

The aforementioned methods are not designed to produce a numerical predictor of CLV but only to score the customers according to their potential profitability. Furthermore, these methods disregard the fact that customers' past behaviors are, many times, the result of past company activities. To overcome some of the aforementioned limitations, Fader, Hardie, & Lee (2005a) describe a model for CLV prediction that uses RFM as input variables based on the Pareto/NBD framework (Schmittlein et al., 1987), which will be discussed next.

5.4.2.2 *Pareto/NBD*

The Pareto/NBD model (Schmittlein et al., 1987) aims at predicting individual customer's purchase behavior based on their past purchase patterns. More specifically, for each customer, based on the recency (t) and frequency (X) of the purchases as well as the length of the relationship between the customer and the company (T), the model estimates the expected future number of purchases. The model is based on 5 assumptions:

1. While active, a customer makes purchases following a Poisson process with rate λ,
2. The purchase rate λ differs between customers and is distributed according to a gamma distribution across the customer base,
3. The duration of the active period of the customer is exponentially distributed with a death rate μ,
4. The death rate μ differs between customers and is distributed according to a gamma distribution across the customer base, and
5. The death rate and the purchase rates are independent.

Based on these assumptions, the authors find that the customers "deaths" for a sample follow a Pareto distribution of the second kind (Johnson & Kotz, 1970), while the number of purchases made by an active customer follows a negative binomial distribution (Ehrenberg, 1972)—hence the name Pareto/NBD.

Schmittlein et al. (1987) suggest two approaches to estimate the parameters of these distributions based on customers' past behaviors: maximum likelihood and fitting observed moments. In case a model without prior data is needed, Schmittlein et al. (1987) also discuss the possibility of handpicking the parameters based on management judgments. Once the parameters have been identified, each customer's future number of purchases is predicted using the two aforementioned distributions and the customer's X, t, and T.

One of the main issues with the Pareto/NBD is its computational complexity (Fader et al., 2005b), as the estimation requires multiple evaluations of the Gauss hypergeometric function. This problem is mitigated by the modified BG/NBD model proposed by Fader et al. (2005b), which models the customer activity using a beta-geometric model that is easier to implement efficiently.

Both aforementioned models are able to predict the future number of purchases for a given customer and they can, for instance, be used to count expected active users at a given point in time. However, these methods do not model the value of each purchase; therefore, they cannot directly predict the CLV.

Reinartz and Kumar (2000, 2003), in their studies on profitable lifetime duration, employ Schmittlein et al.'s (1987) model to calculate the number of time periods in which a customer will perform a purchase. The authors transform the continuous probability that a customer is active into a dichotomous measure of whether the customer is active or inactive at a given point in time. Given a probability threshold, it is possible to identify a customer's future date of churn, which, combined with the first date of the customer relationship, gives an expected customer relationship duration. This duration, expressed as a number of periods n, is used to calculate the customer's lifetime value using the formula defined by Berger and Nasr (1998) and described in Equation 5.1.

Schmittlein and Peterson (1994) propose an extension of the original Pareto/NBD model in which the future monetary value of each transaction is sampled from a normal distribution centered around the mean monetary value of a cohort. However, Fader et al. (2005a) observe that—in the data they analyzed—there are large differences between mean, mode, and median, indicating that the distribution of the monetary values is highly skewed. Therefore, the authors propose to model the average transaction value using an adapted version of the gamma-gamma model proposed by Colombo and Jiang (1999).

One of the main strengths and, at the same, one of the main limitations of the Pareto/NBD or BG/NBD models, is that they rely on a small number of purely transactional data. This is a strength in that it makes the model general enough to be easily applied in different contexts. At the same time, the resulting model will always risk to be suboptimal, as it disregards potentially relevant information. Singh, Borle, and Jain (2009) address this limitation and propose an estimation framework that can flexibly incorporate multiple statistical distributions and consider a number of covariates, such as age or gender.

Glady et al. (2009) address another important limitation of the aforementioned models: they all assume independence between the frequency of transactions and the profit per transaction. The authors of the study demonstrate that such an assumption does not hold in multiple real-world datasets and propose a modified Pareto/Dependent model that performs better than Pareto/NBD in such circumstances.

5.4.3 Markov Chain Models

Pfeifer and Carraway (2000) proposed an alternative approach to CLV prediction, suggesting to model the customer relationship as a Markov chain model (MCM) in which the different states of the model represent different conditions of the relationship between the customer and the company in terms of transactions and customer activity. The transition probabilities between states represent the probability of a customer to move from one condition to the other one, for example, for a customer to make a purchase or to churn.

Figure 5.2 shows an example of a simple Markov chain model representing the possible states of the relationship between a customer and the company and the valid transitions between the states. In the depicted case, the states are based on the recency of the last purchase (e.g., r1 corresponds to recency equal to one), and there are only five valid stages before churn. However, as in the examples reported by

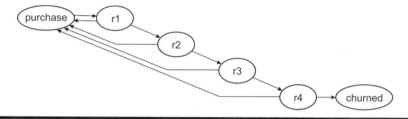

Figure 5.2 **Simple customer relationship Markov chain model. States r1 to r4 represent different values of recency from 1 to 4.**

Pfeifer and Carraway (2000), the states in a real-world scenario are based on a multitude of factors, and there are many more valid transitions, each with their own probability. While Pfeifer and Carraway (2000) show how it is possible to calculate CLV using a MCM representation of the customer relationship with a given set of states and transaction probabilities, Etzion, Fisher, and Wasserkrug (2004) focus on the process of learning the states and the transitions from past customer data. The process requires identification of the variables determining the states of the model, to define their ranges, and to discretize them.

At this point, the transition probabilities between the states can be calculated via the following three steps:

1. Initialize a transition matrix—that is, a square matrix that contains the probability of transitioning between one state and another one—with zeros in all cells;
2. For each customer performing a transition between a state *i* and a state *j*, the matrix cell identified by *ij* is incremented; and
3. At the end of the processing, each line of the matrix is normalized to the [0,1] range using a min-max normalization.

The resulting matrix can be used, as suggested by Pfeifer and Carraway (2000), to calculate CLV for a customer in any given state.

Ching, Ng, Wong, and Altman (2004) employ the same approach to build multiple transition matrices that describe the customer behaviors in different market conditions—for instance, with or without a promotion—finding that the transition matrices differ and so do the CLV and the customer retention. The authors further showcase how to use stochastic dynamic programming to estimate the optimal promotion strategy that optimizes CLV given the previously found transition matrices and a set of constraints on the possessive budget.

5.4.4 Supervised Learning Models

The general principle at the core of all supervised learning algorithms is to learn a function between some example input and output data, for instance, between past customer behavior and their recorded lifetime value. This example data is usually called training data, and the function resulting from this training phase—the model—is used to predict the target variable (e.g., CLV) on newly collected data. This procedure is not dissimilar to some of the MCM-based approaches described previously (Etzion et al., 2004). However, the models presented in this section differ from MCM models in that they trade explanatory power for the possibility of capturing more complex behaviors using some form of computational black-box model.

This means that the resulting models are less useful for informing the business about specific customers' preferences, but they can potentially be more accurate and be deployed, for instance, for marketing automation. It is important to note that this is not a hard distinction, and many models described in this and the previous sections include a mix of explanatory and black-box models.

An example of a model incorporating different learning algorithms is the one proposed by Haenlein et al. (2007). The authors describe an approach to CLV prediction that uses a combination of classification and regression tree (CART) analysis (Breiman, 2017) and MCM. First, the customers are divided into age groups. Second, a regression tree model is built for each age group to predict the profit for a customer within that group. Afterward, the transition probabilities between the groups are modeled as a Markov chain so that the model is able to follow the transitions of the customers throughout their lifetime. The resulting lifetime value is calculated as a discounted sum of each of the CLVs predicted in the possible customer states weighted by the transition probabilities.

Cheng et al. (2012) approached CLV prediction in a similar way, but they extended the model by building a different Markov chain for each period of the customer relationship. Each chain includes a number of states depending on the activity level of the customers in that specific period. The total CLV for a customer is calculated by summing the predicted CLVs over the different states and periods weighted by the transition probabilities and the survival probability of each period. An artificial neural network is then used to predict the profit contribution of a customer at a given state, while the survival probability in each period is calculated using a logistic regression model.

Within the context of free-to-play games, supervised learning methods have been employed in a number of studies. Compared to the previously mentioned approaches, supervised learning offers two key advantages that makes it particularly interesting for the free-to-play games industry: the ability to leverage a wide variety of data about the customer behavior and the ability to make predictions about CLV for players who are not yet customers, that is, who have not yet made a single purchase.

The first aspect is important, as in the free-to-play games industry, customers are also players and the data describing their gaming behavior is much richer and at a much higher frequency compared to their purchase behavior data. Furthermore, there are a number of studies that show how past in-game behavior is a predictor of future in-game behavior (Mahlmann, Drachen, Togelius, Canossa, & Yannakakis, 2010), of player preferences (Burelli & Yannakakis, 2015), and of the probability of making a purchase within the game (Hanner & Zarnekow, 2015).

The second aspect is partially related to the first one. Since the predictions can also be based on non-purchase-related data, it is potentially possible to perform predictions also for players who have not yet made a purchase and who may never make one. As described in Section 5.3.4, the majority of free-to-play players do not make any in-game purchase and generate little to no revenue. In such a context, it is important that a model that predicts CLV is able to discern which customers will be making a purchase before the first one is actually made.

In one of the first studies on the application of supervised learning for CLV prediction in free-to-play games, Alves et al. (2014) present a performance comparison of linear and non-linear models for the prediction of CLV. The dataset used for the study contains in-game events from the first 7 days of gameplay from about 38 million players with the input variables including data about player spending, gameplay, game progression, social interactions, success metrics, and game settings preferences. The target variable is the amount of revenue generated by each player after 180 days. The results of the study show that an ensemble of two artificial neural networks using the absolute-differences technique outperformed the other methods in terms of mean square error in a 10-fold cross-validated comparison.

A related study is presented by Sifa et al. (2015) in their article on purchase behavior prediction in mobile free-to-play games. Similar to Alves et al. (2014), the authors present a comparative study of multiple supervised learning algorithms. However, the objective of the prediction is slightly different, as the authors argue that CLV prediction is a combination of three prediction tasks: predicting whether players will ever make a purchase, predicting the number of purchases, and predicting the value of each purchase. The results of the study show that, for the classification task, the models having the best performance are tree-based models—such as random forest and decision tree classifiers[7]—and that it is extremely valuable to resample the dataset, as players performing purchases are extremely underrepresented. For this purpose, the authors employ the SMOTE-NC (Chawla, Bowyer, Hall, & Kegelmeyer, 2002) method to oversample the "converted" user's data points.

In a latter article, Sifa et al. (2018) reported on a study that attempted to predict CLV in one single step, more in line with the approach presented by Alves et al. (2014). The study evaluated the performance of a deep neural network in predicting day 360 cumulative undiscounted revenue per player, and it compared the results against a number of algorithms, such as random forest and linear regression. The results of the comparison show that the deep neural network outperforms the other regression algorithms in terms of normalized root mean square error.

Furthermore, the authors demonstrate how to adapt SMOTE-NC to resample the dataset and to reduce the imbalance between customers who made a purchase

---

[7] Machine learning methods based on decision trees are briefly reviewed in Chapter 6.

and customers who did not. This process requires a number of adjustments to the standard implementation of SMOTE-NC, as the original algorithm is designed for classification problems, while a direct prediction of CLV is a regression problem.

5.5 Software Packages

In Section 5.4, we gave an overview of the current state-of-the art in CLV prediction, mostly from an academic perspective, listing and explaining a number of scientific articles describing the main approaches to solve the prediction problem. However, most of the algorithms presented so far have been implemented, to different degrees, in software packages that can be applied to easily perform CLV predictions on new datasets. In this article, we identify three main packages that can either be used directly to predict CLV or that can be used to construct a model for CLV prediction. The software packages are Lifetimes (Davidson-Pilon, 2018) and BTYD (Dziurzynski, Wadsworth, & McCarthy, 2014) that implement some of the algorithms presented in Section 5.4.2, and scikit-learn (Mueller, 2018), a popular machine learning package for the Python programming language that can be used to implement the models presented in Section 5.4.4. While alternative packages such as Keras (Chollet, 2018) or XGBoost (Cho, 2018) can also be used to develop supervised learning models, most of them are compatible with scikit-learn, for which reason this package was chosen for this chapter. To build and operate with MCMs, there are a large number of different alternatives for both the Python and the R language, for example, the DTMC pack (Spedicato, 2017) and PyMC3 (Salvatier, Wiecki, & Fonnesbeck, 2016). However, these packages are designed to offer functionalities that go far beyond the code needed to implement the models presented in Section 5.4.3, which can be easily implemented using standard algebra functionalities. For this reason, MCM packages are not covered in this section.

5.5.1 Lifetimes/BTYD

The Lifetimes (Davidson-Pilon, 2018) and BTYD (Dziurzynski et al., 2014) packages are both software implementations of the Pareto/NBD, BG/NBD, and gamma-gamma models. They allow learning of the parameters of the various distributions from past purchases data and predicting future purchase numbers and the purchase values for new customers. In this section, we will give a sample of how to train and produce predictions with Lifetimes; however, the procedure is very similar for the BTYD software package.

The main components of the Lifetimes package are the classes `BetaGeoFitter` and `GammaGammaFitter`. The first class (`BetaGeoFitter`) contains all the logic necessary to fit a BG/NBD model from transactional data in the format of purchase recency, purchase frequency, and current age of the customer in terms of customer relationship duration. It is also possible to alternatively fit a Pareto/NBD model using the `ParetoNBDFitter` class instead. Given a dataset with correctly formatted inputs[8], the code to fit the `BetaGeoFitter` is given in Listing 5.1.

LISTING 5.1 FITTING OF THE BETA-GEOMETRIC DISTRIBUTION TO PREDICT PURCHASE NUMBERS USING THE LIFETIMES LIBRARY

```
from lifetimes import BetaGeoFitter

bgf = BetaGeoFitter(penalizer_coef=0.0)
bgf.fit(data['frequency'], data['recency'], data ['T'])
```

Icon source: Icon made from www.flaticon.com. Full icon credit listed at the end of the References section on p. 107.

The second class (GammaGammaFitter) provides all the methods necessary to fit a gamma-gamma model and can be used, in combination with the BetaGeoFitter, to predict the CLV. The gamma-gamma model is also trained on transactional data containing the frequency and the total monetary value of the purchases made by each customer.

The code to fit the gamma-gamma model is shown in Listing 5.2, while the code to perform CLV predictions on new data using the previously fit models is given in Listing 5.3. The time and discount rate depend on the parameters of the specific prediction to be performed.

LISTING 5.2 FITTING OF THE GAMMA-GAMMA DISTRIBUTION FOR PURCHASE VALUE PREDICTION USING THE LIFETIMES LIBRARY

```
from lifetimes import GammaGammaFitter

returning_customers_summary = data[data['frequency']>0]
ggf = GammaGammaFitter(penalizer_coef=0)
ggf.fit(returning_customers_summary['frequency'],
returning_customers_summary['monetary_value'])
```

Icon source: Icon made from www.flaticon.com. Full icon credit listed at the end of the References section on p. 107.

Further documentation and tutorials about the two packages can be found on their project web pages[9,10].

---

[8] The package provides a function named summary_data_from_transaction_data that allows one to produce correctly formatted data for the algorithm from a list of transactions.

[9] https://github.com/CamDavidsonPilon/lifetimes (Accessed: December 2018)

[10] https://cran.r-project.org/web/packages/BTYD/index.html (Accessed: December 2018)

LISTING 5.3   CLV PREDICTION USING THE LIFETIMES LIBRARY IMPLEMENTATION OF THE BG/NBD MODEL

```
ggf.customer_lifetime_value(
      bgf,
      new_data['frequency'],
      new_data['recency'],
      new_data['T'],
      new_data['monetary_value'],
      time=180,
      discount_rate=0.01)
```

Icon source: Icon made from www.flaticon.com. Full icon credit listed at the end of the References section on p. 107.

5.5.2 Scikit-Learn

Scikit-learn (Mueller, 2018) is a library for the Python programming language that provides functionalities to perform supervised and unsupervised learning tasks. The supervised learning part of the library implements a wide variety of algorithms ranging from linear models to tree-based methods for both classification and regression. In the following, we will show how to use scikit-learn to build a regression model based on the Random Forest algorithm similar to the one presented in Alves et al. (2014) and Sifa et al. (2018).

Random Forest (Breiman, 2001) is an ensemble algorithm that combines a number of tree predictors trained on different portions of the data. The output of the model is generally either the mode or the mean of the outputs of the different tree predictors depending on whether the task is a classification or a regression task. Scikit-learn implements this class of algorithms through the RandomForestRegressor and

LISTING 5.4   TRAINING OF A RANDOM FOREST REGRESSOR FOR CLV PREDICTION WITH THE SCIKIT-LEARN LIBRARY

```
from sklearn.ensemble import RandomForestRegressor

X = data['number_of_sessions','number_of_rounds',
         'number_of_days','number_of_purchases',
         'total_purchase_amount']
y = data["day_360_CLV"]
model = RandomForestRegressor(n_estimators=100)
model.fit(X, y)
```

Icon source: Icon made from www.flaticon.com. Full icon credit listed at the end of the References section on p. 107.

RandomForestClassifier classes; for the purpose of this article, we will show how to use the RandomForestRegressor to predict CLV through regression.

Given a dataset, similar to the one used in Sifa et al. (2018), containing one entry per player with summary data about his or her in-game behavior, the code to fit the RandomForestRegressor is provided in Listing 5.4.

For readability, the number of features selected as inputs is reduced in comparison to Sifa et al. (2018). Furthermore, the number of trees in the ensemble (100 in the example in Listing 5.4) has been chosen without any specific motivation, as no precise description is included in the article. Both the size of the ensemble and maximum depth of the trees—as well as the other parameters of the ensemble—are problem specific and should be selected either algorithmically or through extensive experimentation. The code necessary to perform CLV prediction using the previously fit model is shown in Listing 5.5.

LISTING 5.5   CLV PREDICTION USING A RANDOM FOREST REGRESSOR FROM THE SCIKIT-LEARN LIBRARY

```
X = new_data['number_of_sessions', 'number_of_rounds',
'number_of_days', 'number_of_purchases',
'total_purchase_amount']
y = model.predict(X)
```

Icon source: Icon made from www.flaticon.com. Full icon credit listed at the end of the References section on p. 107.

The resulting array *y* will contain the predicted CLVs. The scikit-learn library also includes a number of functionalities to estimate the prediction error and to perform different forms of validation and testing, for instance, *k*-folds cross-validation. More information can be found on the project's documentation page.[11]

5.6 Conclusions

In this chapter, we have described the applications of CLV prediction in the free-to-play games and other industries, and we attempted to give a comprehensive description of the different methods that are currently used to predict CLV. We have identified a number of activities that can benefit from an accurate prediction ranging from customer acquisition to market segmentation, and we have described how the need for such prediction is even more important in free-to-play games due to

---

[11] https://scikit-learn.org/stable/documentation.html (Accessed: December 2018)

the characteristics of the market and the customer relationship (e.g., incredibly high competition in user acquisition and very low number of paying customers compared to the player base).

In Section 5.4, we have identified four main groups of methods for the prediction within the literature: average based, Pareto/NBD and derivatives, Markov chain and supervised learning models. The methods that are currently dominant within the free-to-play games industry are either average based or some form of Pareto/NBD. However, there is an emerging trend in recent years with more studies being published on the application of different supervised learning algorithms to CLV prediction.

These methods have a number of advantages over classical statistical methods in this context, as they make no assumptions about the distributions of the input data and easily allow multiple covariates to be included in the model. Furthermore, in an industry with such a low rate of conversion to paying users, being able to predict revenue from a player who has not yet made any purchase has the potential to be very useful, for instance, for early estimation of the profitability of a player acquisition campaign.

Based on the analysis presented and in light of the recent improvements within the field of machine learning, we close the article by proposing a number of possible interesting future directions for CLV prediction research.

Deep learning: One group of supervised learning algorithms that has only been minimally explored in one of the most recent articles (Sifa et al., 2018) is deep neural networks.[12] The work by Sifa et al. (2018) does not give an in-depth description of the deep multi-layer perceptron used; however, in the absence of other information, we can assume that the model was based on a standard fully connected feed-forward neural network with multiple hidden layers. Given the results achieved with a relatively simple architecture, it would be interesting to test more advanced deep learning techniques such as auto-encoders for feature extraction (Vincent, Larochelle, Bengio, & Manzagol, 2008) or deep convolutional neural networks (Krizhevsky, Sutskever, & Hinton, 2012).

Time series: All of the models presented in this chapter act on some form of summary data representing the behavior of customers/players up to a given point in time. While some of these summary representations do include some notion of the temporal aspect of the behaviors (e.g., the recency and frequency features in RFM-based models), these cannot capture any particular sequence of purchases or any sequence of in-game events that is

---

[12] Deep learning techniques (also with application to CLV) are covered in Chapter 6.

connected to the probability that a player will perform a purchase or not. One possible approach to leverage this kind of information is to treat player behavior data a time series and perform some form of time-series regression or classification to predict CLV or a purchase event. Within the aforementioned deep learning field, algorithms such as long short-term memory networks (Hochreiter & Schmidhuber, 1997) or the more recent temporal convolution networks (Elbayad, Besacier, & Verbeek, 2018) could be used to process the data and perform CLV predictions.

Transfer learning and lifelong learning: Game developers in the mobile free-to-play market are challenged with the increasing need to manage a multitude of games live at the same time. These games often have very long lifetimes and, throughout their lifetimes, the games are adjusted and evolved. In consequence of this game evolution and due to changes in the customer acquisition initiatives over time, the player base changes as well. This adds a new dimension to the problem of CLV prediction, as the models need to be constantly updated and new models need to be built quickly for new versions of the games and for new games. Within this scenario, research in cross-game player behavior analysis (Martínez, Garbarino, & Yannakakis, 2011), transfer learning (Yosinski, Clune, Bengio, & Lipson, 2014), and lifelong machine learning (Silver, Yang, & Li, 2013) and their application to CLV prediction will become increasingly important.

References

Aeron, H., Bhaskar, T., Sundararajan, R., Kumar, A., & Moorthy, J. (2008). A metric for customer lifetime value of credit card customers. *Journal of Database Marketing & Customer Strategy Management, 15*(3), 153–168.

Alha, K., Koskinen, E., Paavilainen, J., Hamari, J., & Kinnunen, J. (2014). Free-to-play games: Professionals' perspectives. *Proceedings of Nordic DiGRA*, 1–14. Finland: Digital Games Research Association.

Alves, J., Lange, S., Lenz, M., & Riedmiller, M. (2014). Case study: Behavioral prediction of future revenues in freemium games. In *Workshop New Challenges in Neural Computation 2014* (pp. 26–69).

Baden-Fuller, C., & Haefliger, S. (2013). Business models and technological innovation. *Long Range Planning, 46*(6), 419–426.

Berger, P. D., & Nasr, N. I. (1998). Customer lifetime value: Marketing models and applications. *Journal of Interactive Marketing, 12*(1), 17–30.

Berger, P. D., Weinberg, B., & Hanna, R. C. (2003). Customer lifetime value determination and strategic implications for a cruise-ship company. *Journal of Database Marketing & Customer Strategy Management, 11*(1), 40–52.

Blattberg, R. C., & Deighton, J. (1996). Manage marketing by the customer equity test. *Harvard Business Review, 74*(4), 136.

Breiman, L. (2001). Random forests. *Machine Learning, 45*(1), 5–32.

Breiman, L. (2017). *Classification and Regression Trees*. New York: Routledge.

Burelli, P., & Yannakakis, G. N. (2015). Adaptive virtual camera control trough player modelling. *User Modelling and User-Adapted Interaction*, *25*(2), 155–183.

Chawla, N. V., Bowyer, K. W., Hall, L. O., & Kegelmeyer, W. P. (2002). SMOTE: Synthetic minority over-sampling technique. *Journal of Artificial Intelligence Research*, *16*, 321–357.

Cheng, C. J., Chiu, S. W., Cheng, C. B., & Wu, J. Y. (2012). Customer lifetime value prediction by a Markov chain-based data mining model: Application to an auto repair and maintenance company in Taiwan. *Scientia Iranica*, *19*(3), 849–855.

Ching, W. K., Ng, M. K., Wong, K. K., & Altman, E. (2004). Customer lifetime value: Stochastic optimization approach. *Journal of the Operational Research Society*, *55*(8), 860–868.

Cho, H. (2018). XGBoost Python Package. Retrieved from https://pypi.org/project/xgboost/

Chollet, F. (2018). Keras: Deep learning for humans. Retrieved from https://pypi.org/project/Keras/

Colombo, R., & Jiang, W. (1999). A stochastic RFM model. *Journal of Interactive Marketing*, *13*(3), 2–12.

Davidson-Pilon, C. (2018). Lifetimes: Measure customer lifetime value in Python. Retrieved from https://pypi.org/project/Lifetimes/

Dickson, P. R., & Ginter, J. L. (1987). Market segmentation, product differentiation, and marketing strategy. *The Journal of Marketing, 51*, 1–10.

Donkers, B., Verhoef, P. C., & de Jong, M. (2003). Predicting customer lifetime value in multi-service industries (ERIM Report Series Reference No. ERS-2003-038-MKT). Retrieved from https://ssrn.com/abstract=411666

Drachen, A., El-Nasr, M. S., & Canossa, A. (2013). Game analytics: The basics. In M. S. El-Nasr, A. Drachen, & A. Canossa (Eds.), *Game Analytics: Maximizing the Value of Player Data* (pp. 13–40). London, UK: Springer.

Dwyer, F. R. (1997). Customer lifetime valuation to support marketing decision making. *Journal of Direct Marketing*, *11*(4), 6–13.

Dziurzynski, L., Wadsworth, E., & McCarthy, D. (2014). BTYD: Implementing Buy 'Til You Die Models. Retrieved from https://cran.r-project.org/package=BTYD

Ehrenberg, A. S. C. (1972). *Repeat Buying: Theory and Applications*. Amsterdam, the Netherlands: North-Holland.

Elbayad, M., Besacier, L., & Verbeek, J. (2018). Pervasive attention: 2D convolutional neural networks for sequence-to-sequence prediction. In *Proceedings of the SIGNLL Conference on Computational Natural Language Learning*. Retrieved from http://arxiv.org/abs/1808.03867

Etzion, O., Fisher, A., & Wasserkrug, S. (2004). e-CLV: A modelling approach for customer lifetime evaluation in e-commerce domains, with an application and case study for online auctions. In *IEEE International Conference on e-Technology, e-Commerce and e-Service* (pp. 149–156). IEEE.

Fader, P. S., Hardie, B. G., & Lee, K. L. (2005a). RFM and CLV: Using iso-value curves for customer base analysis. *Journal of Marketing Research*, *42*(4), 415–430.

Fader, P. S., Hardie, B. G., & Lee, K. L. (2005b). "Counting your customers" the easy way: An alternative to the Pareto/NBD model. *Marketing Science*, *24*(2), 275–284.

Glady, N., Baesens, B., & Croux, C. (2009). A modified Pareto/NBD approach for predicting customer lifetime value. *Expert Systems with Applications, 36*(2, Part 1), 2062–2071.

Gupta, S., Hanssens, D., Hardie, B., Kahn, W., Kumar, V., Lin, N., ... & Sriram, S. (2006). Modeling customer lifetime value. *Journal of Service Research, 9*(2), 139–155.

Gupta, S., & Lehmann, D. R. (2006). Customer lifetime value and firm valuation. *Journal of Relationship Marketing, 5*(2–3), 87–110.

Haenlein, M., Kaplan, A. M., & Beeser, A. J. (2007). A model to determine customer lifetime value in a retail banking context. *European Management Journal, 25*(3), 221–234.

Hanner, N., & Zarnekow, R. (2015). Purchasing behavior in free to play games: Concepts and empirical validation. In *Proceedings of the 48th Hawaii International Conference on System Sciences* (pp. 3326–3335). IEEE.

Harrison, B. E., & Roberts, D. L. (2014). Analytics-driven dynamic game adaption for player retention in a 2-dimensional adventure game. In *Proceedings of the Conference on Artificial Intelligence and Interactive Digital Entertainment* (pp. 23–29). AAAI.

Hochreiter, S., & Schmidhuber, J. (1997). Long short-term memory. *Neural Computation, 9*(8), 1735–1780.

Hughes, A. M. (2000). *Strategic Database Marketing: The Masterplan for Starting and Managing a Profitable Customer-Based Marketing Program*. New York: McGraw-Hill.

Hwang, H., Jung, T., & Suh, E. (2004). An LTV model and customer segmentation based on customer value: A case study on the wireless telecommunication industry. *Expert Systems with Applications, 26*(2), 181–188.

Jackson, B. B. (1985). *Winning and Keeping Industrial Customers*. Lexington, MA: Lexington Books.

Jain, D., & Singh, S. S. (2002). Customer lifetime value research in marketing: A review and future directions. *Journal of Interactive Marketing, 16*(2), 34–46.

Johnson, N. L., & Kotz, S. (1970). *Continuous Univariate Distributions (Vol. 1)*. New York: John Wiley & Sons.

Kaplan, E. L., & Meier, P. (1958). Nonparametric estimation from incomplete observations. *Journal of the American Statistical Association, 53*(282), 457–481.

Khajvand, M., Zolfaghar, K., Ashoori, S., & Alizadeh, S. (2011). Estimating customer lifetime value based on RFM analysis of customer purchase behavior: Case study. *Procedia Computer Science, 3*, 57–63.

Koetsier, J. (2017). The best Android game has just 4.5% user retention after 30 days. Retrieved from https://www.forbes.com/sites/johnkoetsier/2017/10/20/the-very-best-android-game-has-just-4-5-user-retention-after-30-days/

Krizhevsky, A., Sutskever, I., & Hinton, G. E. (2012). Imagenet classification with deep convolutional neural networks. In *Advances in Neural Information Processing Systems 25 (NIPS 2012)* (pp. 1097–1105), New York: Curran Associates.

Kumar, V. (2010). A customer lifetime value-based approach to marketing in the multichannel, multimedia retailing environment. *Journal of Interactive Marketing, 24*(2), 71–85.

Kumar, V., Ramani, G., & Bohling, T. (2004). Customer lifetime value approaches and best practice applications. *Journal of Interactive Marketing, 18*(3), 60–72.

Lachowetz, T., McDonald, M., Sutton, W., & Clark, J. (2001). The National Basketball Association: Application of customer lifetime value. *Sport Marketing Quarterly, 10*(3), 181–184.

Mahlmann, T., Drachen, A., Togelius, J., Canossa, A., & Yannakakis, G. N. (2010). Predicting player behavior in Tomb Raider: Underworld. In *IEEE Symposium on Computational Intelligence and Games* (pp. 178–185). IEEE.

Malhotra, N. K. (2007). Review of marketing research. In N. K. Malhotra (Ed.), *Review of Marketing Research* (pp. v–v). Bradford, UK: Emerald Group Publishing Limited.

Malthouse, E. C., & Blattberg, R. C. (2005). Can we predict customer lifetime value? *Journal of Interactive Marketing, 19*(1), 2–16.

Martínez, H. P., Garbarino, M., & Yannakakis, G. N. (2011). Generic physiological features as predictors of player experience. In *International Conference on Affective Computing and Intelligent Interaction* (pp. 267–276). Berlin, Germany: Springer.

Mueller, A. (2018). Scikit-learn: A set of python modules for machine learning and data mining. Retrieved from https://pypi.org/project/scikit-learn/

Mulhern, F. J. (1999). Customer profitability analysis: Measurement, concentration, and research directions. *Journal of Interactive Marketing, 13*(1), 25–40.

Nieborg, D. B. (2015). Crushing candy: The free-to-play game in its connective commodity form. *Social Media + Society, 1*(2), 2056305115621932.

Periáñez, Á., Saas, A., Guitart, A., & Magne, C. (2016). Churn prediction in mobile social games: Towards a complete assessment using survival ensembles. In *2016 IEEE International Conference on Data Science and Advanced Analytics (DSAA)* (pp. 564–573). IEEE.

Pfeifer, P. E., & Carraway, R. L. (2000). Modeling customer relationships as Markov chains. *Journal of Interactive Marketing, 14*(2), 43–55.

Pfeifer, P. E., Haskins, M. E., & Conroy, R. M. (2005). Customer lifetime value, customer profitability, and the treatment of acquisition spending. *Journal of Managerial Issues, 17*(1), 11–25.

Reinartz, W. J., & Kumar, V. (2000). On the profitability of long-life customers in a non-contractual setting: An empirical investigation and implications for marketing. *Journal of Marketing, 64*(4), 17–35.

Reinartz, W. J., & Kumar, V. (2003). The impact of customer relationship characteristics on profitable lifetime duration. *Journal of Marketing, 67*(1), 77–99.

Rosset, S., Neumann, E., Eick, U., & Vatnik, N. (2003). Customer lifetime value models for decision support. *Data Mining and Knowledge Discovery, 7*(3), 321–339.

Rosset, S., Neumann, E., Eick, U., Vatnik, N., & Idan, Y. (2002). Customer lifetime value modeling and its use for customer retention planning. In *Proceedings of the Eighth ACM SIGKDD International Conference on Knowledge Discovery and Data Mining* (pp. 332–340). New York : ACM.

Runge, J. (2014). The golden curve: Determining player value in freemium apps. Retrieved from https://gameanalytics.com/blog/golden-curve-determining-player-value-freemium-apps.html

Runge, J., Gao, P., Garcin, F., & Faltings, B. (2014). Churn prediction for high-value players in casual social games. In *IEEE Conference on Computational Intelligence and Games* (pp. 1–8). IEEE.

Salvatier, J., Wiecki, T. V., & Fonnesbeck, C. (2016). Probabilistic programming in Python using PyMC3. *Peer J Computer Science, 2*, e55.

Schmittlein, D. C., Morrison, D. G., & Colombo, R. (1987). Counting your customers: Who-are they and what will they do next? *Management Science, 33*(1), 1–24.

Schmittlein, D. C., & Peterson, R. A. (1994). Customer base analysis: An industrial purchase process application. *Marketing Science, 13*(1), 41–67.

Seufert, E. B. (2013). Two methods for modeling LTV with a spreadsheet. Presentation at the Slush Conference 2013. Retrieved from https://www.slideshare.net/EricSeufert/ltv-spreadsheet-models-eric-seufert

Shankar, V., & Balasubramanian, S. (2009). Mobile marketing: A synthesis and prognosis. *Journal of Interactive Marketing, 23*(2), 118–129.

Shen, C. C., & Chuang, H. M. (2009). A study on the applications of data mining techniques to enhance customer lifetime value. *WSEAS Transactions on Information Science and Applications, 6*(2), 319–328.

Shih, Y. Y., & Liu, C. Y. (2003). A method for customer lifetime value ranking—Combining the analytic hierarchy process and clustering analysis. *Journal of Database Marketing & Customer Strategy Management, 11*(2), 159–172.

Sifa, R., Hadiji, F., Runge, J., Drachen, A., Kersting, K., & Bauckhage, C. (2015). Predicting purchase decisions in mobile free-to-play games. In *Proceedings of the Conference on Artificial Intelligence and Interactive Digital Entertainment* (pp. 79–85). Menlo Park, CA: AAAI.

Sifa, R., Runge, J., Bauckhage, C., & Klapper, D. (2018). Customer lifetime value prediction in non-contractual freemium settings: Chasing high-value users using deep neural networks and SMOTE. In *Proceedings of the 51st Hawaii International Conference on System Sciences* (pp. 923–932). Honolulu, HI: ScholarSpace.

Silver, D. L., Yang, Q., & Li, L. (2013). Lifelong machine learning systems: Beyond learning algorithms. In *AAAI Spring Symposium* (pp. 49–55). Menlo Park, CA: AAAI Press.

Singh, S. S., Borle, S., & Jain, D. C. (2009). A generalized framework for estimating customer lifetime value when customer lifetimes are not observed. *QME, 7*(2), 181–205.

Spedicato, G. A. (2017). Discrete time Markov chains with R. *The R Journal, 9*(2), 84–104.

Tactile Games. (2018). *Bee Brilliant Blast* [Mobile game]. Copenhagen, Denmark: Tactile Games.

Venkatesan, R., & Kumar, V. (2004). A customer lifetime value framework for customer selection and resource allocation strategy. *Journal of Marketing, 68*(4), 106–125.

Verhoef, P. C., & Donkers, B. (2001). Predicting customer potential value an application in the insurance industry. *Decision Support Systems, 32*(2), 189–199.

Vincent, P., Larochelle, H., Bengio, Y., & Manzagol, P. A. (2008). Extracting and composing robust features with denoising autoencoders. In *Proceedings of the 25th international conference on Machine learning* (pp. 1096–1103). New York : ACM.

Yosinski, J., Clune, J., Bengio, Y., & Lipson, H. (2014). How transferable are features in deep neural networks? In *Proceedings of the 27th International Conference on Neural Information Processing Systems, 2* (pp. 3320–3328). Cambridge, MA: MIT Press.

Icon Source

listing.png:

Chapter 6

Advanced Data Science Models for Player Behavioral Prediction

África Periáñez, Anna Guitart, Pei Pei Chen,
and Ana Fernández del Río

Contents

6.1 Introduction

The video game industry is experiencing a paradigm shift. Today's games are always connected to the Internet, which allows developers to both actively interact with their players and collect vast amounts of data on their behavior in real time. It is not exaggerated to say that we are witnessing a true revolution, one that affects traditional platforms and emerging mobile games alike and that creates plenty of new opportunities and challenges for data science research and business applications. If we want to take full advantage of this new scenario, we need to develop suitable machine learning methods to model and predict player behavior.

Modern titles allow players to perform a rich variety of in-game actions through which they can effectively express highly nuanced motivations and emotions. Developers are not only competing for players' money but also for their time, and the biggest challenge is to retain users with very diverse tastes, desires, and interests. This can only be achieved if we are able to profile players individually and present them with personalized contents, such as actions, promotions, or rewards, they are likely to find appealing.

Because of the constant and continued relationship between player and game (which can last for years) and the exceptional level of granularity of the collected records, game data emerges as an ideal testing ground to explore not only social and consumer dynamics, but also different aspects of users' personalities, such as addictions and motivations. This allows researchers to develop sophisticated machine learning and statistical models that can predict with a high level of accuracy almost every action of each player.

In this chapter, we discuss some of the modern business challenges faced by game studios and examine machine learning-based data science approaches that can be used to tackle them. The machine learning methods presented in this chapter are easily parallelizable and computationally efficient, scale to large datasets, adapt to different kinds of players and games, and allow an intuitive visualization of the results. Due to these virtues, they can be readily applied in operational business settings, and perhaps the day they will be available for all users across game studios is not that far away.

In particular, in Section 6.2 we show that conditional inference survival ensembles serve to predict which players are going to leave the game soon, giving developers the chance to implement actions to try to retain them. On the other hand, in Section 6.3 we present a comparative study of different parametric and deep-learning models that can be used to estimate customer lifetime value,[1] namely the total amount of money each player will spend in the game until they quit. The results suggest that convolutional neural networks (a special type of deep neural network) produce the most accurate forecasts and, moreover, are particularly effective in pinpointing potential top spenders.

6.2 Predicting Churn and Player Life Expectancy with Ensemble Learning

Reducing "churn" (i.e., preventing players from leaving the game[2]) is essential to increase player engagement and maximize game monetization. Fortunately, by using sophisticated churn prediction models (Bertens, Guitart, & Periáñez, 2017; Periáñez, Saas, Guitart, & Magne, 2016), it is possible to predict sufficiently in advance—actually, for some games, almost from the very moment the user joins the game—when and in which part of the game a certain player is going to quit. This, in turn, allows developers to take preventive actions targeted at retaining potential churners, such as sending a particular reward to a player, or developing the game following a personalized approach.

Churn prediction is a challenge common to a variety of sectors, such as telecommunications (Amin et al., 2019; Huang, Kechadi, & Buckley, 2012; Tamaddoni Jahromi, Sepehri, Teimourpour, & Choobdar, 2010), finance and banking (He, Shi, Wan, & Zhao, 2014; Kumar & Ravi, 2008; Zorić, 2016), e-commerce (Chen, Chiu, & Chang, 2005; Yoon, Koehler, & Ghobarah, 2010; Yu, Guo, Guo, & Huang, 2011), and insurance (Morik & Köpcke, 2004; Smith, Willis, & Brooks, 2000), and has been thoroughly investigated in the last decade. For a comprehensive list of papers exploring churn prediction in different sectors, we refer the reader to Verbeke, Martens, Mues, and Baesens (2011).

In the gaming field, pioneering studies were performed by Ding, Gao, and Chen (2015), Hadiji et al. (2014), Kawale, Pal, and Srivastava (2009), and Runge, Gao, Garcin, and Faltings (2014). Defining churn in this field is particularly challenging since the relationship with the user is non-contractual and, as a result, there is no fixed date when it should end. Usually, churn is defined by specifying a period of inactivity after which the player is supposed to have quit the game. The length

---

[1] Customer lifetime value is discussed in depth in Chapter 5.

[2] Churn is a reoccurring concept throughout this book. For example, Chapter 5 discusses churn in the context of customer lifetime value, while Chapter 9 briefly discusses the usefulness of community metrics for understanding churn.

of such a period will differ among titles and game genres and ranges from 3 days in highly casual games to more than 60 days in some massively multiplayer online titles.

Even though different approaches can be used to predict when a player will abandon a game, those based on survival analysis appear as the most suitable ones due to the natural ability of this technique to deal with censoring (incomplete observations), a complication that is inherent in churn. By combining survival models and ensemble learning techniques, it is possible to obtain highly accurate prediction results. In this section, we will explore this avenue and present a method to predict churn based on conditional inference survival ensembles.

The proposed method is able to accurately predict when and at which game level each player will leave the game, also providing a reliable estimate of their accumulated playtime until that moment. Further, it is robust to different data distributions, applicable to a wide range of response variables, and can be efficiently parallelized. All these features make this model very well-suited to perform churn prediction analyses in real time, even in games with millions of daily active users.

6.2.1 Survival Analysis

Survival analysis is a set of statistical methods used to predict the time until the occurrence of a certain event of interest as well as its relationship with various factors. Originally it was used to predict lifetime expectancies in the medical and biological fields (Fleming & Lin, 2000; Hougaard, 1999; Li & Ma, 2013), with the event of interest being the decease of an individual. However, more recently these methods began to be employed in other sectors, such as telecommunications (Lu, 2002), banking (Stepanova & Thomas, 2002), and insurance (Fu & Wang, 2014), in order to foresee customer attrition.

The video game industry can also greatly benefit from survival analysis, as it may help developers to predict and reduce churn. In this case, the event of interest is a certain player leaving the game. However, the information on churn extracted from game datasets is necessarily incomplete since a substantial number of players will not have quit during the timespan covered by the dataset. In other words, the data only reflects whether or not the event of interest occurs before a certain time t. When this happens, the data is said to be "censored." One of the reasons why survival analysis is so useful is because it is naturally suited to deal with such censored data.

We start by introducing some terminology and notation. The time-to-event outcome, that is, the time elapsed until the event of interest, is called the "survival time." We can define a survival function $S(t)$, which gives the probability that a player is alive at time t. The survival function can be evaluated using the nonparametric Kaplan–Meier estimator (Kaplan & Meier, 1958), with the churn probability directly calculated from the collected (censored) survival times.

Now assume that k players churn at different times $t_1 < t_2 < t_3 < \ldots < t_k$ during the timespan T of the study. Since these churn events are taken to be independent of each other (Clark, Bradburn, Love, & Altman, 2003), we can calculate the cumulative survival probability simply by multiplying the probabilities of surviving from one of these times to the next:

$$S\left(t_j\right) = S\left(t_{j-1}\right)\left(1 - \frac{d_j}{n_j}\right), \quad S(0) = 1.$$

Here, n_j and d_j are the number of players alive before t_j and leaving the game at that moment. It is easy to see that $S(t_j)$ is a step function that changes its value precisely at those times when some player churns.

A more detailed analysis will allow for the existence of more than one possible failure event. The alternative events are known as "competing risks" (Prentice et al., 1978) and may prevent the observation of the main event of interest. For instance, in this study we are concerned with the primary cause of churn, namely the loss of interest in the game. However, this is not the only reason why a player may stop playing the game. It could also be that they lost their phone or they do not have any credit left. These alternative causes are regarded as competing risk events.

The impact of multiple covariates or predictors—variables that we expect to be correlated with the player's reason for leaving the game—can be investigated through parametric (e.g., accelerated failure time models (Marubini & Valsecchi, 2004)) or semiparametric survival techniques, such as the regression method for censored observations (Powell, 1984) or the Cox proportional hazards model (Cox, 1972; Cox & Oakes, 1984). According to the latter, the hazard function $h_k(t)$ for k individual players and p covariate vectors $x_{k,i}(i = 1, \ldots, p)$ can be written as

$$h_k\left(t\right) = h_0\left(t\right)\exp\left(\beta_1 x_{k,1} + \ldots + \beta_p x_{k,p}\right),$$

where $h_0(t)$ is the baseline hazard, and β_i are the regression coefficients. The Cox model and its extensions (Therneau & Grambsch, 2000) can be used with censored data and permit an intuitive interpretation of the impact of the different features (i.e., covariates). The hazard function is not assumed to follow any particular statistical distribution (rather it is fitted from the data), and the censoring problem is solved by maximizing the partial likelihood.

Therefore, the above techniques present a series of appealing characteristics. However, they also have a major drawback: they assume there exists a fixed relationship between the output and the variables (which are supposed to be additive and constant over time) and that this relation should be explicitly specified, which entails laborious and time-consuming efforts in terms of model selection and evaluation. Moreover, in spite of being semiparametric, these methods have some trouble scaling to large datasets, even though alternative "regularized" Cox regression models (Mittal, Madigan, Burd, & Suchard, 2013) trying to fix this issue have been proposed. Still, these models rely on restrictive assumptions that are not easily satisfied.

In parametric approaches such as accelerated failure time models (Marubini & Valsecchi, 2004), the data is assumed to follow some previously specified distribution (e.g., Weibull, log-normal, exponential). The problem with these methods is that real data often does not follow any of these particular distributions accurately enough, and thus they yield suboptimal results.

As we will see in what follows, all these drawbacks can be solved by employing machine learning algorithms. Hence, machine learning methods currently constitute the best approach to efficiently cope with censored data problems.

6.2.2 Survival Trees and Ensembles

In this section, we will review machine learning methods based on decision trees. Our ultimate goal is to introduce the so-called survival ensembles, a sophisticated tree-based technique that offers great promise for the prediction of churn.

6.2.2.1 Decision Trees

Decision trees were introduced by Morgan and Sonquist (1963) and became popular in the 1980s thanks to classification and regression trees (CART) (Breiman, Friedman, Stone, & Olshen, 1984; Quinlan, 1986; Salzberg, 1994), nonparametric techniques whose main idea is to recursively split the feature space, grouping subjects that are more homogeneous in terms of the outcome variable and separating those that exhibit larger differences. The splitting starts by dividing the root node, which contains all the data, into several child nodes (usually two, in which case we talk of binary trees) by minimizing a metric called "impurity." Such minimization ensures maximum homogeneity within each node, with typical choices for the impurity measure being the cross-entropy or the sum of squared errors. As a very simple example of these methods, we can consider a continuous variable X and a binary split achieved by checking whether $X \leq d$ is satisfied for a certain constant d.

6.2.2.2 Survival Trees

Survival trees are binary trees grown by recursively partitioning the sample space based on a certain statistical survival criterion, such as the cumulative hazard function or a Kaplan–Meier estimator. The principle that guides the splitting is to maximize the survival difference between the two child nodes. At each node, the algorithm examines all predictor variables x_i and possible splits in order to find the combination that maximizes the survival difference. As a result, individuals with similar survival characteristics are grouped together. As the tree grows, these groups become more and more homogeneous in terms of survival expectancy (which increases the difference between branches).

Survival trees constitute a powerful classification tool and can be used to model censored data. The idea of using tree-based models to handle censoring can be traced back to Ciampi, Bush, Gospodarowicz, and Till (1981) and Marubini, Morabito, and Valsecchi (1983), while the first survival tree was famously introduced by Gordon and Olshen (1985). In their model, a Kaplan–Meier estimator survival function was computed at every node using Wasserstein metrics as a discrepancy measure. We refer the reader to Bou-Hamad, Larocque, and Ben-Ameur (2011) for a comprehensive review of different types of survival trees.

However, the results produced by a single tree may suffer from instability, meaning that small changes in the data could result in significantly different predictions (Kretowska, 2014), a discrepancy that is mainly related to the prediction of risk factors. As we proceed to discuss, this issue can be solved if we employ multiple survival trees.

6.2.2.3 Survival Ensembles

The possibility of using an ensemble of tree-based models instead of a single one was originally suggested by Breiman (1996, 2001) in terms of the well-known random forests. Since then, ensemble models have been shown to yield accurate prediction results in various real-world applications (Zhang & Ma, 2012).

In case the underlying algorithm is some kind of survival tree, the techniques exploiting this idea are known as survival forests or survival ensembles. In other words, survival ensembles are machine learning methods based on growing a set of survival trees. The two main examples are random survival forests, introduced by Ishwaran, Kogalur, Blackstone, and Lauer (2008), and conditional inference survival ensembles, developed by Hothorn, Hornik, and Zeileis (2006) by building on previous work (Hothorn, Bühlmann, Dudoit, Molinaro, & Van Der Laan, 2005; Hothorn, Lausen, Benner, & Radespiel-Tröger, 2004).

Random survival forests are based on Nelson–Aalen estimates (Aalen, 1978; Nelson, 1972). The splitting criterion is the maximum of the log-rank statistical test, which leads to biased results as it favors covariates with many possible splits (Wright, Dankowski, & Ziegler, 2017).

On the other hand, conditional inference survival ensembles rely on a weighted Kaplan–Meier function, which is based on the measurements employed to train the model. The ensemble survival function (Mogensen, Ishwaran, & Gerds, 2012) can be expressed as

$$S^{\text{conditional}}\left(t\,|\,x_i\right) = \prod\left(1 - \frac{\sum_{n=1}^{N} T_n\left(dt, x_i\right)}{\sum_{n=1}^{N} Q_n\left(t, x_i\right)}\right)$$

where $n = 1, \ldots, N$ is the number of trees within the ensembles, and x_i are the different covariates. In the node where x_i is located, T_n accounts for the uncensored events until time t, and Q_n for the number of individuals at risk at t. Two other distinctive features of this technique are that it assigns additional weight to the nodes that have more subjects at risk and that it uses linear rank statistics as the splitting criterion to grow the trees.

Conditional inference survival ensembles constitute a promising approach to deal with the censoring nature of the churn prediction problem. Moreover, they also solve some of the issues inherent to the other methods presented in this section. For example, it is more flexible than the traditional Cox regression model and does not suffer from the typical instability of survival trees. In addition, the bias problem affecting random survival forests can be fixed by choosing a method that does not overfit and that provides robust information on the importance of the different covariates. For these reasons, we will explore this method more closely in the following.

6.2.3 Data Selection, Modeling, and Validation

In this section, we illustrate the capabilities of a method based on conditional inference survival ensembles using real data from the mobile game *Age of Ishtaria* (Silicon Studio, 2014), a role-playing, freemium, and social mobile game.

6.2.3.1 Data Selection and Kaplan–Meier Visualization

The selected data sample ranges from September 2014 (when the game was released) to May 2017 and includes 2.1 million users. For this particular title—and following Periáñez et al. (2016)—we consider that a player has churned after nine consecutive days without connecting.[3] We divided players into three different groups according to their paying behavior, namely "whales" (i.e., top spenders), paying users (PUs) (players who spend some money, but not nearly as much as whales), and non-paying users.

Figure 6.1 shows the Kaplan–Meier survival curves for these different groups as a function of time and level. It can be seen that non-paying users have a much lower survival probability than either PUs or whales. In fact, about 80% of them churn the very first day they connect to the game (cf. Figure 6.1a). On the contrary, whales are typically much more engaged with a churn rate that remains below 50% even after 400 days. Survival probabilities can also be displayed as a function of game level (Figure 6.1b), with whales presenting—as could have been expected—much higher survival probabilities in advanced levels. These curves constitute a prime example of how player behavior—in this case, engagement—can be quantified.

---

[3] As previously discussed, other games may require different churn criteria.

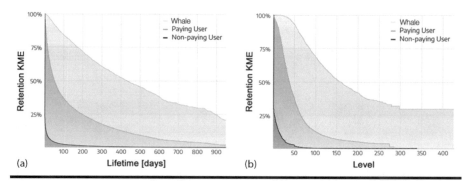

Figure 6.1 Cumulative survival probability computed using Kaplan–Meier estimates as (a) a function of time and (b) game level. Players were stratified into three groups by their expenditure: whales (top spenders), paying users, and non-paying users.

Predictions were generated only for whales, that is, the highest-value players who provide more than 50% of the revenue. For the game and time span considered, this condition results in a subset of 6,136 players. We chose the input features based on two requirements. They should: (1) capture the complex dynamics of the data, and (2) be easily generalizable to other titles—as the model should be applicable to various kinds of games. With this in mind, we studied different behavioral data of each player (e.g., daily logins, purchases, playtime, level-ups, click counts, gained experience, and social interactions) that can be obtained from their action log. This data is not only available in most games but also contains the essential information to understand different playstyles. The present feature computation is parallelizable over all players by using multiple cores (each of which focuses on a different subset of players) on a single machine.

6.2.3.2 *Conditional Inference Survival Ensembles*

In order to model game churn and predict when and where (at which level) whales will abandon the game, we used conditional inference survival ensembles composed of 1,000 trees (we found this number to be the optimal choice in terms of performance and training time). We can further understand how conditional inference trees work through the toy example depicted in Figure 6.2, which illustrates a simple splitting with four terminal nodes. We also show the Kaplan–Meier survival curves representing the survival probabilities of the n players grouped in each of these nodes, which exhibit significant differences among them. In this example, the root node is split according to the last level reached by the player: users are grouped on the right or left child node depending on whether they got past game level 110 or not. These two child nodes are further divided, with one of the partitions

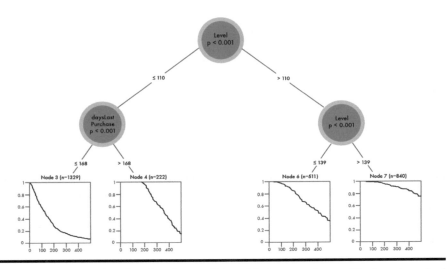

Figure 6.2 Example of a simple conditional inference tree with four terminal nodes. The Kaplan–Meier survival curves for the *n* players grouped in each of these nodes are also shown.

also based on level and the other on the number of days since the player made their last in-game purchase (called "daysLastPurchase" in Figure 6.2).

This toy model yields a survival function for each player, which indicates the probability that they churn—as a function of time and level—since they registered in the game. Figure 6.3 shows an example of these Kaplan–Meier

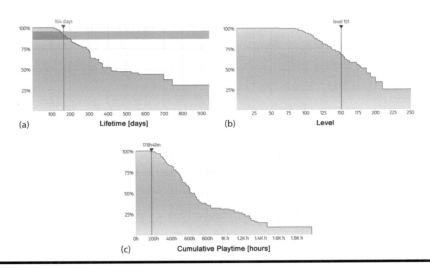

Figure 6.3 Predicted survival curves as a function of (a) time (days), (b) level, and (c) playtime (hours) for a particular player obtained using a conditional inference survival ensemble model.

survival functions with the probability of churn being plotted against time (in days), game level, and playtime (in hours).

6.2.3.3 Model Validation

Assessing the accuracy of our predictions poses some difficulties, since conventional methods to visualize and evaluate prediction performances are not suitable due to the existence of censoring (Mogensen et al., 2012). Figure 6.4a, 6.4c, 6.4e show a set of scatter plots comparing the predictions of our conditional inference survival ensemble model (in terms of total lifetime, last level reached, and cumulative playtime) with the actual observed data. As can be seen from the mean-difference plots in Figure 6.4b, 6.4d, 6.4f, there is a good agreement between the predicted and measured survival times and levels, especially when the values of these variables are not too large. This means that the model is able to pinpoint those whales who are going to abandon the game prematurely, after a relatively short lifetime/playtime or at an unusually early stage. Such information is essential in order to increase player retention and monetization.

The prediction accuracy can be further evaluated using the integrated Brier score (IBS) (Brier, 1950; Mogensen et al., 2012), which is also valuable for comparing the proposed method to other existing techniques. In Table 6.1, we show the IBS (computed using bootstrap cross-validation with replacement over 1,000 samples) for the conditional inference survival ensemble technique, the Cox regression model, and the Kaplan–Meier estimates. As we can see, our method outperforms Cox regression (the lower the IBS value, the better the prediction accuracy) in all three—lifetime, level, and playtime—predictions.

These results demonstrate that conditional inference survival ensembles can be used to accurately model and predict churn as they produce reliable estimates of when, at which level, and after how much playtime a certain player will leave the game. Moreover, they show that our method is robust against different data distributions (even if we consider nonlinear outcomes, as game level) and applicable to different kinds of response variables.

While Cox regression also performs relatively well (as per the results in Table 6.1 on p. 123), the problems mentioned above—namely that it requires a lot of human effort and has troubles scaling to large datasets—make it unsuitable in an operational production environment. The proposed survival ensemble model not only circumvents these issues but also presents several other advantages: it can be easily adapted to different types of games and is parallelizable over multiple cores and over multiple machines. Using this method, developers can efficiently obtain survival probability curves for each player to predict when and where they are going to quit the game in real time. This will give developers the chance to devise actions to retain potential churners.

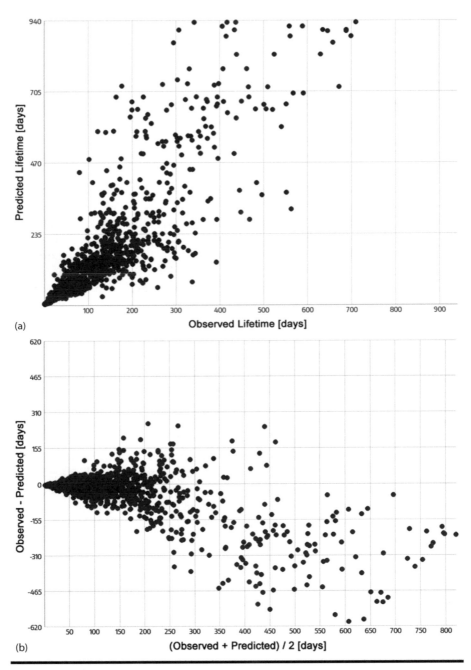

Figure 6.4 Comparison between the predictions of our conditional inference survival ensemble model and the actual observed data in terms of total time since registration (a), maximum level reached (c), and cumulative playtime (e). The corresponding mean-difference plots (b, d, f) are shown. *(Continued)*

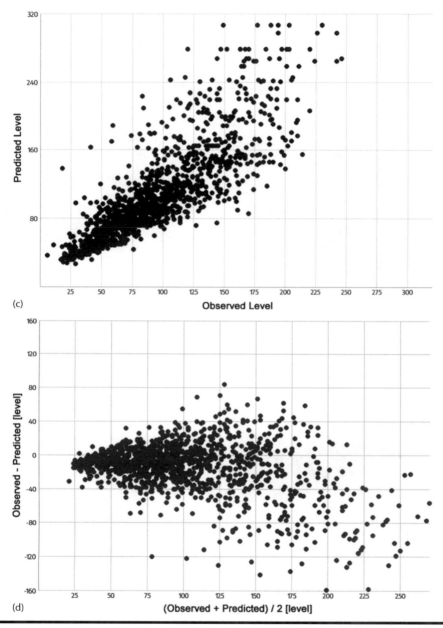

(c)

(d)

Figure 6.4 (Continued)   Comparison between the predictions of our conditional inference survival ensemble model and the actual observed data in terms of total time since registration (a, b), maximum level reached (c, d), and cumulative play-time (e, f). The corresponding mean-difference plots are shown on the right.

(Continued)

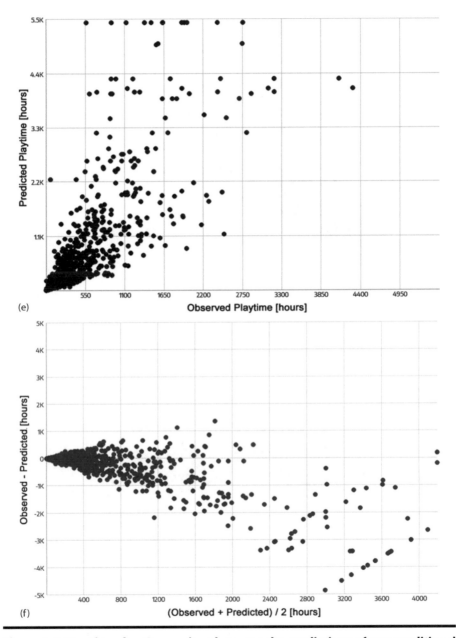

(e)

(f)

Figure 6.4 (Continued) Comparison between the predictions of our conditional inference survival ensemble model and the actual observed data in terms of total time since registration (a, b), maximum level reached (c, d), and cumulative playtime (e, f). The corresponding mean-difference plots are shown on the right.

(*Continued*)

Table 6.1 Integrated Brier Score (IBS) for Different Methods, Showing That the Survival Ensemble Model Yields the Most Accurate Predictions

	IBS		
Model	*Lifetime*	*Level*	*Playtime*
Survival ensemble	0.013	0.019	0.012
Cox regression	0.014	0.026	0.014
Kaplan–Meier	0.085	0.106	0.100

6.3 A Machine Learning-Based Lifetime Value Computation: Deep Learning and Parametric Models

Machine learning can also be of great help in assessing the lifetime value of video game players. Lifetime value (LTV), also referred to as customer lifetime value (CLV), is an estimate of the expected revenue customers will generate over their entire relationship with a service (Pfeifer, Haskins, & Conroy, 2005). Since it serves to identify potential high-value users, it is a useful measure for deciding on future investments, user retention strategies, as well as marketing and promotion campaigns (Farris, Bendle, Pfeifer, & Reibstein, 2010).

Lifetime value was first introduced in the context of marketing (Dwyer, 1997; Berger & Nasr, 1998; Hoekstra & Huizingh, 1999; Shaw & Stone, 1988) and has been used in many different fields, including video games (Davidovici-Nora, 2013; Luton, 2013). Even though the most recent works on LTV prediction make use of machine learning methods (see, e.g., Chamberlain, Cardoso, Liu, Pagliari, and Deisenroth (2017) and Tkachenko (2015) who apply random forests and deep Q-learning, respectively), only a handful of studies related to video games have exploited such techniques. For instance, Sifa et al. (2015) proposed a binary classification model to predict whether a player will purchase an in-game item and a regression model to estimate the number of future purchases by each player. Voigt and Hinz (2016) combined machine learning methods with the synthetic minority oversampling technique (SMOTE) to predict LTV for individual players. Drachen et al. (2018) computed the LTV of mobile game players through a two-step process (first classifying whether players are PUs or not and then predicting their monetary value) that employs different machine learning algorithms, such as random forests and extreme gradient boosting. Sifa, Runge, Bauckhage, and Klapper (2018) also explored various machine learning methods—including deep neural networks—combined with SMOTE to foresee the cumulative spend of each user during one year.

In this section, we start by reviewing the main approaches and models used to compute LTV. We will, however, keep the discussion brief—focusing only on details necessary to follow the remainder of this section—as customer lifetime value models have already been discussed in detail in Chapter 5. Then, we present the results of a recent study that compared the performance of parametric models (such as Pareto/NBD) and deep learning methods in predicting the economic value of individual video game players (Chen, Guitart, del Río, & Periáñez, 2018). As we will see, convolutional neural networks (CNNs) emerge as the most efficient way of tackling this problem because they not only provide the most accurate results but also reduce computation times (since they can work directly with raw sequential data) and are especially well-suited to identify potential whales.

6.3.1 Historical and Predictive Approaches to Compute Lifetime Value

Models to calculate LTV can be divided into two broad classes: Historical approaches compute the value of the different customers by considering their past transactions only, without trying to predict what they will do in the future. In contrast, predictive schemes try to model the purchasing behavior of users to infer their future actions. In these models, LTV is estimated from the predicted purchasing dynamics and lifetime expectancy of each client.

Historical LTV computations generally make use of the recency, frequency, monetary value (RFM) model (Fader, Hardie, & Lee, 2005b) that groups users based on the recency, frequency, and monetary value of their past purchases. The fundamental assumption of this method is that customers with more recent or frequent transactions or who spent larger amounts of money are more likely to keep on purchasing in the future.

Predictive approaches are usually implemented by means of probabilistic or parametric models, which assume a repeated purchase pattern until the end of the business relationship, that is, until the player churns in the context of video games. For this reason, these are also referred to as "buy till you die" (BTYD) models (Schmittlein, Morrison, & Colombo, 1987).

Probabilistic models apply to non-contractual settings with continuous purchase opportunities (the customer can purchase at any time). Actually, these conditions occur in many business contexts, such as online shopping, grocery purchases, movie rentals, and also in free-to-play or freemium games, which have lately become one of the major business models in the video game industry. These games can be downloaded and played without paying, and generate revenue mainly through in-app purchases of items or services (e.g., getting rid of ads).

Therefore, parametric formulations can be used to predict LTV in free-to-play games. In what follows, we will briefly introduce the most popular model of this kind—the Pareto/NBD model—and some of its extensions.

6.3.1.1 Pareto/Negative Binomial Distribution Model

The Pareto/NBD model (Schmittlein et al., 1987) combines two parametric distributions: the Pareto distribution is used to obtain a binary classification of whether users are active or not, while the negative binomial distribution (NBD) serves to estimate the purchase frequency (Fader & Hardie, 2005). This model makes the following assumptions:

- The number of transactions made by a customer in a given time follows a Poisson distribution, with each customer having his or her own transaction rate.
- Customer lifetimes follow an exponential distribution, with each customer having their own dropout (churn) rate.
- Transaction and dropout rates vary independently across customers, and their heterogeneity is modeled by means of gamma distributions (Wheat & Morrison, 1990). The shape and scale parameters of these two distributions are the four parameters that will be employed (along with the client's transaction history) to predict future purchase behavior (Fader & Hardie, 2005; Schmittlein et al., 1987).

The NBD and Pareto distributions are obtained as the continuous mixture of the Poisson and exponential distributions of all customers, respectively.

This model requires only two quantities to describe the transaction history of each customer: their frequency (the number of purchases they made during the observation period, which must also be specified for each client) and recency (the time of their last purchase).

With all this information, we can derive the maximum likelihood function of the model, whose maximization yields the four relevant parameters mentioned above, as well as expressions for the expected number of purchases and the probability of being active for every customer, conditional on their transaction history. Such expressions allow the estimation of the future purchasing behavior of customers. By adding a gamma-gamma model[4] for the monetary value of each transaction, their LTV can finally be obtained (Fader et al., 2005b).

6.3.1.2 Other Parametric Models

Other parametric models use different probability distributions (which may be better suited for certain problems) to model the dropout and transaction rates. In this chapter, we will consider models that use:

- The beta-geometric (BG) distribution (Gupta, 1991; Platzer & Reutterer, 2016) instead of the Pareto distribution. These models involve simplifications that optimize computation efficiency without sacrificing significant predictive power.

---

[4] Gamma-gamma models are also covered in Chapter 5.

■ The condensed negative binomial distribution (CNBD) (Chatfield & Goodhardt, 1973) instead of the NBD distribution. Models with such a modification take more details of the clients' transaction history into account, specifically purchase regularity.

The first of those extensions was the BG/NBD (Fader, Hardie, & Lee, 2005a) model. The main difference with respect to the Pareto/NBD model is that customers are assumed to defect (churn) immediately after their last purchase, instead of at any moment between their last purchase and the end of the observation period. Such an assumption not only makes the model much easier to implement but also speeds up computations and improves the robustness of the parameter search. The BG/NBD model has a similar ability to fit the data and prediction accuracy as the Pareto/NBD model. It, however, considers (somewhat counterintuitively) that users without repeated purchases cannot defect and are hence considered as active regardless of their time of inactivity. The MBG/NBD model—which uses the Markov–Bernoulli geometric (MBG) distribution (Batislam, Denizel, & Filiztekin, 2007)—removes this inconsistency by allowing for zero repeat purchasers.

More recent parametric methods include the BG/CNBD-k and MBG/CNBD-k formulations (Platzer & Reutterer, 2016; Platzer, 2016), which extend the BG/NBD and MBG/NBD models, respectively. They allow for fixed regularity within transaction timings by considering that they are Erlang-k distributed (Herniter, 1971). When purchase timings are fairly regular, these models may considerably improve forecasting accuracy without increasing computational costs.

6.3.2 Lifetime Value Using Deep Learning Methods

As previously described, the most recent studies on LTV prediction are based on machine learning methods. In particular, deep learning techniques[5] (LeCun, Bengio, & Hinton, 2015) have shown great potential to tackle this and other important problems. For instance, deep neural networks (DNNs) have yielded outstanding results in problems related to image (Esteva et al., 2017) and speech (Graves, Mohamed, & Hinton, 2013), classification of particle physics experimental results (Ciodaro, Deva, De Seixas, & Damazio, 2012), genomics (Xiong et al., 2015), or electronic health records (Rajkomar et al., 2018).

Deep learning can also be used to accurately predict user behavior in video games, and DNNs have been used to predict churn (Kim, Choi, Lee, & Rhee, 2017) or to simulate in-game events (Guitart, Chen, Bertens, & Periáñez, 2018).

---

[5] Deep learning techniques are representation-learning methods that are able to directly assimilate raw data and to automatically find representations to classify data or make predictions. They differ from traditional machine learning methods in that they do not require sophisticated feature engineering processes.

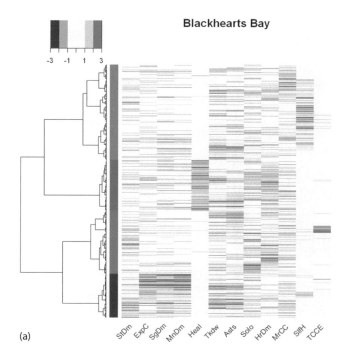

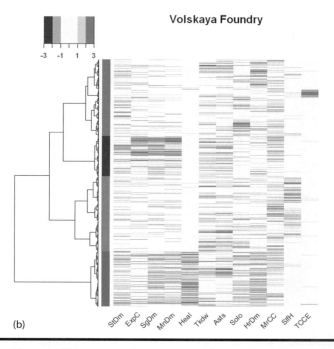

Figure 4.1 Clustered heatmaps of 25,000 participants from winning teams on the (a) Blackhearts Bay and (b) Volskaya Foundry maps (see Table 4.1 on pp. 57–58 for an explanation of the abbreviations). The colored sidebars indicate similarly structured clusters across maps. *(Continued)*

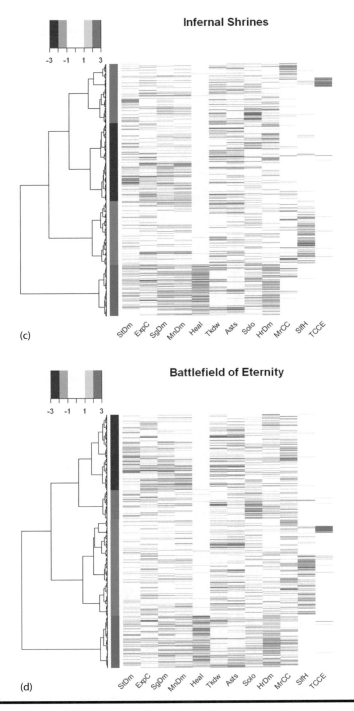

Figure 4.1 (Continued) Clustered heatmaps of 25,000 participants from winning teams on the (c) Infernal Shrines and (d) Battlefield of Eternity maps (see Table 4.1 on pp. 57–58 for an explanation of the abbreviations). The colored sidebars indicate similarly structured clusters across maps.

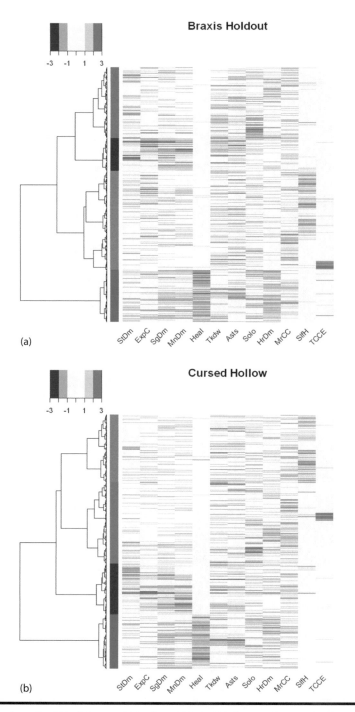

Figure 4A.1   Clustered heatmaps of 25,000 participants from winning teams on the (a) Braxis Holdout and (b) Cursed Hollow maps (see Table 4.1 on pp. 57–58 for an explanation of the abbreviations). The colored sidebars indicate similarly structured clusters across maps.   (*Continued*)

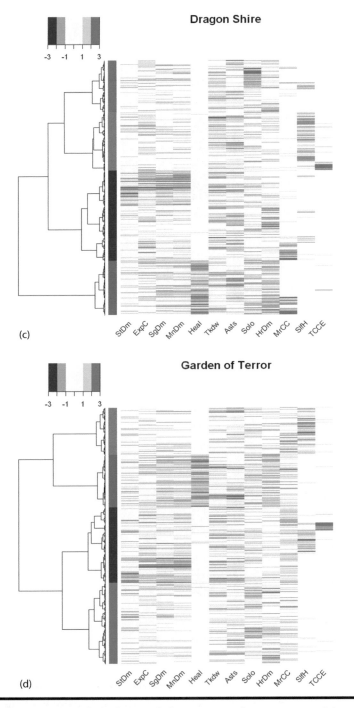

Figure 4A.1 (Continued) Clustered heatmaps of 25,000 participants from winning teams on the (c) Dragon Shire and (d) Garden of Terror maps (see Table 4.1 on pp. 57–58 for an explanation of the abbreviations). The colored side-bars indicate similarly structured clusters across maps. *(Continued)*

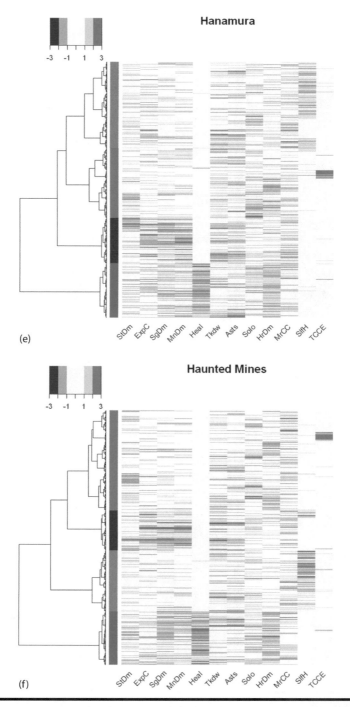

Figure 4A.1 (Continued) Clustered heatmaps of 25,000 participants from winning teams on the (e) Hanamura and (f) Haunted Mines maps (see Table 4.1 on pp. 57–58 for an explanation of the abbreviations). The colored sidebars indicate similarly structured clusters across maps. **(Continued)**

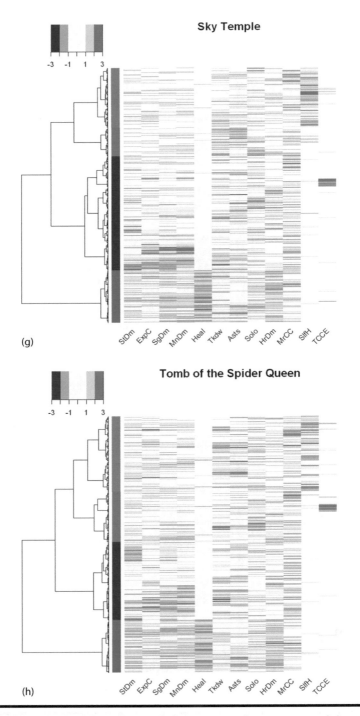

Figure 4A.1 (Continued) Clustered heatmaps of 25,000 participants from winning teams on the **(g)** Sky Temple and **(h)** Tomb of the Spider Queen maps (see Table 4.1 on pp. 57–58 for an explanation of the abbreviations). The colored sidebars indicate similarly structured clusters across maps. *(Continued)*

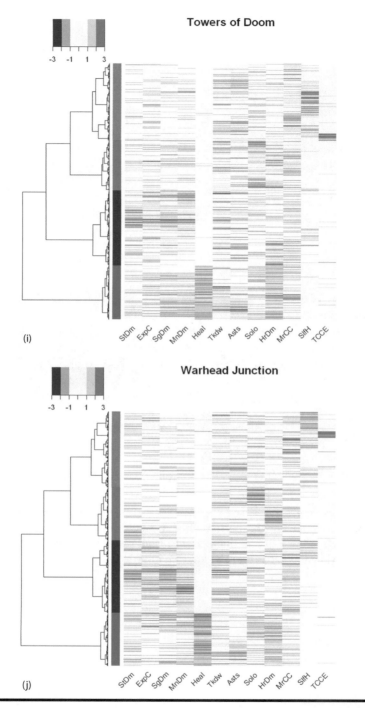

Figure 4A.1 (Continued) Clustered heatmaps of 25,000 participants from winning teams on the (i) Towers of Doom and (j) Warhead Junction maps (see Table 4.1 on pp. 57–58 for an explanation of the abbreviations). The colored side-bars indicate similarly structured clusters across maps.

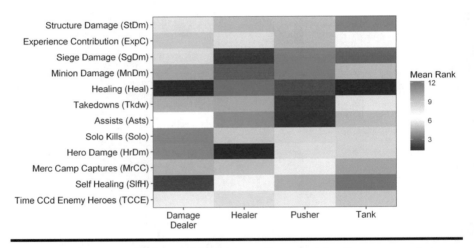

Figure 4.2 Heatmap of the performance attribute metrics (by mean rank across maps) for each of the four identified groups. High ranks (green) indicate higher attribute scores while low ranks (purple) indicate lower attribute scores.

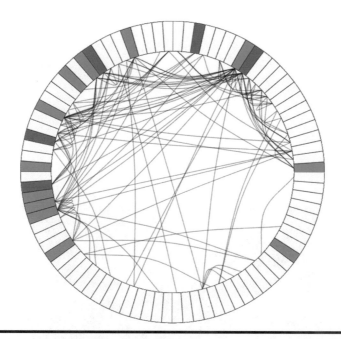

Figure 11.4 A chord diagram showing the internal structure of a clan. Sectors represent the individual members, and arcs show which players have played together. (Courtesy of Günter Wallner.)

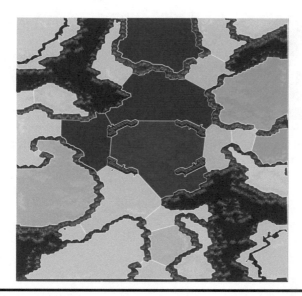

Figure 11.6 A choropleth map showing the number of destroyed units in different regions during a *StarCraft: Brood War* match using a yellow (low number of kills) to red (large number of kills) color gradient.

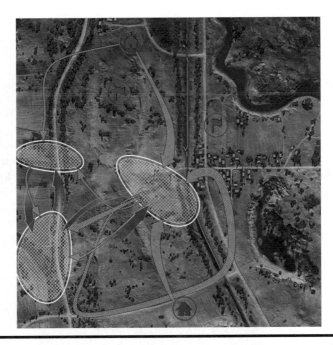

Figure 11.7 Example of a battle map showing troop movements, combat regions, and long-distance attacks. (Courtesy of Günter Wallner.)

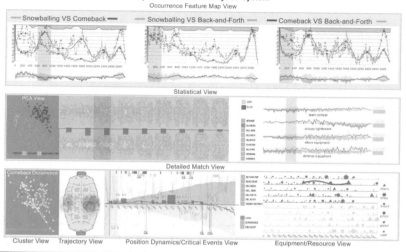

Figure 12.6 Deep MOBA Visual Analytics System. The Occurrence Feature Map View offers a pairwise comparison of the features obtained by the deep model by game occurrence. The PCA View shows the distribution of the three occurrences. Key regions and critical events are detected to give visual clues on both important timestamps and geographical areas (Statistical View). A number of recommended matches of a certain occurrence are displayed in the Cluster View. Users can select one node (a representative match) to view details, including simulating the movements of all players in the Trajectory View, comparing the performance of both teams in the Position Dynamics View, and observe critical events and equipment/resource changes in the Equipment/Resource View.

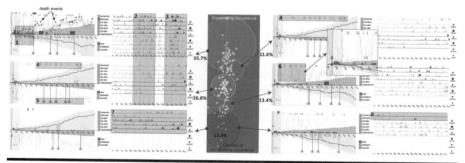

Figure 12.9 *Snowballing* occurrences pattern set. (1) In the initial stage, the team in advantage overwhelms the opponent in several combats (note that the purple nodes indicate death events of the disadvantaged teams, resulting in a significant upgrade of equipment). (2) In the final stage, another upgrade of equipment leads to the final occurrence (3). (4) The sequence of *hitting towers* is mainly conducted by the *snowballing* teams, indicating a passive resistance of the disadvantaged teams. (5) All the light towers of the disadvantaged teams are occupied in all representative matches. (6) The irregular trajectories show that some particular behaviors such as "away from keyboard" may contribute to losing the initial combats. (7, 8) Overwhelming performance by some individual players and an unbalanced number of players may also result in *snowballing*.

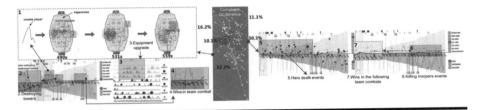

Figure 12.10 (1) Two "green" players return home to their base (indicated by the arrow labeled trajectories), but an opponent (the unwise "purple" player) advances deep into the eventually victorious team's camp (the purple trajectory), chases them alone, and is killed. (2) The two "green" players then destroy two towers (indicated by two dots), followed by (3) an equipment upgrade—represented by the icons—before winning the subsequent team combats and finally making the *comeback* happen (4). (5) In the early stage, the *comeback* team is defeated in most of the *team combats*. However, they kill many troopers (6) that help them to win the following *team combats* (7).

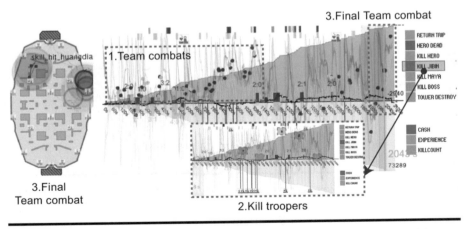

Figure 12.11 In the earlier stages, both teams achieve some success on (1) *team combat, kill heroes,* and (2) *kill troopers*. However, (3) in the final combats, the victorious team wins through a series of *killing hero* events.

While Sifa et al. (2018) also addressed LTV, they focused on estimating the amount spent by each player over one year based on their activity during their first 7 days in the game. In contrast, our aim here is to predict the purchases a player will make until they abandon the game, hence, over a time period that may range from a few days to several years. Below we will show that DNNs cannot only improve LTV prediction in video games—even in production settings—but also add significant value through the early detection of high-value players.

6.3.2.1 Deep Multilayer Perceptron

A deep multilayer perceptron (DMLP) (Bengio, 2009) is a type of DNN with an input layer that receives the data (in our case, features contained in player activity logs), an output layer that yields the prediction result (the LTV), and several hidden layers in between (Schmidhuber, 2015). Layers are formed by neurons with nonlinear activation functions. Every layer (except for the output layer) is fully connected to the next one, that is, each neuron in a layer is connected to all neurons in the next layer. The neural network is optimized through a learning process consisting of multiple iterations or "epochs." In each epoch, weights between nodes are adjusted by means of a gradient descent algorithm, with the purpose of minimizing the value of a certain predefined cost function, such as the root mean square error.

6.3.2.2 Convolutional Neural Networks

A CNN is another type of DNN, formed by one or more convolutional layers that are usually followed by pooling layers (Scherer, Müller, & Behnke, 2010) and fully connected layers (LeCun et al., 1989; Szegedy et al., 2015). In the convolutional layers, filters (kernels) are repeatedly applied over inputs. One of the major advantages of CNNs over DMLPs is their local connectivity: each filter covers several inputs, so each neuron is connected only to a local region of the previous layer (Turaga et al., 2010). Moreover, CNNs are able to learn user behavior directly from raw time series, whereas DMLPs require feature engineering to transform them into structured data.

CNNs have been extensively used in signal and image processing, and also for time series prediction (LeCun & Bengio, 1995). For instance, Yang, Nguyen, San, Li, and Krishnaswamy (2015) used CNNs to perform human activity recognition from time series data acquired by on-body sensors. In contrast, Babu, Zhao, and Li (2016) applied such neural networks to estimate the remaining useful life of system components from sensor data. Finally, Tsantekidis et al. (2017) present a CNN-based method to predict stock prices, using as input time series data on millions of financial exchanges. In this chapter, we will apply CNNs to the prediction of future purchases, using multichannel time series data from player activity logs. In Chapter 12, CNNs are employed to detect characteristic gameplay moments in multiplayer online battle arena games.

6.3.3 Lifetime Value Using Deep Learning and Parametric Models: A Case Study

In what follows, we discuss a study that used a DMLP, a CNN, and the previously discussed parametric models (namely the Pareto/NBD, BG/NBD, BG/CNBD-*k* and MBG/CNBD-*k* models) to predict the in-app purchases of players based on their activity logs and to estimate their economic value (Chen et al., 2018). We start by describing the two DNN models employed in the study.

The DMLP consisted of five fully connected layers: the input layer, three hidden layers, and the output layer. The input layer included 203 nodes (one for each selected feature), while the hidden layers had 300, 200, and 100 neurons. Initial weights were set by Xavier initialization (Glorot & Bengio, 2010), and the network was trained using an adaptive stochastic gradient descent optimization algorithm called Adam (Kingma & Ba, 2015). The activation functions were sigmoids.

The CNN had ten layers (see Figure 6.5): the input layer, three convolutional layers, a max-pooling layer placed after the first convolutional layer to control overfitting (Scherer et al., 2010), a flatten layer, three fully connected layers, and the output layer. The three convolutional layers had 32, 16, and one filter of size seven, three, and one, respectively. The pool size of the max-pooling layer was two. Finally, the three fully connected layers had 300, 150, and 60 nodes. As before, we used Xavier initialization and the Adam optimization algorithm, but instead of sigmoids we used rectifier functions (Glorot, Bordes, & Bengio, 2011) for the activation functions.

6.3.3.1 Dataset and Predictor Variables

As in Section 6.2, the dataset used in this case study comes from the game *Age of Ishtaria* (Silicon Studio, 2014). Since one of our main goals is to find a suitable method to identify whales as soon as possible, we start by taking a look at the characteristics of these top spenders within our dataset. In Figure 6.6 we can see the—noticeably different—probability distributions of total sales (deduced from a kernel density estimation) for whales and the rest of PUs. The horizontal axis represents total sales in yens, and the area under each curve integrates to one. On the

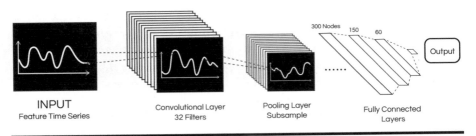

INPUT
Feature Time Series

Convolutional Layer
32 Filters

Pooling Layer
Subsample

300 Nodes   150   60

Output

Fully Connected
Layers

Figure 6.5   Structure of the convolutional neural network used for predicting LTV.

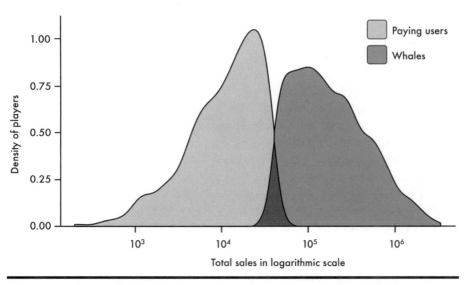

Figure 6.6 **Probability density function of total sales (derived from a kernel density estimation) for whales (top spenders) and the rest of paying users.**

other hand, Figure 6.7 shows the distribution of whales and PUs as a function of their LTV. As expected, there are not many whales with very large LTV—but these users are the most important in terms of revenue.

Our dataset covered approximately 32 months, from September 24, 2014, to May 1, 2017. However, we limited our study on the prediction accuracy

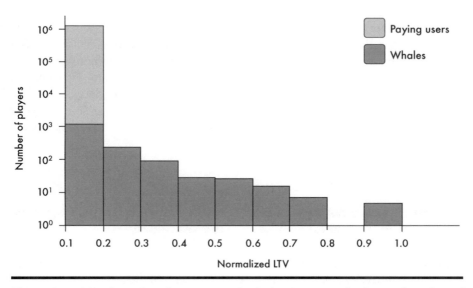

Figure 6.7 **Number of paying users and whales (top spenders) as a function of their normalized lifetime value.**

of the various methods to those paying users who churned between May 1, 2016, and May 1, 2017 (2,505 players), using the data prior to May 1, 2016, to extract the historical RFM information required by the parametric models and the relevant input features for the DNN models. We adopted the same churn definition as introduced in Section 6.2 and considered that a player has abandoned the game after being inactive for 9 days. Inspection of the data supports this definition, as players who remained inactive for 9 days and then became active again—and who were thus incorrectly flagged as churners under this criterion—contribute only marginally (far less than 1%) to the monthly revenue of the game.

For both deep learning models, data from users who left the game before the start of the prediction period was separated into a training set (80% of the players, where 20% of them were used to validate) and a test set (the remaining 20%). At every epoch, the model was first updated using the training set, and second, predictions for the validation set were performed. This process was repeated until prediction errors did not decrease for 20 epochs, after which the weights that yielded the lowest error were adopted. Such an "early stopping" approach helps to prevent overfitting (Prechelt, 1998). The features for the deep learning models consisted of behavior logs for each player, containing information about daily logins, purchases, playtime, level-ups, and other actions. As stressed in Section 6.2, this information is available in most modern games, which ensures the general applicability of the discussed methods. The DMLP model used the statistics of these variables (such as the average daily playing time or the maximum number of level-ups between two consecutive purchases), whereas the CNN model employed their daily time series (covering the whole data period).

On the other hand, parametric models need a fixed prediction horizon,[6] which was set to 365 days. Note that, as previously commented for the Pareto/NBD model, parametric models serve primarily to predict the future number of purchases. However, if we want to estimate LTV, we need a submodel for the monetary value of those transactions. Here we explored two different approaches: either using gamma distributions or simply assigning a fixed value to each purchase made by a certain player, namely the average spend per purchase inferred from his or her transaction history.

6.3.3.2 Results and Discussion

To assess the accuracy of the predictions produced by the different models, the following four error measures were used:

■ The root mean square logarithmic error (RMSLE), which is scale-dependent and sensitive to outliers (Hyndman & Koehler, 2006).

---

[6] Prediction horizons were discussed in more depth in the previous chapter.

- The normalized root mean square error (NRMSE), more appropriate than the RMSLE for comparing datasets with different scales.
- The symmetric mean absolute percentage error (SMAPE), based on the mean of the quotient of the absolute deviations between the observed and predicted values divided by the average of these values.
- The percentage error, computed here as the mean of the deviations divided by the maximum observed value.

The accuracy results for the different models during the training and prediction phases are presented in Tables 6.2 and 6.3, respectively. Even though all models yield predictions with percentage errors less than 10%, both DNN models clearly outperform all parametric models, showing similar NRMSE values to those found by Sifa et al. (2018) for high-value players. Moreover, the significant dip in the RMSLE observed for the deep learning methods suggests that they are more accurate than parametric models at all scales. Remarkably, the results of the DMLP and CNN models are very similar, a fact that is likely due to the large overlap between the features used in each of them.

As for the parametric models, we see that the main differences in performance appeared between those that consider a gamma distribution for the purchase rate (NBD models) and those that allow for regularity within transaction timings (CNBD models). As expected, the latter performed better. In contrast, introducing a gamma-gamma submodel for the spend per transaction (instead of

Table 6.2   Error Measures for the LTV Training for Different Parametric and Deep Learning Models

Model	RMSLE	NRMSE	SMAPE	% Error
Pareto/NBD + average	9.42	1.89	95.87	6.20
Pareto/NBD + gamma	9.43	1.91	96.29	6.24
MGB/CNBD-k + average	3.41	1.72	75.44	5.52
MGB/CNBD-k + gamma	3.55	1.77	78.58	5.71
BG/CNBD-k + average	4.13	1.69	76.82	5.43
BG/CNBD-k + gamma	4.24	1.74	79.83	5.63
BG/NBD + average	9.48	1.89	96.35	6.21
BG/NBD + gamma	9.49	1.92	96.67	6.26
DMLP	1.78	1.07	75.08	3.90
CNN	1.74	1.11	72.75	3.96

Table 6.3   Error Measures for the LTV Prediction for Different Parametric and Deep Learning Models

Model	RMSLE	NRMSE	SMAPE	% Error
Pareto/NBD + average	9.35	1.88	95.65	8.96
Pareto/NBD + gamma	9.37	1.88	96.35	9.01
MGB/CNBD-k + average	3.46	1.68	75.53	7.88
MGB/CNBD-k + gamma	3.61	1.73	79.67	8.08
BG/CNBD-k + average	4.41	1.65	76.22	7.85
BG/CNBD-k + gamma	4.24	1.71	79.72	8.06
BG/NBD + average	9.37	1.88	96.06	8.96
BG/NBD + gamma	9.39	1.88	96.80	9.03
DMLP	1.82	1.12	72.99	5.82
CNN	1.84	1.05	73.76	5.72

simply taking the average of each player's past purchases) does not seem to have any meaningful impact. Therefore, our results do not support the need to introduce such a submodel.

Apart from being less accurate than the deep learning methods, our analysis detected two important problems shared by all parametric models. On the one hand, they often predict no future transactions for players who actually continue purchasing. On the other hand, they systematically underestimate the future spend of the highest-value users. In other words, probabilistic models did not accurately predict the purchasing behavior of whales, and thus are not particularly apt to detect them, which (given the importance of these players) can be seen as a serious shortcoming.

This second problem can be observed in Table 6.4, which compares the prediction errors for all PUs and top spenders (defined as the 20% of players who spent the most during that year). Even though all models yield significantly higher percentage errors when considering only top spenders, the performance of both DNN models is clearly better, with errors that are approximately half as large as in parametric models.

Table 6.4   Prediction Errors for PUs and Top Spenders for Different Parametric and Deep Learning Models

Model	% Error (All PU)	% Error (Top Spenders)
Pareto/NBD + average	8.96	33.35
Pareto/NBD + gamma	9.01	33.39
MGB/CNBD-k + average	7.88	29.61
MGB/CNBD-k + gamma	8.08	30.54
BG/CNBD-k + average	7.85	29.46
BG/CNBD-k + gamma	8.06	30.45
BG/NBD + average	8.96	33.34
BG/NBD + gamma	9.03	33.38
DMLP	5.82	15.76
CNN	5.72	15.64

6.4 Conclusions

In the last few years, both traditional console games and novel mobile games have become always online, allowing game developers to record every single action performed by their players. Such a unique source of information, together with advanced machine learning techniques, opens the door for a comprehensive analysis of player behavior that can be used to predict their actions and to get a thorough understanding of player needs and desires on quantitative grounds.

Reducing user abandonment or churn is a challenge faced by many industries and particularly relevant for the video game sector. Acquisition campaigns to attract new players tend to be expensive, which is why trying to prevent existing users from leaving is normally the most cost-effective approach to increase monetization. To this end, it is essential to identify potential churners beforehand, as this allows developers to implement personalized actions directed toward retaining their most valuable players.

Although there are previous works devoted to churn modeling in video games (Runge et al., 2014; Hadiji et al., 2014; Rothenbuehler, Runge, Garcin, & Faltings, 2015), they—in general—employ methods that yield binary predictions, cannot be readily applied to different data distributions, or are unable to capture the dynamic nature of churn. Moreover, they also face issues of scalability and do not provide predictions at the level of individual players.

In the first part of this chapter, we discussed churn prediction beyond the classical binary approach, exploiting advanced ensemble learning techniques. We have shown that an ensemble model based on survival analysis can accurately predict when and at which game level a player is going to leave the game as well as their cumulative playtime until that moment. The methodology presented provides a comprehensive solution to the churn prediction problem that can be applied to different games and data, is readily implementable in real business settings, and helps to fully understand and anticipate player attrition.

Afterward, we evaluated the performance of machine learning models in the computation of LTV—an estimate of the revenue that a player will generate until they leave the game—and compared it with that of the more traditional parametric models, such as the Pareto/NDB model and its extensions.

It is hardly surprising that deep learning models outperformed simpler parametric models, since the former use much more detailed data and (especially in the case of the DMLP) computational resources. More noteworthy, the difference in performance is especially acute in the case of top spenders, whose purchasing behavior is poorly predicted by probabilistic models. This is of critical importance, considering that one of the primary objectives of LTV prediction in video games is the early detection of whales.

Deep learning models not only present advantages in terms of accuracy but also from an operational point of view. The ultimate goal is to engineer a model that can be run daily in production settings and is able to analyze the large datasets generated by players since they join a game. CNN models emerge as promising candidates, as these networks can assimilate raw data, not requiring the pre-processing or feature engineering demanded by the DMLP or Pareto/NDB models. This can translate into significant savings in computational time, which may prove essential in the case of AAA games, where datasets can be really huge—containing up to petabytes of data.

In future work, we will investigate the sensitivity of our predictions to the forecast horizon (with the aim of automatically finding the optimal horizon for each game) and to the size of the training set (trying to find the minimum size that still results in accurate predictions). We also plan to investigate other deep learning structures, such as long short-term memory (LSTM) networks (Hochreiter & Schmidhuber, 1997), which can learn feature representations from time-series data with a long-term view.

In short, we have shown that machine learning models are capable of teasing out significant information on the future behavior of individual players from the large datasets generated by video games. The predictions produced by these models can prove invaluable to developers, as they could help to reduce player attrition, boost conversion rates, and maximize the playing time and lifetime value of individual users. Moreover, studios may take advantage of such forecasts to increase the appeal of their games through player-focused data-driven development. As all these possibilities should result in a significantly increased game monetization, we cannot but conclude that the future of video games is closely intertwined with machine learning.

Acknowledgments

We would like to thank Javier Grande for his great help editing this chapter and Vitor Santos for his support with data visualization.

References

Aalen, O. (1978). Nonparametric inference for a family of counting processes. *The Annals of Statistics, 6*(4), 701–726.

Amin, A., Al-Obeidat, F., Shah, B., Adnan, A., Loo, J., & Anwar, S. (2019). Customer churn prediction in telecommunication industry using data certainty. *Journal of Business Research, 94*, 290–301.

Babu, G. S., Zhao, P., & Li, X. L. (2016). Deep convolutional neural network-based regression approach for estimation of remaining useful life. In *International Conference on Database Systems for Advanced Applications* (pp. 214–228). Cham, Switzerland: Springer.

Batislam, E. P., Denizel, M., & Filiztekin, A. (2007). Empirical validation and comparison of models for customer base analysis. *International Journal of Research in Marketing, 24*(3), 201–209.

Bengio, Y. (2009). Learning deep architectures for AI. *Foundations and Trends® in Machine Learning, 2*(1), 1–127.

Berger, P. D., & Nasr, N. I. (1998). Customer lifetime value: Marketing models and applications. *Journal of Interactive Marketing, 12*(1), 17–30.

Bertens, P., Guitart, A., & Periáñez, Á. (2017). Games and big data: A scalable multi-dimensional churn prediction model. In *IEEE Conference on Computational Intelligence and Games* (pp. 33–36). IEEE.

Bou-Hamad, I., Larocque, D., & Ben-Ameur, H. (2011). A review of survival trees. *Statistics Surveys, 5*, 44–71.

Breiman, L. (1996). Bagging predictors. *Machine Learning, 24*(2), 123–140.

Breiman, L. (2001). Random forests. *Machine Learning, 45*(1), 5–32.

Breiman, L., Friedman, J., Stone, C. J., & Olshen, R. A. (1984). *Classification and regression trees*. Boca Raton, FL: CRC press.

Brier, G. W. (1950). Verification of forecasts expressed in terms of probability. *Monthly Weather Review, 78*(1), 1–3.

Chamberlain, B. P., Cardoso, A., Liu, C. H., Pagliari, R., & Deisenroth, M. P. (2017). Customer lifetime value prediction using embeddings. In *Proceedings of the 23rd ACM SIGKDD International Conference on Knowledge Discovery and Data Mining* (pp. 1753–1762). ACM Press.

Chatfield, C., & Goodhardt, G. J. (1973). A consumer purchasing model with Erlang inter-purchase times. *Journal of the American Statistical Association, 68*(344), 828–835.

Chen, M. C., Chiu, A. L., & Chang, H. H. (2005). Mining changes in customer behavior in retail marketing. *Expert Systems with Applications, 28*(4), 773–781.

Chen, P. P., Guitart, A., del Río, A. F., & Periáñez, Á. (2018). Customer lifetime value in video games using deep learning and parametric models. Retrieved from https://arxiv.org/abs/1811.12799

Ciampi, A., Bush, R. S., Gospodarowicz, M., & Till, J. E. (1981). An approach to classifying prognostic factors related to survival experience for non-Hodgkin's lymphoma patients: Based on a series of 982 patients: 1967–1975. *Cancer, 47*(3), 621–627.

Ciodaro, T., Deva, D., De Seixas, J. M., & Damazio, D. (2012). Online particle detection with neural networks based on topological calorimetry information. In *Journal of Physics: Conference Series, 368*(1), 012030.

Clark, T. G., Bradburn, M. J., Love, S. B., & Altman, D. G. (2003). Survival analysis part I: Basic concepts and first analyses. *British Journal of Cancer, 89*, 232–238.

Cox, D. (1972). Regression models and life-tables. *Journal of the Royal Statistical Society. Series B (Methodological), 34*(2), 187–220.

Cox, D. R., & Oakes, D. (1984). *Analysis of survival data*. Boca Raton, FL: CRC Press.

Davidovici-Nora, M. (2013). Innovation in business models in the video game industry: Free-To-Play or the gaming experience as a service. *The Computer Games Journal, 2*(3), 22–51.

Ding, J., Gao, D., & Chen, X. (2015). Alone in the game: Dynamic spread of churn behavior in a large social network a longitudinal study in MMORPG. *International Journal of Smart Home, 9*(3), 35–44.

Drachen, A., Pastor, M., Liu, A., Fontaine, D. J., Chang, Y., Runge, J., … Klabjan, D. (2018). To be or not to be… social: Incorporating simple social features in mobile game customer lifetime value predictions. In *Proceedings of the Australasian Computer Science Week Multiconference* (Article no. 40). ACM Press.

Dwyer, F. R. (1997). Customer lifetime valuation to support marketing decision making. *Journal of Direct Marketing, 11*(4), 6–13.

Esteva, A., Kuprel, B., Novoa, R. A., Ko, J., Swetter, S. M., Blau, H. M., & Thrun, S. (2017). Dermatologist-level classification of skin cancer with deep neural networks. *Nature, 542*, 115.

Fader, P. S., & Hardie, B. G. S. (2005). *A note on deriving the Pareto/NBD model and related expressions*. Retrieved from http://www.brucehardie.com/notes/009/pareto_nbd_derivations_2005-11-05.pdf

Fader, P. S., Hardie, B. G., & Lee, K. L. (2005a). "Counting your customers" the easy way: An alternative to the Pareto/NBD model. *Marketing Science, 24*(2), 275–284.

Fader, P. S., Hardie, B. G., & Lee, K. L. (2005b). RFM and CLV: Using iso-value curves for customer base analysis. *Journal of Marketing Research, 42*(4), 415–430.

Farris, P. W., Bendle, N., Pfeifer, P., & Reibstein, D. (2010). *Marketing metrics: The definitive guide to measuring marketing performance*. Upper Saddle River, NJ: Pearson Education.

Fleming, T. R., & Lin, D. Y. (2000). Survival analysis in clinical trials: past developments and future directions. *Biometrics, 56*(4), 971–983.

Fu, L., & Wang, H. (2014). Estimating insurance attrition using survival analysis. *Variance, 8*(1), 55–72.

Glorot, X., & Bengio, Y. (2010). Understanding the difficulty of training deep feedforward neural networks. In *Proceedings of the Thirteenth International Conference on Artificial Intelligence and Statistics* (pp. 249–256). Sardinia, Italy: PMLR.

Glorot, X., Bordes, A., & Bengio, Y. (2011). Deep sparse rectifier neural networks. In *Proceedings of the fourteenth International Conference on Artificial Intelligence and Statistics* (pp. 315–323).

Gordon, L., & Olshen, R. A. (1985). Tree-structured survival analysis. *Cancer Treatment Reports*, *69*(10), 1065–1069.

Graves, A., Mohamed, A. R., & Hinton, G. (2013). Speech recognition with deep recurrent neural networks. In *2013 IEEE international conference on Acoustics, speech and signal processing* (pp. 6645–6649). IEEE.

Guitart, A., Chen, P. P., Bertens, P., & Periáñez, Á. (2018). Forecasting player behavioral data and simulating in-game events. In *Future of Information and Communication Conference* (pp. 274–293). Cham, Switzerland: Springer.

Gupta, S. (1991). Stochastic models of interpurchase time with time-dependent covariates. *Journal of Marketing Research*, *28*(1), 1–15.

Hadiji, F., Sifa, R., Drachen, A., Thurau, C., Kersting, K., & Bauckhage, C. (2014). Predicting player churn in the wild. In *IEEE Conference on Computational intelligence and games (CIG)*, (pp. 1–8). IEEE.

He, B., Shi, Y., Wan, Q., & Zhao, X. (2014). Prediction of customer attrition of commercial banks based on SVM model. *Procedia Computer Science, 31*, 423–430.

Herniter, J. (1971). A probablistic market model of purchase timing and brand selection. *Management Science, 18*(4-part-ii), P-102–P-113.

Hochreiter, S., & Schmidhuber, J. (1997). Long short-term memory. *Neural Computation*, *9*(8), 1735–1780.

Hoekstra, J. C., & Huizingh, E. K. (1999). The lifetime value concept in customer-based marketing. *Journal of Market-Focused Management, 3*(3–4), 257–274.

Hothorn, T., Bühlmann, P., Dudoit, S., Molinaro, A., & Van Der Laan, M. J. (2005). Survival ensembles. *Biostatistics, 7*(3), 355–373.

Hothorn, T., Hornik, K., & Zeileis, A. (2006). Unbiased recursive partitioning: A conditional inference framework. *Journal of Computational and Graphical Statistics, 15*(3), 651–674.

Hothorn, T., Lausen, B., Benner, A., & Radespiel-Tröger, M. (2004). Bagging survival trees. *Statistics in Medicine, 23*(1), 77–91.

Hougaard, P. (1999). Fundamentals of survival data. *Biometrics, 55*(1), 13–22.

Huang, B., Kechadi, M. T., & Buckley, B. (2012). Customer churn prediction in telecommunications. *Expert Systems with Applications, 39*(1), 1414–1425.

Hyndman, R. J., & Koehler, A. B. (2006). Another look at measures of forecast accuracy. *International Journal of Forecasting, 22*(4), 679–688.

Ishwaran, H., Kogalur, U. B., Blackstone, E. H., & Lauer, M. S. (2008). Random survival forests. *The Annals of Applied Statistics, 2*(3), 841–860.

Kaplan, E. L., & Meier, P. (1958). Nonparametric estimation from incomplete observations. *Journal of the American Statistical Association, 53*(282), 457–481.

Kawale, J., Pal, A., & Srivastava, J. (2009). Churn prediction in MMORPGs: A social influence-based approach. In *International Conference on Computational Science and Engineering* (pp. 423–428). IEEE.

Kim, S., Choi, D., Lee, E., & Rhee, W. (2017). Churn prediction of mobile and online casual games using play log data. *PLoS One, 12*(7), e0180735.

Kingma, D. P., & Ba, J. (2015). Adam: A method for stochastic optimization. *In Proceedings of the 3rd international conference on learning representations.* Retrieved from https://arxiv.org/abs/1412.6980

Kretowska, M. (2014). Comparison of tree-based ensembles in application to censored data. In *International Conference on Artificial Intelligence and Soft Computing* (pp. 551–560). Cham, Switzerland: Springer.

Kumar, D. A., & Ravi, V. (2008). Predicting credit card customer churn in banks using data mining. *International Journal of Data Analysis Techniques and Strategies, 1*(1), 4–28.

LeCun, Y., & Bengio, Y. (1995). Convolutional networks for images, speech, and time series. In M. A. Arbib (Ed.), *The handbook of brain theory and neural networks* (pp. 276–279). Cambridge, MA: MIT Press.

LeCun, Y., Bengio, Y., & Hinton, G. (2015). Deep learning. *Nature, 521*, 436–444.

LeCun, Y., Boser, B., Denker, J. S., Henderson, D., Howard, R. E., Hubbard, W., & Jackel, L. D. (1989). Backpropagation applied to handwritten zip code recognition. *Neural Computation, 1*(4), 541–551.

Li, J., & Ma, S. (2013). *Survival analysis in medicine and genetics.* CRC Press.

Lu, J. (2002). Predicting customer churn in the telecommunications industry—An application of survival analysis modeling using SAS. *SAS User Group International (SUGI27) Online Proceedings*, 114–127.

Luton, W. (2013). *Free-to-play: Making money from games you give away.* San Francisco, CA: New Riders.

Marubini, E., Morabito, A., & Valsecchi, M. G. (1983). Prognostic factors and risk groups: Some results given by using an algorithm suitable for censored survival data. *Statistics in Medicine, 2*(2), 295–303.

Marubini, E., & Valsecchi, M. G. (2004). *Analysing survival data from clinical trials and observational studies.* Chichester, UK: John Wiley & Sons.

Mittal, S., Madigan, D., Burd, R. S., & Suchard, M. A. (2013). High-dimensional, massive sample-size Cox proportional hazards regression for survival analysis. *Biostatistics, 15*(2), 207–221.

Mogensen, U. B., Ishwaran, H., & Gerds, T. A. (2012). Evaluating random forests for survival analysis using prediction error curves. *Journal of Statistical Software, 50*(11), 1–23.

Morgan, J. N., & Sonquist, J. A. (1963). Problems in the analysis of survey data, and a proposal. *Journal of the American Statistical Association, 58*(302), 415–434.

Morik, K., & Köpcke, H. (2004). Analysing customer churn in insurance data—A case study. In *European Conference on Principles of Data Mining and Knowledge Discovery* (pp. 325–336). Berlin, Germany: Springer.

Nelson, W. (1972). Theory and applications of hazard plotting for censored failure data. *Technometrics, 14*(4), 945–966.

Periáñez, Á., Saas, A., Guitart, A., & Magne, C. (2016). Churn prediction in mobile social games: Towards a complete assessment using survival ensembles. In *IEEE International Conference on Data Science and Advanced Analytics* (pp. 564–573). IEEE.

Pfeifer, P. E., Haskins, M. E., & Conroy, R. M. (2005). Customer lifetime value, customer profitability, and the treatment of acquisition spending. *Journal of Managerial Issues, 17*(1), 11–25.

Platzer, M. (2016). *Customer base analysis with BTYDplus.* Retrieved from https://rdrr.io/cran/BTYDplus/f/inst/doc/BTYDplus-HowTo.pdf

Platzer, M., & Reutterer, T. (2016). Ticking away the moments: Timing regularity helps to better predict customer activity. *Marketing Science, 35*(5), 779–799.

Powell, J. L. (1984). Least absolute deviations estimation for the censored regression model. *Journal of Econometrics, 25*(3), 303–325.

Prechelt, L. (1998). Early stopping-but when? In *Neural Networks: Tricks of the trade* (pp. 55–69). Berlin, Germany: Springer.

Prentice, R. L., Kalbfleisch, J. D., Peterson Jr, A. V., Flournoy, N., Farewell, V. T., & Breslow, N. E. (1978). The analysis of failure times in the presence of competing risks. *Biometrics, 34*(4), 541–554.

Quinlan, J. R. (1986). Induction of decision trees. *Machine learning, 1*(1), 81–106.

Rajkomar, A., Oren, E., Chen, K., Dai, A. M., Hajaj, N., Hardt, M., … Dean, J. (2018). Scalable and accurate deep learning with electronic health records. *npj Digital Medicine, 1*(1), 18.

Rothenbuehler, P., Runge, J., Garcin, F., & Faltings, B. (2015). Hidden Markov models for churn prediction. In *SAI Intelligent Systems Conference* (pp. 723–730). IEEE.

Runge, J., Gao, P., Garcin, F., & Faltings, B. (2014). Churn prediction for high-value players in casual social games. In *IEEE Conference on Computational Intelligence and Games* (pp. 1–8). IEEE.

Salzberg, S. L. (1994). [Review of the book *C4.5: Programs for Machine Learning*, by J. R. Quinlan]. *Machine Learning, 16*(3), 235–240.

Scherer, D., Müller, A., & Behnke, S. (2010). Evaluation of pooling operations in convolutional architectures for object recognition. In *Artificial Neural Networks–ICANN 2010* (pp. 92–101). Berlin, Germany: Springer.

Schmidhuber, J. (2015). Deep learning in neural networks: An overview. *Neural Networks, 61*, 85–117.

Schmittlein, D. C., Morrison, D. G., & Colombo, R. (1987). Counting your customers: Who are they and what will they do next? *Management Science, 33*(1), 1–24.

Shaw, R., & Stone, M. (1988). *Database marketing*. Aldershot, UK: Gower.

Sifa, R., Hadiji, F., Runge, J., Drachen, A., Kersting, K., & Bauckhage, C. (2015). Predicting purchase decisions in mobile free-to-play games. In *Proceedings of the Conference on Artificial Intelligence and Interactive Digital Entertainment* (pp. 79–85). AAAI.

Sifa, R., Runge, J., Bauckhage, C., & Klapper, D. (2018). Customer lifetime value prediction in non-contractual freemium settings: Chasing high-value users using deep neural networks and SMOTE. In *Proceedings of the 51st Hawaii International Conference on System Sciences* (pp. 923–932).

Silicon Studio (2014). *Age of Ishtaria* [Mobile game]. Tokyo, Japan: Silicon Studio.

Smith, K. A., Willis, R. J., & Brooks, M. (2000). An analysis of customer retention and insurance claim patterns using data mining: A case study. *Journal of the Operational Research Society, 51*(5), 532–541.

Stepanova, M., & Thomas, L. (2002). Survival analysis methods for personal loan data. *Operations Research, 50*(2), 277–289.

Szegedy, C., Liu, W., Jia, Y., Sermanet, P., Reed, S., Anguelov, D., … & Rabinovich, A. (2015). Going deeper with convolutions. In *Proceedings of the IEEE Conference on Computer Vision and Pattern Recognition* (pp. 1–9).

Tamaddoni Jahromi, A., Sepehri, M. M., Teimourpour, B., & Choobdar, S. (2010). Modeling customer churn in a non-contractual setting: The case of telecommunications service providers. *Journal of Strategic Marketing, 18*(7), 587–598.

Therneau, T. M., & Grambsch, P. M. (2000). *Modeling survival data: Extending the Cox model*. New York, NY: Springer Science+Business Media.

Tkachenko, Y. (2015). *Autonomous CRM control via CLV approximation with deep reinforcement learning in discrete and continuous action space*. Retrieved from https://arxiv.org/abs/1504.01840

Tsantekidis, A., Passalis, N., Tefas, A., Kanniainen, J., Gabbouj, M., & Iosifidis, A. (2017). Forecasting stock prices from the limit order book using convolutional neural networks. In *IEEE 19th Conference on Business Informatics* (pp. 7–12). IEEE.

Turaga, S. C., Murray, J. F., Jain, V., Roth, F., Helmstaedter, M., Briggman, K., … Seung, H. S. (2010). Convolutional networks can learn to generate affinity graphs for image segmentation. *Neural Computation, 22*(2), 511–538.

Verbeke, W., Martens, D., Mues, C., & Baesens, B. (2011). Building comprehensible customer churn prediction models with advanced rule induction techniques. *Expert Systems with Applications, 38*(3), 2354–2364.

Voigt, S., & Hinz, O. (2016). Making digital freemium business models a success: Predicting customers' lifetime value via initial purchase information. *Business & Information Systems Engineering, 58*(2), 107–118.

Wheat, R. D., & Morrison, D. G. (1990). Estimating purchase regularity with two inter-purchase times. *Journal of Marketing Research, 27*(1), 87–93.

Wright, M. N., Dankowski, T., & Ziegler, A. (2017). Unbiased split variable selection for random survival forests using maximally selected rank statistics. *Statistics in Medicine, 36*(8), 1272–1284.

Xiong, H. Y., Alipanahi, B., Lee, L. J., Bretschneider, H., Merico, D., Yuen, R. K., ... & Frey, B. J. (2015). The human splicing code reveals new insights into the genetic determinants of disease. *Science, 347*(6218).

Yang, J. B., Nguyen, M. N., San, P. P., Li, X. L., & Krishnaswamy, S. (2015). Deep convolutional neural networks on multichannel time series for human activity recognition. In *Proceedings of the Twenty-Fourth International Joint Conference on Artificial Intelligence* (pp. 3995–4001).

Yoon, S., Koehler, J., & Ghobarah, A. (2010). Prediction of advertiser churn for Google AdWords. In *JSM Proceedings*. Alexandria, VA: American Statistical Association.

Yu, X., Guo, S., Guo, J., & Huang, X. (2011). An extended support vector machine forecasting framework for customer churn in e-commerce. *Expert Systems with Applications, 38*(3), 1425–1430.

Zhang, C., & Ma, Y. (Eds.). (2012). *Ensemble machine learning: Methods and applications*. New York, NY: Springer Science+Business Media.

Zorić, A. B. (2016). Predicting customer churn in banking industry using neural networks. *Interdisciplinary Description of Complex Systems: INDECS, 14*(2), 116–124.

Chapter 7

Integrating Social and Textual Analytics into Game Analytics

Lareina Milambiling, Michael Katchabaw, and Damir Slogar

Contents

7.1 Introduction

It has been recently said that the world's most valuable resource is no longer oil but rather data (The Economist, 2017). Its true worth, however, is not realized until it has been mined, refined, and processed into a more useful form—knowledge. To do so, powerful analytics techniques are essential to the modern organization. In the games industry, this has given rise to what is referred to as game analytics (El-Nasr, Drachen, & Canossa, 2013; Lovato, 2015). Analytics can be applied to every aspect of a game, including its development, marketing, user acquisition, play, and monetization. Currently, game analytics is dominated by an ingest, store, process, analyze, and present approach (Wiger, 2015; Weber, 2018a, 2018b) to deliver key insights to decision-makers (Tabor & Vrdoljak, 2016). That said, richer and deeper analytics methods based on machine learning[1] and data mining are beginning to emerge in the marketplace (Grosso, 2017; Kerr, 2017), and research activity in these directions is also on the rise, as discussed in (El-Nasr, Drachen, & Canossa, 2013; Latysheva, 2017).

While considerable efforts have been spent leveraging various quantitative approaches in this space, surprisingly little effort has been expended on analyzing and correlating textual artifacts created by players before, during, and after play. Existing work such as Albrechtslund (2010); Jordan, Buente, Silva, & Rosenbaum (2016); Seay, Jerome, Lee, & Kraut (2004); and Warmelink & Siitonen (2011) mainly took a qualitative approach.

The reality is that textual artifacts are commonplace, found in reviews, message board comments, postings on social media such as Facebook or Twitter, e-mail communications with developers, and so forth. These artifacts have the potential to provide significant insight into both the player and their play in ways that have yet to be explored. Do these artifacts correlate with metrics of engagement, retention, conversion, or churn? What are the predictive qualities of these artifacts? What are their limitations? Not knowing the answers to these questions represents a tremendous gap in current approaches to game analytics, a gap that can only be addressed through integrating social and textual analytics driven by computational linguistics into the traditional game analytics pipeline.

---

[1] Machine learning techniques are discussed in Chapter 6.

This chapter provides a thorough and detailed treatment of this topic, delving into both theoretical and practical aspects of integrating social and textual analytics into modern game analytics. This chapter divides this treatment into sections as follows:

- **Background**: Introduces the reader to game analytics, social analytics, and textual analytics, providing motivation and discussing the current state-of-the-art in these areas.
- **Integration Framework**: An examination of how to integrate social and textual analytics into a traditional game analytics pipeline, delving into design and architectural considerations. This resulted in the creation of the Framework for the Integration of Social and Textual Analytics (FISATA).
- **Implementation Guide**: With the framework in mind, this section discusses practical aspects of implementing FISATA, using our mobile gaming data systems at Big Blue Bubble and our musical world-builder game, *My Singing Monsters* (Big Blue Bubble, 2012), as a baseline and foundation for this work.
- **Case Study**: With implementation in hand, a comprehensive case study was conducted on *My Singing Monsters* player data accumulated over a three-and-a-half-year period, including traditional metrics and key performance indicators, as well as social media artifacts mined using the Hootsuite analytics tool. An extensive analysis was conducted using this integrated dataset, exploring retention, engagement, purchase behavior, and other measures of player activity in this context. This section presents the methodologies, data, analysis, and results from this case study in detail.
- **Conclusions**: A conclusion to the chapter, discussing key takeaways and plans for future work in this area.

7.2 Background

Game analytics is a rapidly growing and increasingly important quantitative element of game development in which player and play data is analyzed to discover actionable information that could guide monetization and future development activities. Over time, game analytics has evolved from a handful of simple metrics and statistics to leverage more complex and powerful analytical techniques, borrowing from allied disciplines such as data analytics, big data, and business intelligence. The problem space too has shifted over time; no longer is it solely about converting users or generating revenue. Indeed, there is a growing interest in general game design improvement and optimization. Consequently, we are increasingly seeing game analytics applied across the industry, and these trends are only growing stronger (El-Nasr, Drachen, & Canossa, 2013).

7.2.1 Traditional Metrics and Key Performance Indicators

Game analytics started at first with a single, simple metric, downloads (Yamparala, 2014). While providing a basic number yielding some indication of player base, this metric on its own is of limited usefulness (El-Nasr, Drachen, & Canossa, 2013). Over time, more robust sets of metrics were employed to measure players and their play, such as the pirate metrics (acquisition, activation, retention, referral, and revenue, in short AARRR) (Yamparala, 2014). Such metrics can track players from their initial exposure to the game (acquisition) through to their conversion (revenue), providing much more valuable information. A similar set of metrics (but without such a catchy acronym), which serve as key performance indicators that are essential to game analytics, was discussed by Williams (2015).

Other key performance indicators are now used to provide more detail, especially of play activity. These include download/upgrade actions, activity, activity time, recency, ratings, churn, loading time, behavior flow, and crashes/exceptions (Yamparala, 2015). Lifetime value (LTV) has also emerged as one of the most important metrics for games[2] (MacMillan, 2017) and can assist in the calculation or prediction of other key metrics, such as return on investment (ROI) or return on advertising spending (ROAS). The evolution and maturation of analytics is reflected in the growing availability of industry-standard tools to assist in collecting, analyzing, and understanding these metrics. Such tools include Flurry, Google Analytics, Localytics, Kissmetrics, deltaDNA, and others (El-Nasr, Drachen, & Canossa, 2013; Tabor & Vrdoljak, 2016; Roseboom, 2017).

Growing attention has been given to game analytics in the broader research community, with developers investigating new metrics, as well as new approaches to collection, mining, analysis, evaluation, and visualization. A compendium of novel work and contributions from this community can be found in El-Nasr, Drachen, & Canossa (2013).

Studying the literature and tools in this area identifies a considerable gap and opportunity for research and exploration: computational linguistics analysis. Players create a variety of textual artifacts before, during, and after play. These artifacts can be found in reviews, message board comments, postings on social media such as Facebook or Twitter, e-mail communications with developers, and the like, and have the potential to provide deeper insight into both the player and their play in ways that have yet to be thoroughly explored. That said, work toward analyzing and correlating textual artifacts created by players is much harder to come by in the literature than more traditional quantitative approaches to analytics. However, there do exist some qualitative accounts, such as the work of Albrechtslund (2010); Jordan, Buente, Silva, & Rosenbaum (2016); Seay, Jerome, Lee, & Kraut (2004); and Warmelink & Siitonen (2011). While this work provides valuable results from an analytics perspective, it unfortunately yields few insights into the construction of reusable and transferable systems and supports to enable such work in other games in the future.

---

[2] See also Chapters 5 and 6.

Regardless, this initial work clearly demonstrates the benefits of leveraging computational linguistics analysis in the analysis of games. To shed further light on the possibilities presented in such an approach, it is important to first examine the state-of-the-art methods currently found in the discipline of computational linguistics.

7.2.2 Textual Methods and Computational Linguistics

In order to provide proper computational linguistic analysis of the textual artifacts, methods from the fields of text normalization, social media linguistic analysis, text mining, and information retrieval are needed. Here we provide an overview of these fields and discuss the rationale for their integration into broader efforts for game analytics.

7.2.2.1 Text Normalization and Social Media Linguistic Analysis

The nature of the information and data frequently encountered in the gaming space is a newer type of linguistic structure, one that has developed over the last several years and has yet to be thoroughly analyzed: social media. Social media language involves the use of many non-standard spellings and syntax; therefore prior to textual analysis, text normalization is required, based on recently found patterns in social media wordplay and brevity.

Text normalization is a method for conversion of text that includes non-standard words, such as numbers, abbreviations, and misspellings, into normal words. Such non-standard words include abbreviation expansion (including novel abbreviations), expansion of numbers into "number names," correction of misspellings, and disambiguation in cases where there is ambiguity. This method can aid in drawing together different versions of the same word or phrases into one type for ease of analysis. In order to understand how to model a text normalization system for this data, the use of recent social media linguistic analysis is needed.

The majority of linguistic research thus far has investigated formal writing and conversation transcripts, many of which conform to standard language syntax, vocabulary, and orthography (Moseley, 2013). The linguistic analysis of social media language, as well as textual data from blog posts, e-mails, text messages, comments on articles, photos, and videos, is still a new and exciting field. Therefore, navigating the unique syntax, semantics, and brevity patterns of social media, and aligning the aforementioned methods with these aspects, can be a challenge in itself.

Moseley (2013) outlines nine types of abbreviations performed by social media users:

1. Single character, for example: "see" → "c"
2. Word end, for example: "why" → "y"
3. Drop vowels, for example: "should" → "shld"

4. Word begin, for example: "schedule" → "sched"
5. You to U, for example: "your" → "ur"
6. Drop last character, for example: "saying" → "sayin"
7. Repeat letter, for example: "food" → "fooooooood"
8. Contraction, for example: "birthday" → "b'day"
9. Th to D, for example: "this" → "dis"

Further work has been done by McMillan (2014), describing more types of word-play used by social media users (examples provided by McMillan (2014), all taken from Twitter):

1. Phonemic character substitution, for example: "everyone" → "everyl" or "tomorrow" → "2morrow"
2. Acronyms, for example: "laugh out loud" → "lol" or "oh my God" → "omg"
3. Vowel deletion (similar to drop vowels type above), for example: "please" → "pls" or "goodnight" → "gnite"
4. Part of words, for example: "definitely" → "def" or "shout out" → "s/o"
5. Extra letters (similar to repeat letter rule above), for example: "yes" → "… YEESSSSSS"
6. Prepositional because, for example: "Cuddle sesh in the library. Because friendship and emotions" -@HaleySoehn or "Can't study because sleep but can't sleep because study"-@OhlookitsNiamh
7. "I can't even" and variations
8. "That X tho," for example: "That Game of Thrones episode tho. HODOR." -@notcoolraul
9. DFGHJKL (or, nonsense), for example: "…oh. my. god…THIS IS AMAZING AND I AM SO HAPPY AND WEIRDLY PROUD AND UGH JUST SO MANY FEELSDFGHJKL" -@ConnorFranta

Often users use a combination of these abbreviations and wordplay with formal spellings of words; therefore, to correctly identify patterns within the data, a method to recognize multiple forms as the same meaning would require text normalization methods.

Computer-mediated communication also differs from other means of communication in that it lacks prosodic and facial expression, and users have developed several strategies to make up for this deficit (McMillan, 2014). McMillan explains that users use a combination of capitalization and punctuation for marking prosody. Again, this would be something to consider when creating text normalization rules for social media data.

Additionally, what would need to be considered for text normalization are extra-linguistic strategies, often found in social media posts, such as emotions and symbols (e.g., "=" to say "is" or "equivalent") that are used even when any transient linguistic synonyms would not be grammatical (McMillan, 2014).

Therefore, text normalization would be required when dealing with the varying and novel structural patterns found in social media data. However, mixing both formal spellings and differing brevity techniques and prosodic strategies is not unique to social media but can increasingly be found in other forms of communication as well. Consequently, text normalization in accordance with the above outlined social media wordplay types would also aid in capturing the necessary sentiments in communication contexts different from social media.

7.2.2.2 Text Mining and Sentiment Analysis

Text mining is naturally an extension of the field of data mining. Hearst (2004) points out that the metaphor of "mining" is in fact not a very good metaphor for what people in the field of data mining actually do. This metaphor implies that they are extracting and discovering new factoids within their inventory databases; however, what is truly being done by data mining applications tends to be (semi-) automated discovery of trends and patterns across very large datasets, typically for the purposes of decision-making (Hearst, 2004). In the case of text mining, on the other hand, Hearst argues that the mining metaphor that implies the extraction and discovery of factoids from inventory databases can be taken seriously. This is done by discovering or deriving new information from data, finding patterns across datasets, and/or separating signal from noise.

In particular, a specific summarization technique used with text mining would be most useful toward the gaming space: sentiment analysis (Konchady, 2006). Text mining not only makes it easier to find relevant information in a data collection, but this method of summarization also reduces the time a researcher must spend browsing to locate useful text, answer a question, or categorize a document (Konchady, 2006). Previously, this technique has been used to classify news articles into three groups: objective, subjective, neutral. Objective articles present a series of facts related to an event; subjective articles express opinions, ideas, or beliefs; and mixed (neutral) articles consist of part fact and part opinion (Konchady, 2006). More specifically, this classification can be accomplished through the categorization of parts of speech, entities, and word senses and establishing classification features that support an objective or subjective classification. Once these features are known, a naive Bayes classifier (Murphy, 2006) can be applied to estimate the probability that a sentence is subjective (or objective) given the presence or absence of these features (Konchady, 2006). This technique can be simplified by looking at the identification of subjective sentences alone. Some words are more commonly found in subjective rather than objective sentences. For example, the presence of one or more adjectives is frequently a useful indicator of a subjective sentence (Konchady, 2006).

Subjective sentences can be further classified into a positive, negative, or neutral category based on the type of adjectives found in the sentences (e.g., depraved and aggravating are negative adjectives, and genuine and lucky are positive adjectives) (Konchady, 2006). Given the nature of social media posts, one can typically assume that social media entries should be considered subjective, and the focus of work shifts to classifying the social media entries as positive, negative, or neutral (Konchady, 2006). This can be done using the aforementioned word classification to categorize the opinion of sentences in the social media entries. This begins with seed words of manually identified positive and negative adjectives and proceeds with the assumption that words of the same category tend to co-occur in sentences; further word classifications could be done using a likelihood ratio for the occurrence of two words in a phrase (Konchady, 2006).

Applying these techniques, sentences can be classified as positive, negative, or neutral from the average per-word log-likelihood ratio (Konchady, 2006). Building from these techniques, we can then classify the obtained social media entries, providing ease of understanding and analysis of users' opinions by developers for game analytics, opening up many possibilities that previously did not exist. Can aggregate player reactions on social media be mapped to changes in a game's key performance indicators? Are individual player sentiments reflected in their behavior in-game? Do they have any predictive qualities? Given its ability to shed light on these and other important questions, integrating sentiment analysis into game analytics has significant potential.

That said, there are complexities, however, that need to be considered to effectively use sentiment analysis. For example, domain slang can be an issue, as words can take on other meanings in different contexts, as noted by Bertone and Burghardt (2017) and supported by Drescher et al. (2018). This can be particularly the case for games, where game worlds have different rules, norms, customs, and objectives than the real world, and so the meaning of words can change accordingly in these contexts. This does not make sentiment analysis impossible, but it certainly makes it much less straightforward in practice than it is in theory (Drescher et al., 2018).

7.2.2.3 Information Retrieval

Information retrieval differs from text mining in that information retrieval helps users find information that satisfies their needs rather than looking for new discoveries or deriving new information from the current data (Hearst, 2004). The typical problem solved by information retrieval is not that the desired information is not known, but rather that the desired information coexists with many other valid pieces of information. Given the nature of the gaming space, these methods would be useful as well should a developer wish to find specific analytical information for their current needs. This method would help developers retrieve specific information when needed and perform certain tasks.

In recent years, research has studied the integration of language-oriented methods with statistically based methods in information retrieval (Tzoukermann, Klavans, & Strzalkowski, 2004). Many natural language processing applications

Figure 7.1   Traditional metrics workflow.

in information retrieval focus on linguistic techniques to obtain better linguistically motivated indexing, while others attempt to exploit semantic information. The motivations and differing approaches behind these methods can both offer valuable insight as to how to approach and design our textual analytics process.

7.2.2.4 Tools Development

Based on this research, a number of tools and libraries are under active development, including Apache OpenNLP, Python NLTK and TextBlob, R's NLP and TM modules, and GATE.[3] These show considerable promise and could be adapted for use when integrating social and textual analytics into game analytics. Some commercial products (e.g., Hootsuite) are also emerging in this space. Such tools can be quite powerful and useful but can be prohibitively expensive solutions for some applications.

7.3 Integration Framework

As noted above, the traditional workflow for metrics for game analytics is a simple ingest, store, process, analyze, and present pipeline (Wiger, 2015; Weber, 2018a, 2018b). This basic approach is depicted in Figure 7.1. The various phases of this workflow operate as follows:

- **Ingest:** At this point, raw data is taken in from the game, typically in some portable format like JSON or XML, through some form of API (application programming interface) gateway. Often the data is provided through a web service but could be a more specialized reporting/notification/message queuing service as well. This process of ingestion is also sometimes referred to as ETL (extract, transform, and load),[4] as data may be pulled from multiple sources and the target of ingestion is some kind of data store.

---

[3] Throughout the chapter, we will refer to existing tools, data formats, scripting languages, and services that can be used to implement the various aspects of the presented framework. These are summarized in the appendix of this chapter.

[4] See, for example, Kimball & Caserta (2011) for a practical guide on how to design and build ETL systems.

- **Store:** Ingested data is stored at this point for future processing and usage. This could be a structured database, an unstructured document or object store, data lake, or some combination of these approaches, providing persistence to some or all of the data ingested into the workflow. Data stored in this fashion can be used repeatedly for a variety of purposes later in the metrics workflow.
- **Process:** Data is taken from the store[5] and processed to prepare it for analysis. This processing can include a variety of filtering, cleaning, normalization, and aggregation operations to get the data into a form suitable for analysis.
- **Analyze:** At this point, the processed data is analyzed. This analysis can be relatively simple, producing basic key performance indicators, or richer or more complex, including a variety of techniques from data mining and machine learning.
- **Present:** Results from analyses are presented for ultimate dissemination and usage. This can be in a variety of tabular or graphical representations, depending on user need and application.[6]

In theory, integrating social and textual analytics into this workflow could be as simple as augmenting each stage of the traditional metrics workflow presented in Figure 7.1. After all, the ingest, store, process, analyze, and present processes all have their counterparts in social and textual analytics. That said, the natures of these processes are quite unlike, requiring different techniques, algorithms, and resources, and so it is likely better to have a separate framework for social and textual analytics that has separate, distinct points of integration with the more traditional metrics workflow. We call this approach FISATA. This approach is depicted in Figure 7.2 and described below.

To provide input to FISATA, a number of *Drivers/Collectors* are required to ingest data. Each Driver/Collector interfaces with a different source of social and textual information and can include sources such as Facebook, Twitter, and IMAP/POP (for e-mail access). Using standard APIs, software development kits, and protocols, these Drivers/Collectors will be able to retrieve textual information and distribute it into the framework for analysis.

Integrations will also be provided to bring together information made available from other analytics tools and systems with the framework. These will typically use the traditional metrics workflow as discussed above. This could include proprietary solutions but could also include industry standard tools, such as Flurry, Google Analytics, Unity Analytics, and the like, as these tools have various mechanisms for exporting and importing data, as well as connecting with other data sources and consumers.

---

[5] Data can also be streamed for processing as it is ingested to allow for more real-time or near-real-time analyses of the data.

[6] Visualization techniques for representing gameplay data are discussed in detail in Chapter 11.

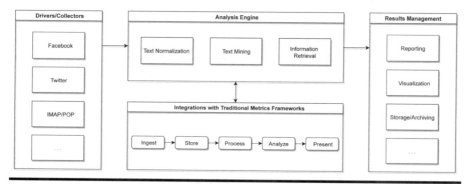

Figure 7.2   Framework for the Integration of Social and Textual Analytics (FISATA).

By providing these Integrations, social and textual information can be correlated with and help inform the analyses performed using traditional metrics data and key performance indicators.

The core of FISATA is the *Analysis Engine*. It provides numerous cognitive linguistics and textual analytics algorithms to extract meaningful information from data provided by the Drivers/Collectors. Interactions with the various Integrations will bring in data from other tools and systems to augment analyses and link social and textual data time-wise or contextually with other metrics and will also allow results from the Analysis Engine to be pushed back to these same tools and systems.

Lastly, *Results Management* will take the products of the Analysis Engine and make them available in various forms to assist in a variety of decision-making processes. This includes reports of quantitative results or raw data (tables, spreadsheets, etc.), various forms of visualization (both static and interactive), and storage or archiving of results for future use.

As such, FISATA is modular, flexible, and extensible. It allows for a variety of sources, analytical methodologies, and outputs from the system and does so in a dynamic fashion, enabling development of the various pieces of the framework to be staggered, while still ensuring that the framework is usable even without full implementation of the entire framework. A discussion of how this has been done in the current work is presented in more detail in the next section.

7.4 Implementation Guide

Implementing the FISATA framework from scratch would present numerous challenges and require significant resources. Fortunately, hosted services and off-the-shelf software (both open source and commercial) can deliver much of the required infrastructure and functionality, allowing researchers to focus on the particular analyses being conducted. As an example, in this chapter, we discuss the approach we have taken at Big Blue Bubble in the construction of our game analytics systems.

Figure 7.3   An implementation of the traditional metrics workflow.

Big Blue Bubble is one of the top independent mobile game developers in Canada. At Big Blue Bubble, our focus on high quality, free-to-play/freemium games led to extensive research and development in game analytics, resulting in a sophisticated and scalable infrastructure to support our many titles, including our flagship brand, *My Singing Monsters* (Big Blue Bubble, 2012), which will be discussed further in the case study in the next section.

7.4.1 Traditional Metrics Workflow

At Big Blue Bubble, our traditional metrics workflow is based on hosted Amazon services, similar to Wiger (2015). While other services could be utilized instead, such as Google DataFlow (Weber, 2018a), the use of Amazon for delivering game-play services made this the logical choice for development. The implementation of our workflow, based on the approach depicted in Figure 7.1, is illustrated in Figure 7.3 and discussed below in further detail.

For collection of metric events, two internally developed, proprietary metrics packages are instrumented into game code: Artemis on the client side and Reaper on the server side (for co-located services). Metrics data is transmitted for ingestion via a secure channel in JSON format. Client events are ingested through a web API gateway and into a queuing/notification service (SNS/SQS), while server events are ingested directly into SNS/SQS, as they do not need to pass through the gateway first.

After ingestion, data is first stored in Amazon's S3 in its original JSON form. This allows for massive amounts of data to be stored for later use efficiently and cost effectively. That said, JSON data in S3 is not an optimal data store to be running queries against for analytics, and so this data is staged on a daily/nightly basis into a Redshift database for more efficient querying later.[7]

Prior to analysis, stored data is processed using a variety of algorithms and Lambda functions.[8] This cleans and filters the data, fills in gaps, and removes extraneous and/or erroneous data records that would pose a threat to the analysis. As some processing operations would need to be applied to the same data every day

---

[7] Data required to support real-time or near-real-time analyses and dashboarding is streamed and staged into Redshift on a more continuous basis.

[8] Amazon's Lambda is a compute service that can execute code, composed of functions, without requiring the provisioning or managing of servers; as such, it is both highly scalable and cost effective at the same time.

to prepare it for analysis, results from these operations may be committed back to storage to reduce or eliminate the need for unnecessary repetitive processing.

Analysis is carried out on Amazon compute servers using EMR, Java, R, Python, and SQL for working with processed data. Results are also staged into Redshift for easy access and later presentation and visualization.

For presentation, a proprietary internal dashboard service, Odin, is used along with a third-party service, Periscope, for both internal and external dissemination of analytics results. Both dashboards pull from the Redshift database to present data in a variety of charts and tables. For one-off analyses and exploratory work, Shiny is used alongside R for reporting.

7.4.2 Integration of Social and Textual Analytics

To support researching and studying our games from a social and textual perspective, we had to augment our traditional metrics workflow at Big Blue Bubble, as shown in Figure 7.3, with additional processes and components to implement FISATA, as discussed in the previous section. The results of this integration are depicted in Figure 7.4 and described below.

As a driver for interfacing with various social networks for the collection of textual artifacts, the Hootsuite analytics tool was used. This permitted the collection of posts and tweets from Facebook and Twitter, with these artifacts stored in a Python dictionary for further analysis. For this work, an IMAP/POP driver was not implemented as e-mail and was not scanned or processed for inclusion at this time.

The analysis engine was written in Python to leverage packages such as the Natural Language Toolkit (NLTK) and TextBlob. Python on its own is a robust language with many features supporting the analytics necessary for this work. Available add-on packages extend the possibilities further, providing a rich library of algorithms and methods for textual analytics. Using this, we could readily

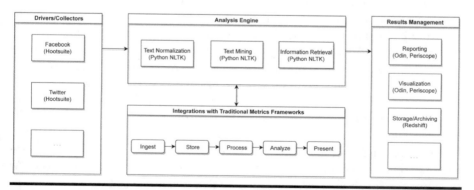

Figure 7.4   Implementation of the Framework for the Integration of Social and Textual Analytics (FISATA).

develop modules for text normalization, text mining, and information retrieval. Doing so is currently the subject of ongoing work.

For integrations with traditional metrics, Amazon backend services were used. In particular, the Redshift database previously discussed provided ready access to metrics data and key performance indicators and provided a storage solution for pushing social and textual metrics back into the pipeline. This then allowed the Odin and Periscope dashboards previously discussed to be used for visualizing, presenting, and managing results from analyses.

A further discussion of these analyses can be found in the case study presented next.

7.5 Case Study

To demonstrate and validate our approach to integrating social and textual analytics into game analytics, we carried out a case study of the implementation of the FISATA framework from the previous section on *My Singing Monsters*, our flagship game at Big Blue Bubble. In this section, we describe the game, outline the analyses conducted using the framework on data gathered from the game and various social channels, and present results from these analyses.

7.5.1 About My Singing Monsters

My Singing Monsters (Big Blue Bubble, 2012) is a casual game played on smartphones and tablets, available on iOS, Android, Amazon, and various other platforms. Initially released in 2012, *My Singing Monsters* is now available in over 180 countries worldwide and has an install base of over 50 million users.

The game itself focuses on a world of singing monsters, as shown in Figure 7.5. The monster world is the universe that the singing monsters inhabit and is powered by the music and elemental power of nature. The monster world is made up of several dimensions and is connected to various other universes in a greater structure called the multiverse. The players interact from the human universe. Players buy, breed, and raise singing monsters to make elaborate multilayered songs. The monsters are kept on islands, with each island building a different song. As a song or songs continue to be sung by monsters, coins and diamonds are earned. Coins and diamonds, in turn, can be used for buying more monsters, buying food for monsters, buying decorations to beautify the islands and make monsters happier, building or upgrading structures that the monsters live in or use, and breeding more monsters. The more monsters a player has, the more coins and diamonds they earn. These actions result in reaching higher game levels. As the player reaches higher levels, additional islands and types of monsters become available to the player as well as new currencies like keys and relics that can be used to unlock even more content.

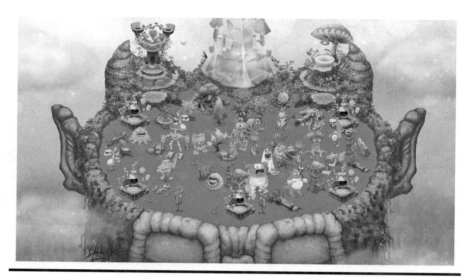

Figure 7.5   Screenshot of *My Singing Monsters*.

My Singing Monsters is a free-to-play/freemium game, with no initial purchase or investment from the player in order to play. The game is monetized through a variety of in-app purchases (IAPs) available to the player as well as both forced and incentivized third-party advertising. In terms of IAPs, players may purchase additional coins, diamonds, food, keys, and relics as the game continues, driving further spending and activities in the game. Making any purchase also permanently removes forced third-party ads during gameplay. Incentivized ads may also be viewed by the player to earn a variety of rewards, including speeding up certain activities, acquiring additional currencies, retrying in-game mini-games, and so on.

Other players can be added as friends through a unique friend code[9] that is used to identify a player. Friends help the player by answering speed-up requests, by liking the player's islands, and by lighting the player's wishing torches to improve their luck and their chances of breeding rarer monster variants. If a player wants other players to befriend them for these benefits, the other players need the player's BBB ID, which has inspired the posting of BBB IDs on Facebook, Twitter, and other social media outlets. As these IDs are internal only to the game, they are on their own not personally identifiable information, and so there is little risk in players sharing them.

7.5.2 Purpose of the Case Study

The general purpose of this case study was to determine what players of *My Singing Monsters* were doing on social media, and to see which, if any, game

---

[9] This code is also referred to as a player's Big Blue Bubble ID or BBB ID.

metrics and key performance indicators correlated with different styles of social media activity. In doing so, it was hoped that by integrating social and textual analytics into ongoing game analytics processes, we at Big Blue Bubble would be able to gain deeper and richer insight into our players, our games, and overall player experience.

7.5.3 General Approach

Using the FISATA framework discussed in the previous section, data was gathered from two social media communication channels related to *My Singing Monsters*. Specifically, these were the *My Singing Monsters* Facebook page and the Big Blue Bubble Twitter account.

From August 2012, when the first post was made, to March 2016, the *My Singing Monsters* Facebook page administrators had posted 2,565 posts. All user comments on these posts were pulled using the framework. In total, 41,402 non-empty comments were pulled.

The Twitter data was pulled using the framework to create a detailed report of Twitter engagement. The resulting report includes tweets with mentions of the *@SingingMonsters* handle and any retweets of *@SingingMonsters* tweets. For the purposes of building a dataset for analysis, only the mentions were used. The input date range for the Twitter mention collection was January 2012 to March 2016. In total, 3,826 non-empty tweet mentions were pulled.

As a result, a total of 45,228 data items were used in creating the dataset for this case study. Only the comments and tweets themselves and their creation dates were ingested in this process. Other personal information (such as user names on the social media sites) was not retrieved during the ingestion stage. This data is never stored for players and would incur new privacy issues if ingested, and so it was neither wanted nor relevant to the study. To link these social and textual artifacts to other game metrics then, the items were scanned for BBB IDs. As noted above, each ID is unique to a player, and players often share their IDs on social channels to build their in-game friend lists. Consequently, each data item was scanned for a potential BBB ID using the regular expression below. Based on the manner in which unique BBB IDs are created, a string was considered a BBB ID if it began with four to eight digits and ended in two lowercase or uppercase letters:

$$[\text{\textbackslash d}]\{4,8\}[\text{a-zA-Z}]\{2\}\text{\textbackslash b}$$

Of the 41,402 collected Facebook comments, 10,764 comments contained one or more BBB IDs (26% of the pulled Facebook comments). Of the 3,826 collected Twitter mentions, only 24 Twitter mentions contained one or more BBB IDs (0.63% of Twitter mentions). In total 3,404 unique IDs were identified in the dataset. In cases where multiple IDs were present in a comment or mention, these were flagged for follow-up processing to attribute the comment or mention to the proper ID manually.[10]

In the sections that follow, we explore a variety of analyses conducted using this dataset.

7.5.4 Activation, Engagement, and Retention of Posters versus Non-Posters

In this section, we study player activation (whether they open the game after they download it), engagement (how frequently they play and how much they play), and retention (how long they play the game until they permanently quit the game). We compare the behavior of posters to that of non-posters to investigate how social media behavior relates to these more traditional game metrics. For our purposes, we treat any player for whom we do not have an attributed comment or mention as a non-poster. Of course, some of these players may have posted without including their BBB ID, but we do not have any way to readily establish linkages in these cases.

We begin by comparing US posters and US non-posters in terms of maximum level reached, average days played, and average money spent on in-app purchases. As users have different monetization trends from country to country, we only compared posters in the US to non-posters in the US initially[11] here (see Figure 7.6). US users comprise 51.3% of all posters and 48% of all non-poster users.

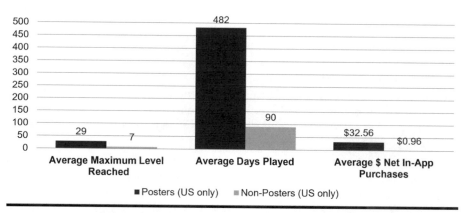

Figure 7.6 US poster versus non-poster behavior.

---

[10] As there were so few of these in our case, this was a quick and straightforward task.

[11] In later analyses, we will relax the US-only restriction and examine players from around the world.

A user's maximum level reached and the average days played are important factors since they give us insight into a user's activation, engagement, and retention. The average amount of IAPs is also very important since this is a main source of revenue for the game. Therefore, by comparing these factors for US posters versus US non-posters, we can see how a difference in social media behavior relates to activation, engagement, retention, and revenue for this geographic region.

In this case, posters play considerably longer and achieve a maximum level over four times higher than non-posters (Figure 7.6). On average, the maximum level reached by a non-poster is 7 whereas the average maximum level reached by a poster is 29. Posters are also retained for 5.4 times longer than non-posters (Figure 7.6). The average number of days a non-poster plays is 90 days, whereas poster average retention is 482 days. Thus, on average, a poster's activation and engagement levels are much higher than a non-poster's, and a poster's retention is much longer than that of a non-poster.

As well, on average, posters spend 33.9 times more money than non-posters (see Figure 7.6). The average amount spent on in-app purchases by non-posters is $0.96, whereas the average amount by posters is $32.56. So, the average revenue earned from a poster is significantly higher than the revenue produced by a non-poster.

Therefore, the average poster reaches higher maximum levels, plays for more days, and spends more on in-app purchases than non-posters. Consequently, posters tend to have more activation and engagement, longer retention, and yield more revenue. Posters are thus clearly an important subset of US users.

Next, we relax the geographic restriction and compare first and last logins of all posters and non-posters from around the world (including the US). Assessing this information helps us further understand how differences in social media behavior affect activation, engagement, and retention.

While acquisition between August 2012 and March 2016 is similar across each month, the majority of posters in this time frame (36%) were acquired in 2013. Eighteen percent of posters (643 users) continued to log in to the game through to July 2016, meaning these posters were still active at that time. These results can be seen in Figure 7.7.

Acquisition of non-posters increased significantly after June 2013 and then increased further in December 2014, consistent with both updates to the game and with active marketing campaigns in place. However, the last login numbers for non-posters show a similar trend; in June 2013, there is a significant increase in last logins per month and a further increase in December 2014. Only 2.1% of all non-posters (865,610 users) have logged in again in July 2016. This can be seen in Figure 7.8.

As a result, a much higher percentage of posters have shown recent activity, have better rates of activation, and have longer retention than non-posters. Again, these results indicate that posters to social media are a subset of users worthy of attention and study around the world.

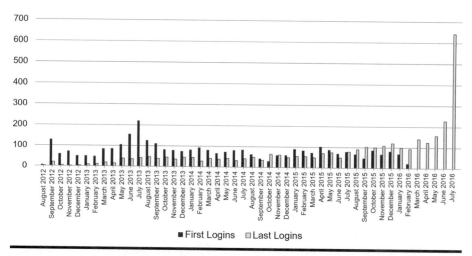

Figure 7.7 First and last login dates of posters that included their BBB ID.

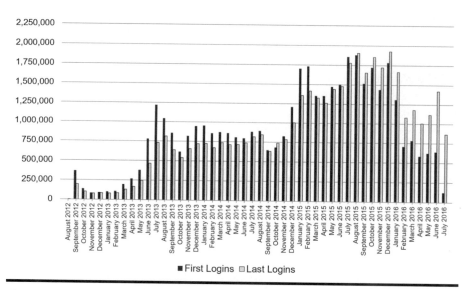

Figure 7.8 First and last login dates of non-posters.

7.5.5 Poster Social Effort

Another interesting relationship to study is that between poster social effort (i.e., posting their BBB ID to find friends) and other metrics. We start by exploring how often posters post their BBB ID to social media. Over 74% of posters only post twice. Just over 13% of posters post thrice, and just over 6% post their BBB ID five or more times. The user with the highest number of posts posted 36 different times. This is shown in Figure 7.9.

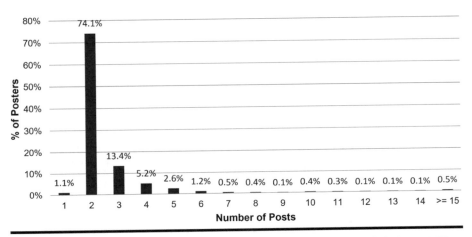

Figure 7.9 Percent of posters and number of posts that included their BBB ID.

We also found that users with more posts had a slightly higher frequency of play (see Figure 7.10, top left). Posters who posted up to three times played 63%–66% of the days they were active (between their first and last logins), whereas posters who posted four or more times played 67%–68% of the days they were active. Therefore, there is a slight correlation. On average, the more social effort made by a user, the higher the frequency in play. Thus, more social effort (i.e., more posts posted) relates to higher activation and engagement.

In addition, we observed that, on average, posters with more posts reach a higher maximum level when playing the game (see Figure 7.10, top right). The average maximum level reached by a poster who posted up to three times is between levels 30–34, whereas the average maximum level reached by a poster who posted four or more times is between levels 37–39. Again, there is a slight correlation here. On average, stronger social effort can be found in posters with higher maximum levels reached. Thus, more social effort again relates with higher activation and engagement.

We also noticed a certain correlation between monster purchases (using in-game currency) and social effort. The average number of monster purchases for a poster who posted once is over 88 purchases, and for a poster who posted two posts, the average number of monster purchases is over 92 monsters. However, for three or four posts, the average jumps up to between 108 and 111 monster purchases, and for five or more posts, the average rises to over 136 purchases (see Figure 7.10, bottom). Therefore, on average, the more posts a poster has made, the more purchases they have made. So, again, this indicates a correlation between more social effort and higher activation and engagement.

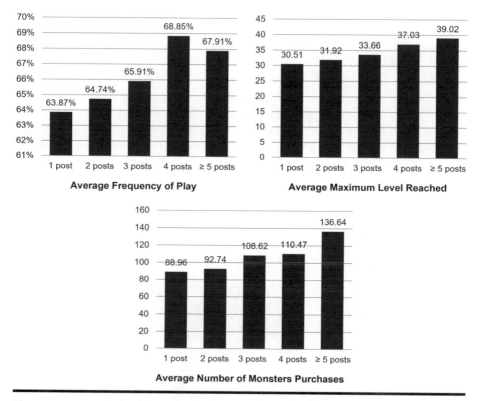

Figure 7.10 Social effort versus frequency of play (top left), maximum level reached (top right), and monster purchases (bottom).

7.5.6 Sentiment Analysis

In this section, we assess the sentiment of user comments and tweets to determine if there is any correlation between sentiment and activation, engagement, retention, or revenue metrics.

Using the features of TextBlob integrated within the FISATA framework, we acquired the sentiment of all of the attributed comments and tweets created by the posters. TextBlob's sentiment analysis tool gives the polarity of the sentence and the subjectivity. While this is not perfect, it can still give us a general sense of the attitudes of the user posts. Here we focus only on the polarity rating of each comment or tweet.

The polarity score is given within the range [–1, 1], with –1 being the most negative a comment or tweet's sentiment can be, 1 being the most positive, and 0 being a neutral sentiment. We calculated an overall sentiment for each user by averaging the polarity for all of their comments/tweets. For the 1,765 users in this analysis, 63 users have an overall sentiment with negative polarity, 819 have an overall sentiment with positive polarity, and 883 users have posts with overall neutral sentiment (see Figure 7.11).

Therefore, while significantly more users have an overall positive sentiment than negative, the majority of users' posts indicate a neutral sentiment.

In Figure 7.12, we compare each user's sentiments to their maximum level reached, days retained, and game currency purchases. Again, these are factors that give insight into a user's activation, engagement, and retention. From Figure 7.12 (left), we see more polarized sentiments and less neutrality from users that have reached higher levels. This is understandable, as they are probably more engaged, attached, and passionate about the game, and so are more likely to comment with emotion.

Examining Figure 7.12 (middle), we see that the number of days a player remains active in the game (days between first login and last login) is slightly longer

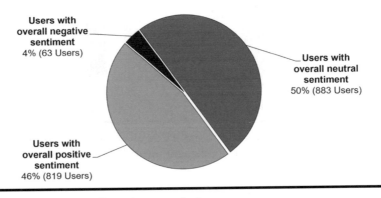

Figure 7.11   User overall sentiment polarity.

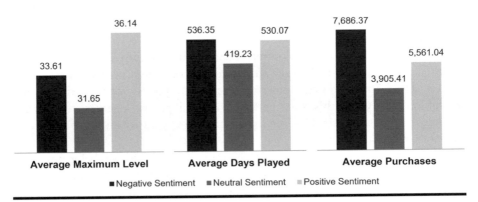

Figure 7.12   User sentiment versus average maximum level reached (left), average days played (middle), and average purchases (right).

for players who have a polarized sentiment than players who have a neutral sentiment. On average, users with an overall negative or positive sentiment in their posts are retained for over 110 more days than users with an overall neutral sentiment. This means that posters with a polarized sentiment have higher retention levels than those with a neutral sentiment.

This does mean that users expressing a negative sentiment tend to be retained better than those with a more positive outlook, which seems counterintuitive. Experience, however, has shown us that users that are retained longer are more engaged with the game, are more passionate about it, and care about it more. They also tend to be more sensitive to developments in the game, which will manifest itself in a negative way through social media when something happens that they do not agree with. It is interesting to note that these users will continue to play even after expressing a negative sentiment, again because of their passion and attachment to the game.

When we look at the average purchases made using in-game currency (diamonds and coins), we see a significant difference in purchase amounts among all three groups (see Figure 7.12, right). Users with polarized sentiment have higher average purchase amounts than users with neutral sentiment. The average purchase amount for users with positive sentiment is over 42% more than the average purchase amount of users with neutral sentiment, and the average purchase amount for users with negative sentiment is almost double the amount of average purchases made by users with neutral sentiment. There is also a considerable difference in average purchase amounts for users with negative sentiment and positive sentiment. Users with negative sentiment on average spent over 38% more than users with positive sentiment. This indicates that users with polarized sentiment, especially those with negative sentiment, have higher levels of activation and engagement, which is quite interesting. While surprising at first, this makes sense again if we were to dig deeper into the psyche of the users. Users spending highly in the game are likely highly engaged and passionate about the game. As such, they are again going to be sensitive about developments to the game that they do not agree with. In fact, their higher spending only builds attachment and sensitivity further, as they are more invested in the experience. As a result, negative sentiments are understandable in such cases. One might expect spending to stop once a negative sentiment has been expressed, but in practice, that is not what is observed. In fact, users tend to spend regardless of prior negative sentiments being expressed, which is perhaps even more interesting. This could be a result of the level of attachment and commitment the users feel toward the game, or their prior investment could also be leading to a sunk cost fallacy.[12] These assumptions are worthy of further investigation.

---

[12] The sunk cost fallacy refers to an irrational economic behavior that manifests itself in a greater tendency to continue a behavior or endeavor once resources (e.g., money, time, effort) have been invested (cf. Arkes & Blumer, 1985).

7.6 Conclusions

Social and textual analytics have the potential to enrich and extend game analytics, providing additional valuable insight to optimize both gameplay and monetization potential. Through a case study of *My Singing Monsters*, our flagship game at Big Blue Bubble, we demonstrated the lessons we can learn from integrating these branches of analytics together under a single analytics framework, called FISATA. These lessons covered various facets of the relationships between social behavior and various key performance indicators, the impact of varying levels of social effort, and the sentiments conveyed by players in their social commentary.

We found relationships between social activity (in particular, activity attached with an in-game identifier) and player engagement, retention, and spending. The amount of social effort expended was aligned with this, with higher levels of social effort observed alongside stronger performance in key metrics. Stronger sentiments tended to be expressed by users who progressed farther, played longer, and spent more, with negative sentiments surprisingly linked to better outcomes than more positive sentiments. These results have shaped the way Big Blue Bubble engages with its community and has led to changes in the social mechanisms in *My Singing Monsters* to encourage and facilitate more social integration, communication, and play. These changes have been well received by the players, judging from their reaction on social media, of course.

While this work already shows great promise and potential for the study of games and game analytics, there is still more that can be done. As such, there are several avenues for continued research in this area. The analyses presented in this chapter are just the beginning; there is so much more that can be explored with the existing dataset given the extent of both the accumulated social content and the game metrics from the same time frame. Given our experience here, we will also explore our other games, applying the analytics framework in different contexts, as we have shown that this can produce valuable, interesting, and—at times—unexpected results. Because of its inherent flexibility, the analytics framework itself can also be further extended through the addition of new drivers for other data sources (e-mail, app store reviews, Instagram, Snapchat, etc.), new analytics algorithms, and so forth. This, in turn, will enable additional and more varied analyses with expanded datasets in the future.

Appendix

This chapter referred to different existing tools, data formats, scripting languages, and services to help with the implementation of the various aspects of the presented, or similar, frameworks. These resources are listed below together with links to their respective websites.

Amazon EMR	https://aws.amazon.com/emr
Amazon Redshift	https://aws.amazon.com/redshift
Amazon S3	https://aws.amazon.com/s3
Amazon Simple Notification Service (SNS)	https://aws.amazon.com/sns
Amazon Simple Queue Service (SQS)	https://aws.amazon.com/sqs
Apache OpenNLP	https://opennlp.apache.org
AWS Lambda	https://aws.amazon.com/lambda
CRAN Task View: Natural Language Processing	https://cran.r-project.org/web/views/ NaturalLanguageProcessing.html
Flurry	http://www.flurry.com/
GATE	https://gate.ac.uk
Google Analytics	https://marketingplatform.google.com/about/ analytics
Hootsuite	https://hootsuite.com
Java	https://www.java.com
JSON	https://www.json.org
Natural Language Toolkit	https://www.nltk.org
Periscope Data	https://www.periscopedata.com
Python	https://www.python.org
R	https://www.r-project.org
Shiny	https://shiny.rstudio.com
SQL	https://www.iso.org/standard/63555.html
TextBlob: Simplified Text Processing	https://textblob.readthedocs.io
Unity Analytics	https://unity.com/solutions/analytics
XML	https://www.w3.org/XML

References

Albrechtslund, A. M. (2010). Gamers telling stories: Understanding narrative practices in an online community. *Convergence, 16*(1), 112–124.

Arkes, H. R., & Blumer, C. (1985). The psychology of sunk cost. *Organizational Behavior and Human Decision Processes, 35*(1), 124–140.

Bertone, A., & Burghardt, D. (2017). A survey on visual analytics for the spatio-temporal exploration of microblogging content. *Journal of Geovisualization and Spatial Analysis, 1*(1), 2.

Big Blue Bubble. (2012). *My Singing Monsters* [Mobile Game]. London, UK: Big Blue Bubble.

Drescher, C., Wallner, G., Kriglstein, S., Sifa, R., Drachen, A., & Pohl, M. (2018). What moves players?: Visual data exploration of twitter and gameplay data. In *Proceedings of the 2018 CHI Conference on Human Factors in Computing Systems* (pp. 560:1–560:13). New York: ACM Press.

El-Nasr, M. S., M., Drachen, A., and Canossa, A. (Eds.) (2013). *Game Analytics: Maximizing the Value of Player Data*. London, UK: Springer.

Grosso, W. (2017). The future of IAP monetization in mobile games. Retrieved from http://www.gamasutra.com/blogs/WilliamGrosso/20170510/297722/The_Future_of_IAP_Monetization_in_Mobile_Games.php.

Hearst, M. (2004). Text data mining. In R. Mitkov (Ed.), *The Oxford Handbook of Computational Linguistics* (pp. 616–628). New York: Oxford University Press.

Jordan, P., Buente, W., Silva, P. A., & Rosenbaum, H. (2016). Selling out the magic circle: Free-to-play games and developer ethics. In *Proceedings of the 1st International Joint Conference of DiGRA and FDG*. Santa Cruz, CA: Digital Games Research Association and Society for the Advancement of the Science of Digital Games.

Kerr, C. (2017). IBM and PlayFab will use machine learning to understand player behavior. Retrieved from http://www.gamasutra.com/view/news/294137/IBM_and_PlayFab_will_use_machine_learning_to_understand_player_behavior.php.

Kimball, R., & Caserta, J. (2011). *The Data Warehouse ETL Toolkit: Practical Techniques for Extracting, Cleaning, Conforming, and Delivering Data*. Indianapolis, IN: John Wiley & Sons.

Konchady, M. (2006). *Text Mining Application Programming*. Boston, MA: Charles River Media.

Latysheva, N. (2017). Understanding and improving games through machine learning. Presentation at the 2017 Games Industry Analytics Forum. Retrieved from https://www.slideshare.net/LaurenCormack/understanding-and-improving-games-through-machine-learning-natasha-latysheva.

Lovato, N. (2015). Everything you need to know about interpreting KPIs. Retrieved from https://gameanalytics.com/blog/everything-need-know-interpreting-kpis.html.

MacMillan, M. (2017). Why LTV is the mother of all metrics for app developers. Retrieved from https://insights.pollen.vc/articles/why-ltv-is-the-mother-of-metrics-for-app-developers.

McMillan, M. (2014). Linguistic strategies for brevity on twitter (Master's Thesis). London, UK: University of Western Ontario.

Moseley, N. (2013). Using word and phrase abbreviation patterns to extract age from twitter microtexts (Master's Thesis, Rochester Institute of Technology, Rochester, NY). Retrieved from http://scholarworks.rit.edu/cgi/viewcontent.cgi?article=5766&context=theses.

Murphy, K. (2006). Naive bayes classifiers. University of British Columbia. Retrieved from https://www.cs.ubc.ca/~murphyk/Teaching/CS340-Fall06/reading/NB.pdf.

Roseboom, I. (2017). Game analytics insight compendium vol.1. Retrieved from https://deltadna.com/resources/dr-rosebooms-game-analytics-insight-compendium-vol-1/.

Seay, A. F., Jerome, W. J., Lee, K. S., & Kraut, R. E. (2004). Project massive: A study of online gaming communities. In *CHI'04 Extended Abstracts on Human Factors in Computing Systems* (pp. 1421–1424). New York: ACM Press.

Tabor, M. & Vrdoljak, M. (Eds.) (2016). *Don't Panic Mobile Developer's Guide to the Galaxy* (16th ed.). Bremen, Germany: Enough Software.

The Economist. (2017). The world's most valuable resource. Retrieved from https://www.economist.com/news/leaders/21721656-data-economy-demands-new-approach-anti-trust-rules-worlds-most-valuable-resource.

Tzoukermann E., Klavans, J., & Strzalkowski, T. (2004). Information retrieval. In R. Mitkov (Ed.), *The Oxford Handbook of Computational Linguistics* (pp. 529–544). New York, Oxford University Press.

Warmelink, H., & Siitonen, M. (2011). Player communities in multiplayer online games: A systematic review of empirical research. In *Proceedings of theDiGRA 2011 Conference*. Finland: Digital Games Research Association.

Weber, B. (2018a). A fully managed game analytics pipeline. Retrieved from https://www.gamasutra.com/blogs/BenWeber/20180401/315962/A_FullyManaged_Game_Analytics_Pipeline.php.

Weber, B. (2018b). A history of game analytics platforms. Retrieved from https://www.gamasutra.com/blogs/BenWeber/20180409/316273/A_History_of_Game_Analytics_Platforms.php.

Wiger, N. (2015). Connecting with your customers—Building successful mobile games through the power of AWS analytics. Presentation at the 2015 Game Developer Conference. Retrieved from https://www.gdcvault.com/play/1021876/Connecting-with-Your-Customers-Building.

Williams, D. (2015). The tenets of community management series: Part 1 of 3. Retrieved from http://www.gamasutra.com/blogs/DmitriWilliams/20150528/244497/The_Tenets_of_Community_Management_Series_Part_1_of_3.php.

Yamparala, P. (2014). Don't market your app if you don't know this—Pirate metrics for mobile apps. Retrieved from http://appentrepreneursassociation.com/dont-market-your-app-if-you-dont-know-this-pirate-metrics-for-mobile-apps.

Yamparala, P. (2015). How you can use analytical tools to find out about the usage rate of your app? Retrieved from http://gamasutra.com/blogs/PuneetYamparala/20150430/242311/How_You_Can_Use_Analytical_Tools_to_Find_Out_About_the_Usage_Rate_of_Your_App.php.

Chapter 8

Social Network Analysis Applied to Game Communities to Identify Key Social Players

Alessandro Canossa and Casper Harteveld

Contents

8.1 Introduction

The game industry is experiencing a paradigm shift that sees games as ongoing services. From the 1970s onward, digital games have been marketed as products with commoditization strategies fitting the "pay once and you are in" business model and with entertainment value between a few hours and a few dozen hours (Sotamaa & Karppi, 2010). That paradigm involved commoditization strategies, such as new versions of popular games, game sequels, expansions, branding and tie-ins to existing intellectual property (IP), licensing IP, and episodic content.

Recently, there have been considerable efforts to push player engagement over the long term, or better, indefinitely ("pay often and you stay in"). Entertainment value is measured in hundreds of hours of playtime and commoditization strategies revolve around subscription-based models, free-to-play games with premium content, free updates, premium downloadable content, and season passes. This push is a paradigm shift in the game industry that no longer sees games as products but rather as services. In an interview, Anne Blondel-Jouin, Vice President of Live Operations at Ubisoft, explained that:

> …games-as-a-service, or live games, refer to games that offer an evolving long-term, entertaining experience for our players. They often have a focus on online competitive multiplayer experiences such as *Tom Clancy's The Division* but they can also include other types of game experiences like *The Crew*. "Live" refers to all the activities and interactions created for the game community including pre- and post-launch as well as regular updates, new content, and events both in-game and out-of-game, etc. throughout the game's lifespan. (Wong, 2017)

This shift entails a different way to understand, contextualize, and leverage player behavior: multiplayer experience can be the main driver for such prolonged retention. With this in mind, the key for maintaining the interest in a game over an extended period of time is to understand the communities of players and the social dimension of play as fundamental elements for a game's extended lifetime. To understand such communities, we suggest employing social network analysis (SNA) tools. In this regard, this chapter presents a case study where we explored players of *Tom Clancy's The Division* (Massive Entertainment, 2016) using tools from social network analysis.

For this study, our aim was to identify and begin to understand influential players in a live game using existing social network analysis methods (modularity, centrality, and prestige measures). Influential players are here defined as players that make exceptional use of social features, such as creating groups for multiplayer sessions. With a focus on identifying influencers, we polled a semi-random sample (246,041 players, roughly 2% of all players) from *Tom Clancy's The Division* (*TCTD*) for our social network analysis. This approach shows that there are extremely influential players and that they have a concrete impact on the communities they help build. This impact is measured in both increased length and frequency of play sessions for all members of a subcommunity that said influential players helped establish. These players are also very different from the "power users"—rather than being characterized by elite performance in the game, they maintain wide-reaching and solid networks of friends and show an active engagement with the multiplayer aspects of a game. They are the "social butterflies," and we present initial evidence that they seem to be essential to the health and livelihood of a game's community.

8.2 Related Work

Prior research on the communities of play and players has employed primarily interview and ethnographic research methods to understand how players interact with each other and the game as a system over time, in particular for so-called massively multiplayer online games (MMOGs) such as *World of Warcraft* (Bartle, 1996; Boellstorff et al., 2012; Pearce, 2011; Taylor, 2009). Other research has used data mining techniques to get insight into team compositions, as we have already seen in Chapter 4, and churn prediction (Hadiji et al., 2014). Increasingly, social network analysis methods are deployed for games (Ang & Zaphiris, 2010; Ducheneaut et al., 2006; Ho & Huang, 2009; Park & Kim, 2014), and similarly to the literature on online communities (Kraut et al., 2012) in general it suggests that there are key members who contribute to keeping the community alive. Pirker et al. (2018) utilized SNA to investigate how patterns of players who play with the same people and those who play with random groups impact performance in the game *Destiny*. In this chapter, we propose to use SNA to identify key players that greatly contribute in creating thriving communities.

8.3 The Game: *Tom Clancy's The Division*

Tom Clancy's The Division (*TCTD*) is an online-only open world action role-playing video game set in a near future New York City in the aftermath of a smallpox pandemic. The player, an agent of the Strategic Homeland Division, must help the group rebuild its operations in Manhattan, investigate the nature of the outbreak, and combat criminal activity in its wake. Released in March 2016, *TCTD* accumulated more than 15 million players becoming the fastest selling new IP of all times. As of April 2017—when the data for this study was polled—there were more than two million active monthly players.

    TCTD is structured with elements of role-playing games combined with collaborative Player versus Environment (PvE) and Player versus Player (PvP) online multiplayer activities. It is possible to play and replay all the story missions with up to four real players in cooperative mode (PvE) or play with a group of players and challenge other players (PvP). In PvP, the activities are: going rogue by killing other players and stealing their loot, extracting newly acquired loot, stopping an extraction in progress and stealing the loot, and clearing landmarks. In PvE, the activities are: completing any of the main or side missions, engaging in search and destroy and high-value target missions, encountering random hostiles and participating in the three incursions, particularly challenging end-game activities.

All activities, both in PvP and PvE, can be completed solo or in groups (Figure 8.1). Groups are composed of the group creator and up to three other players. Groups can be created as a quick-match with random players or with players already connected as friends to the profile through Xbox Live, PlayStation Network, or Uplay accounts[1].

(a)

(b)

Figure 8.1 Screenshots of (a) group play and (b) group management in *Tom Clancy's The Division*. Copyright Ubisoft.

---

[1] Uplay is a multiplayer and communications service for PC, used exclusively by first-party Ubisoft games.

Groups can be created or joined at safe houses and social hubs scattered around the game area or right before beginning any given activity. Ubisoft maintains official forums for all the games published, which are, amongst others, used to find and connect with players for group activities. In fact, the group discussion channel is the third most popular out of eight channels on the *TCTD* official forums.

A playtime segmentation report showed that active players are spending more than 60% of their time playing in groups, while players that quit the game spent less than 37% of their time in groups. Based on that and the existing literature we hypothesized that social dynamics have a massive impact on player retention. Therefore, we explored the communities playing *TCTD* using tools from social network analysis to identify and isolate influential players. We also take a first step in unpacking the playing behavior of these influential players.

8.4 Method

As employees at Ubisoft, we had access to data collected by both the Uplay platform and the *TCTD* game. We first discuss what dataset we used to explore communities of *TCTD* and how we verified it. Then we detail our approach for analyzing this data.

8.4.1 Dataset

To reduce the computational time for this exploratory study, instead of working with the whole dataset from more than 14 million players, we polled a random sample of 200,000 PC players from *TCTD*, and then included all their friends on Uplay that also own *TCTD*, which led to a sample of 246,041 players. We will refer to this sample as the initial sample in the following. We chose PC players only because our access to account data was limited to the Uplay service. Including PS4 and Xbox players would have required special permission from Sony and Microsoft. In addition, we made sure to include the friends of the sampled players, as we were interested in exploring communities and not including their friends would impose an incomplete network. The total population at the time of polling (April 27, 2017) was 14,716,507 players. Therefore, the initial sample constitutes 1.7% of the entire population at that time.

8.4.2 Data Analysis

Our data analysis procedure involved three stages:

1. Influencer identification,
2. Influencer comparison, and
3. Assessing influencer impact on communities.

For the influencer identification, we used data collected from the game *TCTD*, and results were calculated and visualized with Gephi 0.9.1 (Bastian et al., 2009). For the influencer comparison, we used player statistics retrieved from the Uplay player accounts.

8.4.3 Influencer Identification

For the first stage, we utilized the so-called modularity measure (Blondel et al., 2008), which is often used to quantify the presence of community structures in networks (Newman, 2006). Modularity measures the strength of division of a network into clusters (also called groups or communities). It is a scalar value between −1 and 1 and is positive if the number of edges within clusters exceeds the number of expected edges on the basis of chance. With this in mind, a cluster is defined as a region of the network that is strongly connected within (i.e., dense connections between the nodes within a cluster) and relatively sparsely connected to the rest of the network (i.e., sparse connections between nodes in different clusters). Modularity was used to identify communities; after that, we considered two different approaches to identify influential players within these communities.

First, we considered an undirected network with the nodes representing players and the edges modeling their friendship connections. To more closely examine the resulting clusters, we utilized centrality measures. Centrality aims to quantify the "influence" of a particular node within a network. Our aim was to identify within each community which player(s) may be influential. To accomplish this, we considered the following centrality measures: degree (number of links), closeness (easily accessible to all other players, length of the shortest path), betweenness (number of shortest paths to other players), eigenvector, and alpha centrality. While degree centrality counts all connected nodes equally, eigenvector centrality treats connected nodes differently based on their "importance." Alpha centrality is a form of eigenvector centrality that takes into account the external importance given to the individual nodes. A more in-depth discussion of the various centrality measures can, for example, be found in Wasserman and Faust (1994). This first analysis identified players with the largest networks of friends on Uplay.

Second, we considered a directed network, where the nodes again represent the players but where the edges instead represent how groups in *TCTD* are formed (with the arrow pointing from a joiner to a creator). As mentioned earlier, players can create or join a group. Creating a group entails directly inviting friends already in the network of a player or opening a spot for a random player to join the group through quick-matching. Joining a group entails either accepting the invitation of a friend to join the group or taking a spot not filled by a friend of the group creator. The weight of the edges represents the strength of the tie (that is, how many times these players played together), and it is accounted for by prestige measures. Groups can consist of a maximum of four players, so this step of the analysis aggregates data from several sessions over several groups. Identifying influence in directed networks can be accomplished with prestige measures—the equivalent of centrality measures for directed networks (cf. Wasserman & Faust, 1994)—of which we considered the following: in-degree and out-degree (groups created and joined), rank (what fraction of players can be reached via directed paths), and proximity (shortest directed path). The purpose of this second analysis was to assess group-forming behavior.

For all measures considered in both analyses, we explored varying selection criteria (i.e., closeness is larger than 2) and looked at when it levels off (similar to a scree plot) in terms of what players are still considered. These cut-off criteria resulted in 94 communities from the modularity analysis; 1,726 players from the first influencer analysis (most central players) and 832 from the second analysis (most prestigious players with an in-degree prestige of higher than or equal to 3 and a rank prestige higher than or equal to 2). The final step was to look at the intersection of the two analyses: players that are both very central in the friend network and very prestigious group creators. This returned 49 players. These 49 players will be referred to as influential players from now on. Finally, we will look at the relation between the 94 communities identified and the 49 influencers found.

8.4.4 Influencer Comparison

After we identified the influential players, our aim was to get a better understanding of who these influencers are by comparing them to the player population at large and to "power users." We defined a "power user" as a player with at least (a) 70 hours in *TCTD*, (b) 10 friends on Uplay, (c) a Gear Score in the top 5%, and (d) played in groups twice in the week before we polled the sample.

The reason for the 70-hour criterion is to identify players that stick around after the "endgame" (i.e., completing all the story missions). It takes 20–40 hours to complete all the missions,[2] and on average the whole player population has an average playtime of 67 hours and 20 minutes. As *TCTD* is fundamentally a social game, the other two—more arbitrary—criteria were applied. Since, on average, players have 8.60 friends, we set the minimum number for a power user to be 10 friends. The Gear Score is an indicator for how well-equipped players are. Every weapon or piece of gear found after reaching level 30 (the level cap) has a Gear Score value. The higher an item's Gear Score, the stronger the item is, making it a more valuable field asset. The overall Gear Score of players defines their progression after the endgame. We decided to select only the top 5% to ensure that we could capture the top performers in the game. The last criterion, played in groups twice in the week before we polled the sample, was added to ensure that the power users still made extensive use of the multiplayer functionalities of the game.

Applying these criteria to our sample led to 2,102 players (less than 1% of the initial sample) to compare the identified influencers to.

8.4.5 Influencer Impact on Communities

In order to assess the impact that influencers have on the people they play with, we decided to investigate whether there is a change in two variables before and after

---

[2] https://howlongtobeat.com/game.php?id=20073 (Accessed: December 2018).

players begin joining the groups created by the influencers. The variables examined are: average daily playtime (calculated only for days of activity) and the ratio between solo and group play. The first variable—average daily playtime—is a good proxy for engagement, while the second—time spent in solo versus group play—reveals a tendency to value the social dimension of play more. The impact is based on behaviors of players displayed two weeks prior to engaging with influencers and two weeks after that.

8.5 Results

Here we discuss the results of our efforts on influencer identification, comparison, and impact.

8.5.1 Influencer Identification

Figure 8.2 shows the network visualization from our social network analysis. Based on a visual inspection of the network (Figures 8.2 and 8.3), it is noticeable that a number of clusters seems entangled and forms the heart of the community, whereas there are also a number of clusters loosely connected to the rest of the network and located on the periphery of the network. In fact, we can identify three different types of subcommunities: floating, peripheral, and entangled communities (see also Figure 8.3).

- ■ Floating subcommunities are not connected to any other community.
- ■ Peripheral subcommunities have few connections to other communities.
- ■ Entangled subcommunities are very well connected to other communities.

The significance of these observations is that it is less likely that players in floating or peripheral communities have an influence on the *TCTD* community at large. As mentioned earlier, the intersection between the 1,726 players identified by the centrality measures and the 832 players identified by the prestige analysis returned 49 players. We wanted to investigate the relation between these 49 players and the 94 subcommunities identified by the modularity analysis (modularity of 0.933). In fact, these 49 influencers are, not surprisingly, distributed exclusively in the entangled communities at the center of the graph shown in Figure 8.2. We thus decided to look more closely at these 49 players.

8.5.2 Influencer Comparison

In order to further explore the structural differences of the 49 influencers, we compared them against the total population and the 2,102 power users. Table 8.1 gives an overview of the three groups. The comparison is based on the whole lifetime

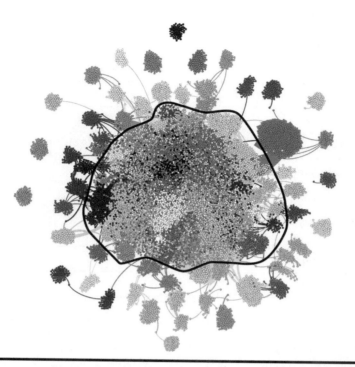

Figure 8.2 Network visualization of the initial sampled 246,041 *TCTD* players. In the center are the entangled communities where the 49 influential players reside (encircled).

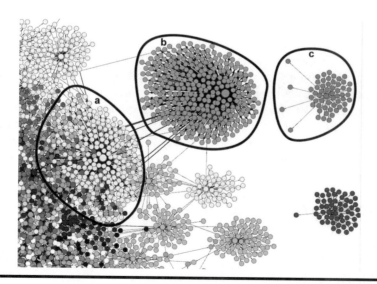

Figure 8.3 Zoomed in network to illustrate from left to right: (a) an entangled community, (b) a peripheral community, and (c) a floating community.

Table 8.1 Comparison of the Three Populations: Influencers, Power Users, and Total Population

	Influencers	Power Users	Total Population
Total # players	49	2,102	14,716,507
# of sessions Avg. (SD)	178 (313)	213 (258)	44 (442.5)
# of friends Avg. (SD)	208 (104)	26.5 (32.4)	8.60 (36.5)
Avg. tot. playtime	119	454	67
Time spent in group/solo play	61%–39%	67%–33%	38%–62%
# of players interacted with in group play	342	27	11
Avg. daily playtime	2.56	3.39	1.56
Forum posts (<10)	22%	8%	0.2%
Forum posts (>10)	8%	2%	0.03%

of players. On average, it turns out that the influencers played 178 sessions from when they started playing (SD = 313) and have 208 friends (SD = 104) on Uplay. In contrast, the 2,102 power users played on average 213 sessions (SD = 258) but only have 26.5 friends (SD = 32.4).

Furthermore, in their lifetime, the 2,102 power users have played in groups at least once with a network of 56,180 different players that are not necessarily their friends, while the 49 influencers in their lifetime have played with at least 16,742 players. That means that on average each power user in their lifetime plays with 27 other players. This is interesting because the number of players that power users interact with in groups (27) is very close to the number of friends (26.5), indicating that power users tend to play almost exclusively with their friends. At the same time, each influencer plays on average with 342 other players, a larger number compared to the number of their friends (208), indicating that influencers play in groups with considerably more players than just their friends. Therefore, the 49 influencers have played with more than ten times the number of players than power users engage with.

Additionally, we aimed to explore non-game-related behaviors, such as posting on the official *TCTD* forums. The success of a game, and thereby the well-being of the community, depends in part on meta-gaming activities, that is, activities that take place outside of the game itself but are about the game, such as discussing strategies, providing tips and suggestions, or sharing experiences. Meta-gaming too relies on the effort of certain individuals (Salovaara et al., 2005), and forums are the prototypical form of meta-gaming. Therefore, if the identified influential players are very active on forums, it will strengthen our findings.

For this effort, we only considered the official Ubisoft forum called "The Division" forums (The Division Forums, n.d.), which at the time of consideration had a population of 26,632 users. This means that less than 1% of the total population of *TCTD* players is active on this site. There are many other dedicated *TCTD* forums; however, it would have been more difficult, if not impossible, to match people posting on these forums with their player statistics. For the official Ubisoft forum, users have to log in with their Uplay account, and therefore we were able to match forum-posting behavior with their player statistics.

Regarding forum-posting behaviors, we restricted ourselves to the quantity of posts per player, not the content of their posts, their length, quality, or even their type (e.g., strategy and tactic discussions, bug reports, feedback). There are other, possibly more accurate metrics to find influencers. For example, Zhao et al. (2014) defined a novel metric using text mining and sentiment analysis[3] that looks at the number of influential responding replies in online health community forums. However, we were only interested in the activity of players on forums and considered the number of posts as a sufficient metric to measure this. From this data, it was evident that influencers engage with the forums almost three times more than even power users.

8.5.3 Influencer Impact on Communities

As mentioned earlier, we wanted to explore the impact of influencers on their respective communities by examining the dynamic chances of behaviors before players begin joining groups created by influencers and after. In order to assess the impact that the influencers have on their communities, we took three steps:

1. We isolated all players that played with influencers (the communities) at least twice in the week before polling the data.
2. We then split the data regarding communities in two: data regarding play behavior corresponding to the 2 weeks before joining the influencers' community and data regarding play behavior for the 2 weeks after joining the influencers' community.
3. We compared daily playtime and time spent in groups before and after joining the communities.

This process yielded the results summarized in Table 8.2. There is a clear change and impact on the behavior of players that join the communities of the identified 49 social players: the daily playtime increases considerably, from a number very close to the general population average to a number very close to the influencers themselves; the amount of time spent in groups increases from the total population average to almost the same amount of the influencers (cf. Table 8.1).

---

[3] Chapter 7 takes a closer look at these methods.

Table 8.2   Changes in the Influencer's Communities Before and After Engaging with Influencers' Created Groups

	Before Joining Community	*After Joining Community*
Daily playtime (hours)	1.77	2.21
Group/solo	41%–59%	59%–41%

8.6 Conclusions

Our aim was to identify and understand influential players in the live game *Tom Clancy's The Division* using existing social network analysis methods. Our results seem to suggest that the identified key members are heavily engaged (as expected) and are characterized by a large number of friends, creating many groups with those friends (as opposed to adding quick-matched players), and a large number of forum posts. At the same time, it is wrong to think of these 49 players as power users. In *TCTD*, power users have reached the level cap of 30 and have achieved a Gear Score in the top 5% (the Gear Score is a numerical rating of the quality of gear collected); the 49 socially influential players identified have a Gear Score in the top 35%. Additionally, power users are not more social than the average, meaning they tend to start groups mostly with their limited number of friends and do not play with quick-matched players. Because of that, the number of friends or groups formed is not sufficient to differentiate players that regularly play with a small number of friends or players that collect large number of friends but do not engage with a lot of them. These facts prove how simple metrics are not sufficient to identify these community leaders. Therefore, social network analysis methods are required to find the exact key members.

Our exploratory study reveals that influential players can be revealed with a combination of modularity and prestige measures. It turns out that these influential players create groups an order of magnitude more than the average player. They play many more sessions (34 times more) and have many more friends (21 times more) than the average player. More importantly, they seem to be the ones who initiate group play and invite others to join. As the sustained lifetime of a game depends in large measure on a healthy, lively community of players engaged with the multiplayer aspects of the game, these players form the invisible social backbone of a game's community. Future research should consider additional steps to identify these players, consider how it generalizes to other live games, and explore how identification will help with community management.

Acknowledgments

This research has been accomplished with the support of Ubisoft, the Games Lab, and the Live Ops team at Massive Entertainment.

References

Ang, C. S., & Zaphiris, P. (2010). Social roles of players in MMORPG guilds: A social network analytic perspective. *Information, Communication & Society, 13*(4), 592–614.

Bartle, R. (1996). Hearts, clubs, diamonds, spades: Players who suit MUDs. *Journal of MUD Research, 1*(1), 19.

Bastian, M., Heymann, S., & Jacomy, M. (2009). Gephi: An open source software for exploring and manipulating networks. *ICWSM, 8*, 361–362.

Blondel, V. D., Guillaume, J. L., Lambiotte, R., & Lefebvre, E. (2008). Fast unfolding of communities in large networks. *Journal of Statistical Mechanics: Theory and Experiment, 2008*(10), P10008.

Boellstorff, T., Nardi, B., Pearce, C., & Taylor, T. L. (2012). *Ethnography and Virtual Worlds: A Handbook of Method.* Princeton, NJ: Princeton University Press.

Division Forums, The (n.d.). Retrieved from http://forums.ubi.com/forumdisplay. php/498-The-Division.

Ducheneaut, N., Yee, N., Nickell, E., & Moore, R. J. (2006). Alone together?: Exploring the social dynamics of massively multiplayer online games. In *Proceedings of the SIGCHI Conference on Human Factors in Computing Systems* (pp. 407–416). New York: ACM Press.

Hadiji, F., Sifa, R., Drachen, A., Thurau, C., Kersting, K., & Bauckhage, C. (2014). Predicting player churn in the wild. In *IEEE Conference on Computational Intelligence and Games* (pp. 1–8). Piscataway, NJ: IEEE.

Ho, S. H., & Huang, C. H. (2009). Exploring success factors of video game communities in hierarchical linear modeling: The perspectives of members and leaders. *Computers in Human Behavior, 25*(3), 761–769.

Kraut, R. E., Resnick, P., Kiesler, S. et al., (2012). *Building Successful Online Communities: Evidence-Based Social Design.* Cambridge, MA: MIT Press.

Massive Entertainment. (2016). *Tom Clancy's The Division* [PC game]. Montreuil, France: Ubisoft.

Newman, M. E. (2006). Modularity and community structure in networks. *Proceedings of the National Academy of Sciences, 103*(23), 8577–8582.

Park, H., & Kim, K. J. (2014). Social network analysis of high-level players in multi-player online battle arena game. In *International Conference on Social Informatics* (pp. 223–226). Cham, Switzerland: Springer.

Pearce, C. (2011). *Communities of Play: Emergent Cultures in Multiplayer Games and Virtual Worlds.* Cambridge, MA: MIT Press.

Pirker, J., Rattinger, A., Drachen, A., & Sifa, R. (2018). Analyzing player networks in Destiny. *Entertainment Computing, 25*, 71–83.

Salovaara, A., Johnson, M., Toiskallio, K., Tiitta, S., & Turpeinen, M. (2005). Playmakers in multiplayer game communities: Their importance and motivations for participation. In *Proceedings of the ACM SIGCHI International Conference on Advances in Computer Entertainment Technology* (pp. 334–337). New York: ACM.

Sotamaa, O., & Karppi, T. (2010). *Games as Services-Final Report* (Tech. Rep.). Tampere, Finland: Tampere University.

Taylor, T. L. (2009). *Play between Worlds: Exploring Online Game Culture*. Cambridge, MA: MIT Press.

Wasserman, S., & Faust, K. (1994). *Social Network Analysis: Methods and Applications*. Cambridge, UK: Cambridge University Press.

Wong, S. (2017). *How Ubisoft Keeps "The Division" and "Rainbow Six Siege" Ahead of the competition*. Retrieved from http://www.alistdaily.com/strategy/ubisoft-keeps -division-rainbow-six-sieg.

Zhao, K., Yen, J., Greer, G., Qiu, B., Mitra, P., & Portier, K. (2014). Finding influential users of online health communities: A new metric based on sentiment influence. *Journal of the American Medical Informatics Association, 21*(e2), e212–e218.

Chapter 9

Methodological and Epistemological Reflections on the Use of Game Analytics toward Understanding the Social Relationships of a Video Game Community

Maude Bonenfant, Patrick Deslauriers, and Issam Heddad

Contents

9.1 Introduction

Researchers in communication studies face many difficulties when they wish to use game analytics methods. Besides the difficulty in accessing in-game databases, this methodology requires training in data sciences since it is based on data processing. However, most communication studies researchers lack such training (Zelenkauskaite & Bucy, 2016). For this reason, there have been few research collaborations between communication and information studies researchers and gaming companies to date (Bonenfant et al., 2017). While these have been valuable in terms of knowledge production, methodological innovation, and technological development, they also encountered various problems (Bonenfant & Meurs, 2018).

In this chapter, we look at the methodological and epistemological challenges we encountered as communication researchers with a background in semiotics when analyzing data collected by a gaming company (Ubisoft). Our central research question is as follows: How can we describe, understand, and qualify a game's community by identifying the social normalization[1] process using game telemetry? In other words, how can we infer the identity relationships,[2] communicational

---

[1] By social normalization, we mean the process through which norms are developed and adopted by a large number of members of a community. These norms are socially defined by the culture and values of the community and, in turn, regulate what is acceptable (implicitly or not) and frowned upon: behaviors, identities, communicational dynamics, metagame, etc.

[2] "Identity relationship" refers to the identity construction of players through their relationships to others. For example, by entering a new community or members experiencing a new social environment and learning to express their identity according to the rules of the group.

dynamics,[3] social norms,[4] and internalized values[5] of gamers by tracking the objective behaviors using methods from game analytics and data collected by a video game company? More precisely, we discuss the possibilities of game analytics and some difficulties encountered in studying player communities when working with data already collected. Game analytics offers many possibilities to gain insight into player communities and provides information that is otherwise unobtainable, for example, with qualitative research methods (i.e., interviews). Automated analysis of written or behavioral data is a valuable method that has many advantages when the conditions for collection, processing, and reporting are optimal. However, the aim of this chapter is to explore the limits of current methods for analyzing video game communities by showing the challenges that communication studies researchers face when using game analytics and data collected in a business context.

In this chapter, we (1) problematize the context of doing research on player communities when using game analytics by discussing advantages and constraints of social network analysis and sentiment analysis. To illustrate the difficulties faced, we (2) briefly present the exploratory research conducted using mixed methods in partnership with Ubisoft Montreal on the game *For Honor* (Ubisoft, 2017), and (3) finally, we give three examples of issues concerning the nature of the collected data in relation to our research objectives involving identity as well as communicational and social questions.

9.2 Context

9.2.1 Shifting from Games-as-a-Product to Games-as-a-Service

In the early 2000s, there was a "shift from [...] games as a retail product towards a more long-term service-based orientation" (Whitson, 2012, p. 4). This is part of a larger context because "as goods become more information-intensive and

---

[3] "Communication dynamics" refers to all messages exchanged verbally or non-verbally (i.e., non-verbal communication) within a community. These exchanges are dynamic because they are constantly reinterpreted according to various communication contexts.

[4] "Social norms" are the social rules, implicit or explicit, that a community formulates in order to regulate interpersonal and social relations. Failure to comply with these rules usually leads to social sanctions that may go as far as being banished by the group.

[5] "Internalized values" refers to values shared by a group that serve as a yardstick for judging the speeches and behaviors of its members and those of outside members. Their role is to legitimize norms by giving them meaning. Values are internalized in the sense that they do not have to be fully explained in order to influence each member of the group on a regular basis.

interactive and are continually upgraded, they change character. They lose their status as products and metamorphose into evolving services" (Rifkin, 2005). This is important because the distribution systems for video games changed from selling material objects in stores to providing intangible services via the Internet. The gaming industry started to slowly move away from a "fire-and-forget" (Sotamaa, 2010) to a software-as-a-service model (Godse & Mulik, 2009), spurred by the popularization of different forms of Internet transactions, such as subscriptions, sale of game components, season passes, and downloadable content. Up until the 2010s, this sales model mostly used "virtual goods" normally found in games such as *FarmVille* (Zynga, 2009). However, from 2010 onward, the games-as-a-service expression started referring more directly to regular updates (or patches) and microtransactions. These transactions occur regularly by continually creating game content in order to sustain the long-term engagement of players.

In recent years, a shift to the games-as-a-service model has been taken place at Ubisoft with investments increasingly being made around this model and games building upon it such as *Rainbow 6 Siege* (Ubisoft, 2015), *The Division* (Massive Entertainment, 2016), and *For Honor* (Ubisoft, 2017). Ubisoft CEO, Yves Guillemot (2017), affirms that "new releases now only represent a part of our business, which is now focused on long-term engagement with our player communities" (p. 3). This long-term engagement also means revenue for Ubisoft who revealed that "for the first time, microtransactions brought in more revenue than digital game sales alone" (McAloon, 2017). As a result, this maintains an active community and keeps the game profitable for the longest possible time (Fields, 2013).

While the games-as-a-service model represents a recent shift in terms of game development, it actually dates farther back when we consider massively multiplayer online role-playing games. Since the end of the 1990s, through his work on massively multiplayer online games, the game designer and design researcher, Raph Koster (1999), has affirmed that games must be considered as services, stating that: "It's a SERVICE. Not a game. It's a WORLD. Not a game. It's a COMMUNITY. Not a game. Anyone who says it's just a game is missing the point." A better knowledge of player communities is essential at this point in order to stimulate their development, keep them active, and motivate purchases on a long-term basis. As Fields (2013) states, "to give customers what they want, we must study how they interact with the games and devices" (p. 66). While the acquisition of players, their retention, and their monetization are keys to a game's success, these phenomena actualize differently depending on the player community. In this chapter, we argue that we can better understand the normalization of players' behaviors by analyzing their identity and their communicational and social relationships. This, in turn, helps explain, among other things, behaviors such as becoming part of a player community, willingness to participate in a game, and the desire to invest time and money.

9.2.2 Predominance of Analytics Tools in the Industry

There are many explanations for the *"quantitative shift in the digital industry"* (Whitson, 2012) following the move from games-as-a-product to games-as-a-service. El-Nasr et al. (2013b) look at the growth in collecting personal data and the use of metrics as necessary information to learn more about players. They give the example of free-to-play games. These productions offer free access to a game and players are encouraged to make microtransactions to further their experience and progression. These new business and gaming models seek to understand player behavior in order to maximize revenue.

Moreover, over the past decade, game analytics and data mining have become increasingly popular and used in the gaming industry as a decision-making tool. The method produces game intelligence objectives that enable decision-makers to act more quickly on different aspects of a game including level design, game design, matchmaking, monetization, and user interface design (Drachen et al., 2012, 2013c). Hence, the role of metrics is ever more central to the various aspects and steps of producing a game (production, alpha, beta, release, post-launch). "Applied right, game telemetry can be a very powerful tool for game development" (Drachen et al., 2013c, p. 206).

But despite the success of such games as *World of Warcraft* (Blizzard Entertainment, 2004), video game business models are not centered around player communities. The evolution of telemetry and game analytics instead relies on consumer metrics (acquisition, retention, monetization, etc.) and gameplay metrics (balance, choice of avatars, missions completed, etc.) as the required elements for successful games. Despite the explosion in quantity of collected data since 2010 and improvements in analytics tools, it is still necessary to prioritize certain information in order to limit the costs of collecting, processing, and reporting data. Moreover, literature on game analytics mainly concerns consumer and gameplay metrics. For example, the book *Game Analytics: Maximizing the Value of Player Data* (El-Nasr et al., 2013a) briefly explains the potential and complexity of communication and socialization metrics without expanding further on the subject. This remains an emerging subject and, as the authors state, clearly deserves a book of its own (Drachen et al., 2013a). In the fast-paced context of video game production and ongoing live operations, the priority rarely goes to data concerning the health of a community or behaviors linked to communication and socialization of players.

Therefore, many questions regarding the understanding of player communities—despite extensive game studies research into identity and social inquiries using computerized data collection—remain. Moreover, business models relying on games-as-a-service principles require healthy player communities and a clear understanding of the identity as well as communicational and social challenges that inspire players to continue with their community.

9.2.3 Community Metrics

At a workshop in 2011, Christou et al., (2013) pointed out the need "to create metrics and methods for evaluating sociability structures and the social player experience" (p. 3240). One way toward achieving this goal are community metrics, which measure interactions between players in-game and out-of-game. This assumes that players discuss and interact on diverse communication platforms made available by the video game company or third-party businesses. Among other things, these metrics observe textual interactions, the number of relationships between players, the time spent as a team with other players, and the items exchanged. They "form an important source of information, applicable in an array of contexts" (Drachen et al., 2013a, p. 23).

Today, with more and more video games online, community metrics are more pertinent, useful, and revealing than ever. For researchers in communication studies who study video games as socialization platforms, the analysis of social data can provide information about technologically mediated communication, implicit or explicit digital relationships between players, and social interaction parameters such as digital self-representation (Olshannikova et al., 2017). Gaming companies can use this information to evaluate a community's social dynamics by learning about the creation, durability, and strength of player connections (friend requests, number of friends, integration in a guild, etc.). It is also helpful in verifying the usage and efficiencies of in-game communication tools (silence, number of words, etc.) and understanding how or why players quit a game without ever returning (churn rate) (Balci & Salah, 2015; Borbora, 2015; Debeauvais et al., 2014). This comprehensive knowledge of a community both in-game and out-of-game is even more important now that an increasing number of AAA games are migrating toward the games-as-a-service model.

9.2.4 Social Network Analysis

Data analytics methods help us understand the context of social interactions in the video gaming field since "from the view of social network analysis, the social environment can be expressed as patterns or regularities in relationships among interacting units" (Wasserman & Faust, 1994, p.3). Social network analysis is one of the most developed branches of data analytics and is as much a tool as it is a theory and a method (Olshannikova et al., 2017). This approach was initially developed in sociology and later applied in other disciplines. It is "concerned with synthesizing the structural attributes of a social network and extracting intelligence from the relationships among the participating entities" (Gandomi & Haider, 2015, p. 142). The social network structure is modeled as a graph that includes nodes, representing individuals, and edges, referring to relationships (Heidemann et al., 2012). This type of analysis helps clarify the role of interpersonal relationships when accessing and disseminating information (Laplante, 2012).

In this regard, many techniques relate to the structure of social networks. They assist researchers using egocentric (Laplante, 2012), community detection (Tang & Liu, 2010), social influence analysis, and link prediction (Gandomi & Haider, 2015) approaches. In combination, they make it possible to identify subgroups not otherwise defined in a larger population. Leaders within these subgroups can also be identified and the links recognized that maintain and strengthen relationships between members over time. For example, the dynamic multiplex network (Jurman, 2016) approach allows many layers of interactions to be represented through time. There are also tools that combine multiple approaches to refine the analysis: CoDEM, for instance, consists of two main processes: (1) evaluating the detected communities, and (2) mining the key nodes inside them (Wang et al., 2014).

Even though these approaches are not often used in production-driven games research, their applications are evident.[6] For instance, Ducheneaut et al. (2006) evaluated the "potential sociability" as well as the strength of links within six or more member guilds. Other researchers used this technique to understand the influence of networks on the churn rate (Kawale et al., 2009). Williams et al. (2006) applied it to study the centrality of an avatar in a *World of Warcraft* guild of players by evaluating the frequency of its participation. The authors explain that "as with any form of social network analysis (Wasserman & Faust, 1994), it is important to understand how the ties between participants were constructed. In our case, we connected individuals based on the time they spent together in a group with their guild mates" (p. 355). However, the authors admit that the technique has limitations: "But although this is a good indicator of the prevalence of joint activities in guilds, it says nothing about the nature of these activities" (Williams et al. 2006, p. 355).

As these examples show, social network analysis is successful in quantifying the links between individuals, evaluating the frequency of exchange, and monitoring the evaluation of a network structure. However, it is not successful in evaluating the relational content in a game. Saint-Charles and Mongeau (2005) define the study of relational content by identifying and analyzing the factors that characterize certain types of interpersonal relationships. This type of study is more qualitative in that it observes factors leading to the creation of relationships, their retention, and their disbandment on the individual level. In other words, it seeks to understand the relational journey of individuals participating in a group (Saint-Charles & Mongeau, 2005; Wellman, 1988).

Social network analysis has the advantage of objectifying the relationships between individuals by representing the network of interpersonal relationships. But the meaning produced by such relationships is not defined, nor are the qualitative characteristics that distinguish each community and subcommunity.

---

[6] For example, Chapter 8 discusses how social network analysis can be used to detect key social players.

Social network analysis presupposes a certain understanding of the notion of "community." In fact, many studies using this approach use the term "cluster" to refer to a community (Girvan & Newman, 2002; Malliaros & Vazirgiannis, 2013), although some recognize the problematic aspect of such use (Bello-Orgaz et al., 2016; Fortunato, 2010). Indeed, from a communication studies point of view, a community cannot be reduced to a "cluster" because a community contains a variety of complementary and opposing characteristics that are not always coherent. Nonetheless, they function together coherently as a whole. For Tönnies (1887), who influenced modern sociology, the community (*Gemeinschaft* in German) is based on "what is common" (goods, interests, goals) and brings together people of a certain homophily. In this sense, the notion of community may include factors such as geographical proximity, national identity, shared language, values and beliefs, and the production and distribution of capital (social, cultural, and symbolic). These elements exemplify the complexity and ambiguity of the notion of community.

Clusters provide input on social ties within a group. It can be very useful to identify them, but they do not help us to better understand the construction of the community's identity, discourses, norms, or values. Therefore, cross-referencing with other types of data (primarily qualitative data) and other methods is necessary to describe communities based on their common characteristics.

9.2.5 Sentiment Analysis

One way to qualify the nature of exchanges between individuals is sentiment analysis[7] (Olshannikova et al., 2017). Understood in the context of content-based analysis (Gandomi & Haider, 2015) "sentiment analysis, or opinion mining, is an active area of study in the field of natural language processing that analyzes people's opinions, sentiments, evaluations, attitudes, and emotions via the computational treatment of subjectivity in text" (Hutto & Gilbert, 2014, p. 217). While the technique was previously reduced to a polarized classification (Nasukawa & Yi, 2003), today, it covers a larger spectrum of analysis (Mullen & Malouf, 2006; Pang & Lee, 2008). Furthermore, thanks to machine learning,[8] it supports an ever more precise classification of different texts. This classification is generally expressed as a lexical features list (such as a list of words). However, to have an accurate list, it must be constructed and validated manually (Hutto & Gilbert, 2014). Hence, "research leveraging sentiment analysis relies heavily on preexisting manually constructed lexicons" (Hutto & Gilbert, 2014, p. 217). Sentiment analysis is applied to a diverse range of study subjects using in-game data. For example, researchers interested in predicting the personality of players in *World of Warcraft* used algorithms created specifically for the application of sentiment analysis on 1,040 pseudonyms of avatars and the guild names they are part of (Shen et al., 2012).

---

[7] Sentiment analysis is also discussed in Chapter 7.
[8] Machine learning is covered as part of Chapter 6.

However, despite the interest in sentiment analysis, this technique is rarely used with textual in-game data in a business context. In addition, it should be noted that players adopt a specific slang, which also means that "the meaning of words as used in a games context can be different, as opposed to being used in the general case" (Drescher et al., 2018, p. 10). There are many reasons for its underutilization with in-game data and, more broadly, the underrepresentation of community metrics in the video game industry. First, as stated earlier in the context of game analytics, gaming companies focus mainly on the customer and on gameplay metrics as the preferred method for analyzing player behavior. Since considerable resources are required to track, collect, process, and report metrics, choices are made to prioritize the company's requirements. To justify research costs, the analyzed data must also provide readily actionable insights. In this sense, customer and gameplay metrics are better suited than community metrics. Indeed, customer and gameplay metrics are easier to interpret, as they are less abstract than "identity relationships, communicational dynamics, and social norms." Thus, it is easier to operationalize and implement data-driven customer and gameplay recommendations in the game development process.

In fact, problems due to social relationships between players are usually complex and difficult to resolve with a patch. It is also difficult to justify the return on investment or even the improved design or enhanced balancing using community metrics. It takes time before the social impacts of a change introduced to a game are felt, and these are difficult to measure. For instance, how can one "measure" the integration of new players in relation to the socialization processes? How can one "measure" the resistance to change among certain expert players in relation to the normalization processes? How can one "measure" the emerging behaviors of creative players in relation to the appropriation processes[9]? In general, it is harder to operationalize community metrics in the context of producing games because they are often reduced to analyzing forums and social media platforms to support the work of community managers (Drachen et al., 2013a).

9.2.6 Responding to Questions in Communication Studies Using Community Metrics

Understanding player communities is difficult to quantify and operationalize because the information is in itself ambiguous, subjective, complex, contextual, and multifactorial. In fact, it is hard to reduce identity and communicational and social questions to a collection of data that is automatically analyzed. In this sense,

> [...] the celebratory promises of big data as "good enough" to produce predictors of social behavior fundamentally ignore a key insight of social

---

[9] "Appropriation" is the process by which players interpret and then use the game in a certain way as opposed to expected use envisioned by the designer.

theory: Aggregated, individual actions cannot, in and of themselves, illustrate the complicated dynamics that produce social interaction— the whole of society is greater than the sum of its parts. (Crawford et al., 2014, p. 1667)

Even if a certain semantic analysis is possible thanks to sentiment analysis techniques, these do not reveal the symbolic meaning inherent in the process of participating in a community. According to Schroeder (2014):

Frequency of words is treated as indicating a certain sentiment or intent without regard to the fact that words may be used in different ways—for example, ironically [...]. As such, Twitter data is treated as if it consists of abstract units, whereas in applied settings, this data would need to be translated into specific populations, targeted in particular times and particular places, and with specific messages. (p. 7)

Meanwhile, segmentation of metrics can cause analytical islands to occur (Zelenkauskaite & Bucy, 2016) where results are detached from the global context in which player communities are analyzed.

For communication studies researchers with a background in semiotics, the meaning is not reduced to a semantic plane but also derives from a syntactic and especially pragmatic one (Morris, 1946; Eco, 1984; Peirce, 1931–1958; Odin, 2011). At the risk of oversimplifying this semiotic approach, we nonetheless insist that the pragmatic approach[10] is limited since it refers to the action between the signs and those who interpret them. This is because the lived context can radically change that interpretation. In any exchange between two or more individuals, a tertiary element representing collective symbols (tiers symbolisant) used by the group intervenes (Quéré, 1982). This is a meta-communicational principle that regulates the communication by neither entirely predefining it nor reducing it to a particular communication. If the rules can be objectified, the symbolic meanings shared by the members of a group are immanent to each context. However, since they are subjectified, they are more or less vague or inconsistent. It is therefore impossible to define the rules in advance since the "tertiary element representing collective symbols" belongs to the social imaginary (Castoriadis, 1975) that is shared by a community. At this level of analysis, there is no longer only the question of networks (social network analysis) or semantics (sentiment analysis) but of the community and pragmatics that community metrics cannot describe, at least not entirely with the methods

---

[10] Pragmatics states that the meaning of an expression lies in its practical consequences, that is to say that its implications and context affects meaning.

and the data currently gathered by the video game industry and to which researchers have access to.

This epistemological difficulty questions "community metrics" as a term, which can be seen as an oxymoron. How can one reconcile the qualitative value of a community with the quantitative representation of the metrics? From a sociological point of view of game studies, the expression "community metrics" is in fact rarely used. This is because qualitative methods often prevail in the field (Consalvo & Dutton, 2006; Boellstorff et al., 2012; Warmeling & Siitonen, 2013). When studies use game analytics as a method, most of them are not really describing a community as much as they are revealing the behaviors of players that are more difficult to identify through qualitative methods (Ducheneaut & Moore, 2004; Ducheneaut et al., 2006; Thurau & Bauckhage, 2010). Other studies focus instead on the psychological profiles of players (Yee et al., 2011; Ducheneaut & Yee, 2013).

Community metrics make it possible to identify behavioral patterns (objectified, rationalized, simplified). However, there are problems in using this method to infer relationships involving identities, communicational dynamics, and social norms since this would require the observation of values that are subjective, affective, and complex. As Kitchin (2014) observes:

> It is one thing to identify patterns; it is another to explain them. This requires social theory and deep contextual knowledge. As such, the pattern is not the end-point but rather a starting point for additional analysis, which almost certainly is going to require other data sets. (p. 8)

In other words, as long as we stay at the semantics and network level, community metrics provides substantial information. However, to comprehend a community in its symbolic relationships requires a mix of qualitative and quantitative methods.

9.3 Mixed-Methods Research with In-Game and Out-of-Game Data

In order to assess the possibilities and limits of what is currently feasible in terms of research with in-game and out-of-game data, we have initiated an exploratory research project conducted in partnership with the Ubisoft's Montreal User Research Lab (MURL) and Ubisoft's La Forge (a space for collaboration between university research and production teams) using a body of data collected between February 15, 2017, and April 15, 2017, on the game *For Honor* (Ubisoft, 2017). The research had two main objectives:

1. To identify the epistemological and methodological problems when using the analytics tools made available to us by MURL, and
2. To build a methodology with mixed methods to help us understand the identity and communicational and social dynamics of the player community.

For Honor is an action and 3D third-person fighting game where 12 heroes (at the launch of the game) from 3 factions (Knights, Vikings, and Samurai) confront one another in close combat. The game is available on PC, PS4, and Xbox One and offers many online game modes, the most popular being "Duel" (1 versus 1, 5 rounds of combat), "Brawl" (2 versus 2, 5 rounds of combat), and "Dominion" (4 versus 4 with objectives). The main objective of this partnership with Ubisoft was to qualify the incipient game community. This was done by

1. Identifying the general characteristics of a community,
2. Describing a number of subcommunities,
3. Analyzing the behavioral normalization processes of these subcommunities,
4. Inferring the values that are promoted through predominant or polarizing discussion subjects, and
5. Identifying the emergent as well as the deviant behaviors.

To do this, we used a mixed-methods approach (Brannen, 2005; Creswell & Plano Clark, 2011; Tashakkori & Teddlie, 2009), cross-referencing the results of the quantitative and qualitative data analyses conducted inside as well as outside the game (cf. Figure 9.1). The methods we used are:

■ Semiotic analysis of the game,
■ Player surveys,
■ Semi-structured interviews with the players,
■ Automated analysis of in-game and out-of-game data, and
■ Manual encoding of out-of-game data from the game's official forum and subreddit.

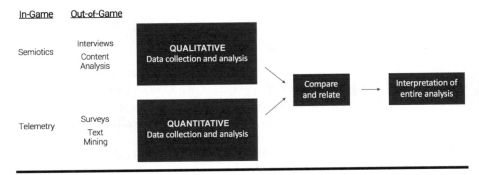

Figure 9.1   Methods used in our research.

In order to understand how the game was designed, we began with a semiotic analysis of *For Honor*. Indeed, we analyzed the organization of the signs in the game interface and the way in which the features allow, favor, prevent, or forbid certain in-game behaviors. This was followed with several questions integrated in a survey created by Ubisoft. This survey was conducted to get the feedback from players on several themes on a large scale. In parallel, semi-structured interviews were conducted with 10 expert players. The collected data served to confirm or refute our results from the two main methods used: the automatic analysis of in-game and out-of-game data as well as the manual encoding of out-of-game data from the game's official forum and subreddit.

In-game telemetry access was provided by Ubisoft Montreal, allowing us to connect directly to the live database and to use the same tools as the studio's game intelligence analysts. Since this was an exploratory research, we did not work on a specific dataset and tested hypothesis. Our explorative approach allowed us to look for ways to use behavioral telemetry data to address the difficulties that arise when understanding gamer communities with the current tools, methods of game analytics, and data collected by a video game company.

Ultimately, our methodology enabled a dynamic interaction between qualitative and quantitative approaches as well as between in-game and out-of-game data. The collected out-of-game information served to prioritize, hierarchize, and define the questions used to analyze in-game data and vice versa. The two analyses were conducted in parallel, and the results were compared and cross-interpreted in order to finalize our conclusions.

9.4 Challenges That Arise from the Nature of the Collected Data Inside the Game

Although mixed methods based on in-game and out-of-game data overcome a certain number of game analysis shortcomings, the exploratory part of the research conducted so far remains confined to a set of challenges on the nature of the collected in-game data in relation to the research objectives. For example, having in-game access to behavioral data collected in a business context does not necessarily integrate the identity as well as communicational and social questions. Complex results must therefore be inferred in order to respond to certain questions. Many researchers, particularly in critical data studies (Bollier, 2010; Boyd & Crawford, 2012; Gitelman, 2013; Dalton & Thatcher, 2014; Kitchin, 2014; Puschmann & Burgess, 2014), have identified certain problems related to specific analysis of results obtained using Big Data, so in this sense the obstacles faced are not new. However, they make it possible to identify the problems that require complementary methods to resolve issues arising from the use of Big Data in the context of game development. In this article, we briefly present three cases where we demonstrate the limits of the in-game data we currently have access to in answering our research questions.

9.4.1 Results Whose Meaning Varies According to Context

In our first case, we show that the interpretation of data depends on the context of its production. A simple digital value does not always allow us to grasp the nuances and complexities of human behaviors. This is because the latent meanings, the intentions, and the desired effects of the players are difficult to quantify or identify based on the objectification of their behaviors. In the case of *For Honor*, we use the example of "Quick Chat" to explain our argument. This communication channel is used in the multiplayer component of the game. It differs from "Text Chat" or "Voice Chat" since it produces predefined announcements or responses to indicate something to teammates or opponents (Toups et al., 2014), using a combination of keys (PC) or buttons (Xbox One and PS4).

The particularity of "Quick Chat" is in the way players misuse and reinterpret the tool (appropriation process). For example, in analyzing the in-game data, we observe that the "Wow!" message is used at the highest frequency (per session average over all players) to communicate courtesy. This represents 35.58% in the dominion mode, 32.66% in the brawl mode, and 23.19% in the duel modes. Do these numbers confirm that the players who play in the dominion or brawl modes are more likely to be positively surprised than the players in the duel mode? Are the players in these two modes more inclined to show respect toward their adversaries who have executed a set of complex commands in order to activate a combat maneuver?

These hypotheses may seem valid at first. However, by referring to the discourses produced by players out-of-game, we can more accurately grasp the nuances of the usage of the term "*Wow!*" In fact, on the consoles, where "Text Chat" does not exist and where the "Voice Chat" is barely used, the main meaning of the "Quick Chat" messages is often distorted by the players. This is a necessary action considering the limited number of messages available on "Quick Chat" and their overall positive connotations. Since players do not have the linguistic means to express negative messages, they creatively use the language available to them. Thus, changing the meaning of certain expressions serves to express emotions that the "Quick Chat" does not make available to players. This is done in various ways, including using the same message consecutively (spam) and using a message in an unusual context (i.e., when we do not expect to see the message or when it is used ironically).

For example, while the single use of the message "*Wow!*" usually expresses amazement, astonishment, or respect for achieving certain actions or moves that are difficult to execute, using the message three consecutive times implies an ironic tone in order to troll, mock, or show frustration toward an adversary or teammate. In this sense, rather than concluding that the positive congratulatory message "Wow!" is more used in the dominion mode, we should look at how the negative trolling message "Wow! Wow! Wow!" is more likely to occur in this mode. Does this not imply that players facing a single enemy in a duel are more respectful toward one another than players in group modes (brawl and dominion)?

As the example shows, despite knowing the quantity of produced messages in each match, game mode, and platform, the context and the intention of the usage is not readily observed with such a method. As time passes, the players develop codes, ways of doing things, and symbolic references. In other words, they normalize certain behaviors (Castronova et al., 2013; Bonenfant et al., 2018). The in-game data is thus limited for understanding the complexity of such phenomenon. Moreover, the interpretation of these data always depends on the context of production, thorough knowledge of the community, the unwritten rules of engagement in the community, and the analysis of its explicit and implicit norms.

9.4.2 Partial and Imprecise Data

Another problem arises when the data is partial or imprecise, an inevitable situation since limited resources make it impossible to capture everything. In the case of *For Honor*, Ubisoft proceeds by using different data collection techniques. In certain events it uses random sampling and in others it uses data collected on the whole population. According to Drachen et al. (2013b), this includes a technique of "deep and shallow combination: collect detailed data but apply a filter at the collection back end, to ensure that detailed (deep) telemetry is collected for a sample of players, but shallow data is collected for all players" (p. 156).

An example that characterizes the sampling problem is that of away from keyboard farming (AFK farming). AFK farming is a deliberate, controversial, and to an extent forbidden tactic that is used to accumulate as much resources as possible (e.g., in-game currency) while expending minimum effort. It is a current tactic in many games to give a certain incentive when a number of tasks or levels is completed. Instead of grinding, which takes a lot of time, or buying in-game resources (microtransactions) to unlock game items more rapidly, some players decide to AFK farm. This behavior is a deviant practice in relation to the expected use of the game (Consalvo, 2009). Normally, the community at large reacts negatively to it because it is perceived as an unfair way of playing. The community may therefore sanction those who use AFK farming. As a result, consciously or unconsciously, the AFK farmers create their own subcommunity. Such information is of great interest in answering questions regarding research on social aspects of the game and its players.

AFK farming is often resolved by detecting idle players. These are players who join a group but do not participate or move. However, the players always find the means to make themselves "invisible" in the face of AFK farming stationary detection techniques. In *For Honor*, certain players have said on social media that they have started to farm by attaching an elastic on the joystick of their controller. This permits their hero to turn in a circle continuously, and hence be "active" during all parts of the game without being detected. This also ensures that the player will capture all the resources offered at the end of a level without actually playing the game.

At the time of our analysis, the positional player data sampling rate used for this event was too small. In this case, it is difficult to detect players who use a rubber band to trick the system. It is then necessary to combine several data sources in order to predict the behavior of a farmer. This includes data from (1) positioning patterns, (2) players who are reported, and (3) patterns of resources accumulation. As Drachen et al. (2013b, p. 159) explain, "even a truly random sample does not guarantee that all values represented will occur in the sample, and runs the risk of missing entire small clusters." This lack of precision restricts one to measure behaviors that reveal certain social characteristics of the community, such as the community's tolerance toward cheating.

9.4.3 Collected Information Aggregated with Other Data

The last example concerns the automatic aggregation of data from many sources. By reducing the details of the results from the data collection process, certain phenomena, or behaviors that are important to a study cannot be detected. The voluntary aggregation of data in order to optimize resources results in loss of information and, more importantly, loss of opportunities to identify certain marginal practices of a community that can eventually be normalized and/or influence other behaviors.

Here we look at daily challenges (sometimes called "dailies"), which is one of the strategies developers use, for example, to keep players strongly engaged. This is a game design element where missions or specific objectives are added to a game's initial winning conditions. These time-dependent challenges can have variable frequencies (e.g., daily, weekly) or be offered at certain dates (e.g., weekend or during a holiday). In *For Honor*, these daily challenges are called "orders." The player can select and accomplish them to gain additional resources. The orders change regularly and are very diverse: get 10 "honorable kills" playing with a Samurai hero, play 5 matches of "death match," and so on.

A particular case occurred when the "revive order" was studied. The objective of this order is to successfully execute five revives during one of many matches. This means that the player has to revive the avatar of a teammate who has died. Initially, the order's intent was to encourage the players to execute more revives while respecting the main objective of the match. However, degenerate strategies (Salen & Zimmerman, 2003) were used by some players when the study was conducted. For example, certain groups of friends developed a tactic to take advantage of the system where the first player intentionally kills their avatar by falling off a cliff. By doing this near their teammate, the player can revive them rapidly. Once the first player conducts five revives, the roles change and it becomes the second player's turn to complete the order. Hence, both players complete the order rapidly and are compensated at the end of the match.

Even if it would be possible to identify this behavior from in-game data, the particularity in our research context is that the data was aggregated in such a way that one cannot distinguish *how* certain players complete certain tasks (revive, 10 honorable kills, etc.). Besides, no information is given about the rate of completion or the time it took to achieve each order. This is because the information gathered by the system denotes the types of orders (daily, weekly, etc.) but gives no details on how the orders were executed by players. This is problematic since the data collection method limits us from knowing if the orders that encourage social interactions (such as the revive order) are more, or less, selected than those oriented toward individualistic behaviors (exceed a large number of personal points, killing minions, etc.). In addition, this aggregation does not tell us if players switch heroes because of orders that require a specific class of heroes. Such information is useful because it would give other indications on the identity relations between players and their avatars.

9.5 Conclusions

One objective of this chapter was to demonstrate the importance of analyzing player communities in the current context of video game development. Understanding these communities is not only important for researchers in communication studies and social sciences but also for the gaming industry due to the shift from a games-as-a-product to a games-as-a-service model. Game analytics partially permits us to analyze the "health" of a community. As we stated at the beginning of this chapter, game analytics offers many benefits, such as gaining insight into player communities and providing information that is otherwise unobtainable. It is a valuable method that has many advantages when the conditions for collection, processing, and reporting are optimal. However, community metrics derived from in-game data in the form currently made accessible by the game industry remain limited for an inquiry that goes beyond social network analysis or sentiment analysis.

The mixed-methods research adopted from various quantitative and qualitative methods makes it possible to overcome the constraints of game analytics by benefiting from the advantages of the qualitative methods used by researchers in semiotics and communication studies. This approach is part of a general movement where the combination of many information sources becomes a necessary practice for refining the analysis of collected data. Similarly, the difficulties signaled in this chapter on the nature of in-game data are not new and confirm what many researchers in game analytics and critical data studied have already identified. What our research contributes is a confirmation of the difficulty of understanding the identity relationships, communication dynamics, social norms, internalized values, and different interpretations by players when using objectively tracked behavioral data gathered through methods of game analytics. We have done this by deploying a mixed-methods research based on questions specific to researchers in communication studies. Moreover, we have provided examples that illustrate the epistemological and methodological limits of automatized analysis of in-game data collected in a business context.

Far from being constraining, these limits demonstrate the interest of pursuing research in game analytics using mixed methods. This is by designing new data collection criteria that make player communities one of the prime objects of study and an important target for the video game industry. To do this, partnerships with the game industry would be advantageous in combining approaches, questions, and intellectual as well as technical means. Likewise, there must be ongoing and even more frequent collaboration between computer science and social science researchers in order to refine the current research tools and methods and to generate new ones. Finally, a vast field of research can be explored since thus far there are very few research mixes using a communicational approach based on game analytics.

References

Balci, K., & Salah, A. A. (2015). Automatic analysis and identification of verbal aggression and abusive behaviours for online social games. *Computers in Human Behavior, 53,* 517–526.

Bello-Orgaz, G., Jung, J. J., & Camacho, D. (2016). Social big data: Recent achievements and new challenges. *Information Fusion, 28,* 45–59.

Blizzard Entertainment. (2004). *World of Warcraft.* [Online video game]. Irvine, CA: Blizzard Entertainment.

Boellstorff, T., Nardi, B., Pearce, C., & Taylor, T. L. (2012). *Ethnography and virtual worlds: A Handbook of Method.* New Jersey: Princeton University Press.

Bollier, D. (2010). *The Promise and Peril of Big Data.* Washington, DC: The Aspen Institute.

Bonenfant, M., Lafrance St-Martin, L. I., Prégent, F., & Crémier, L. (2018). Social systems and behavioral norms: The comparative case study of guild wars II and league of legends. In K. Lakkaraju & G. Sukthankar (Eds.), *Social Interaction in Virtual Worlds.* Cambridge: Cambridge University Press.

Bonenfant, M., & Meurs, M. J. (2018). Collaboration between social sciences and computer science: Towards a cross-disciplinary methodology for studying big social data from online communities. In J. Hunsinger, L. Klastrup & M. Allen (Eds.), *Handbook of Internet Research II.* New York: Springer.

Bonenfant, M., Richert, F., & Deslauriers, P. (2017). Using big data tools and techniques to study a gamer community: Technical, epistemological, and ethical problems. *Loading. The Journal of the Canadian Game Studies Association, 10*(16), 87–108. Retrieved from http://journals.sfu.ca/loading/index.php/loading/article/view/174

Borbora, Z. H. (2015). *Computational analysis of churn in multiplayer online games* (Doctoral Dissertation). Retrieved from the University of Minnesota Digital Conservancy, http://hdl.handle.net/11299/181699.

Boyd, d., & Crawford, K. (2012). Critical questions for big data: Provocations for a cultural, technological, and scholarly phenomenon. *Information, Communication & Society, 15*(5), 662–679.

Brannen, J. (2005). *NCRM methods review papers, NCRM/005. Mixed methods research: A discussion paper.* Discussion Paper. Unpublished manuscript.

Castoriadis, C. (1975). *L'Institution imaginaire de la société.* Paris: Seuil.

Castronova, E., Ross, T. L., & Knowles, I. (2013). Designer, analyst, tinker: How game analytics will contribute to science. In M. S. El-Nasr, A. Drachen, & A. Canossa (Eds.), *Game Analytics: Maximizing the Value of Player Data* (pp. 665–688). London, UK: Springer.

Christou, G., Law, E., Geerts, D., Nacke, L., & Zaphiris, P. (2013). Designing and evaluating sociability in online video games. In *CHI'13 Extended Abstracts on Human Factors in Computing Systems* (pp. 3239–3242). New York: ACM.

Consalvo, M. (2009). *Cheating: Gaining Advantage in Videogames.* Cambridge, MA: The MIT Press.

Consalvo, M., & Dutton, N. (2006). Game analysis: Developing a methodological toolkit for the qualitative study of games. *Game Studies, 6*(1), 1–17. Retrieved from http://gamestudies.org/0601/articles/consalvo_dutton

Crawford, K., Milner, K., & Gray, M. L. (2014). Critiquing big data: Politics, ethics, epistemology. *International Journal of Communication, 8,* 1663–1672.

Creswell, J. W., & Plano Clark, V. L. (2011). The nature of mixed methods research. In J. W. Creswell & V. L. Plano Clark (Eds.), *Designing and Conducting Mixed Methods Research* (pp. 1–18). Thousand Oaks, CA: Sage Publications.

Dalton, C., & Thatcher, J. (2014). What does a critical data studies look like, and why do we care? Seven points for a critical approach to "Big Data." Retrieved from http://societyandspace.org/2014/05/12/what-does-a-critical-data-studies-look-like-and-why-do-w e-care-craig-dalton-and-jim-thatcher/

Debeauvais, T., Lopes, C. V., Yee, N., & Ducheneaut, N. (2014). Retention and progression: Seven months in world of warcraft. In *Proceedings of International Conference on the Foundations of Digital Games.*

Drachen, A., El-Nasr, M. S., & Canossa, A. (2013a). Game analytics: The basics. In M. S. El-Nasr, A. Drachen, & A. Canossa (Eds.), *Game Analytics: Maximizing the Value of Player Data* (pp. 13–40). London, UK: Springer.

Drachen, A., Gagné, A., & El-Nasr, M. S. (2013b). Sampling for game user research. In M. S. El-Nasr, A. Drachen, & A. Canossa (Eds.), *Game Analytics: Maximizing the Value of Player Data* (pp. 143–168). London, UK: Springer.

Drachen, A., Sifa, R., Bauckhage, C., & Thurau, C. (2012). Guns, swords and data: Clustering of player behavior in computer games in the wild. In *IEEE Conference on Computational Intelligence and Games* (pp. 163–170). Piscataway, NJ: IEEE.

Drachen, A., Thurau, C., Togelius, J., Yannakakis, G. N., & Bauckhage, C. (2013c). Game data mining. In M. S. El-Nasr, A. Drachen, & A. Canossa (Eds.), *Game Analytics: Maximizing the Value of Player Data* (pp. 205–254). London, UK: Springer.

Drescher, C., Wallner, G., Kriglstein, S., Sifa, R., Drachen, A. & Pohl, M. (2018). What moves players?: Visual data exploration of Twitter and gameplay data. In *Proceedings of the 2018 CHI Conference on Human Factors in Computing Systems* (560:1–560:13). New York: ACM.

Ducheneaut, N., & Moore, R. J. (2004). The social side of gaming: A study of interaction patterns in a massively multiplayer online game. In *Proceedings of the 2004 ACM Conference on Computer Supported Cooperative Work* (pp. 360–369). New York: ACM.

Ducheneaut, N., & Yee, N. (2013). Data collection in massively multiplayer online games: Methods, analytic obstacles, and case studies. In M. S. El-Nasr, A. Drachen, & A. Canossa (Eds.), *Game Analytics: Maximizing the Value of Player Data* (pp. 641–664). London, UK: Springer.

Ducheneaut, N., Yee, N., Nickell, E., & Moore, R. J. (2006). Alone together?: Exploring the social dynamics of massively multiplayer online games. In *Proceedings of the SIGCHI Conference on Human Factors in Computing Systems* (pp. 407–416). New York: ACM.

Eco, U. (1984). *Sémiotique et philosophie du langage*. Paris: Presses universitaires de France.

El-Nasr, M. S., Drachen, A., & Canossa, A. (2013a). *Game Analytics: Maximizing the Value of Player Data*. London, UK: Springer.

El-Nasr, M. S., Drachen, A., & Canossa, A. (2013b). Introduction. In M. S. El-Nasr, A. Drachen, & A. Canossa (Eds.), *Game Analytics: Maximizing the Value of Player Data* (pp. 3–12). London, UK: Springer.

Fields, T. V. (2013). Game industry metrics terminology and analytics case study. In M. S. El-Nasr, A. Drachen, & A. Canossa (Eds.), *Game Analytics Maximizing the Value of Player Data* (pp. 53–71). London, UK: Springer.

Fortunato, S. (2010). Community detection in graphs. *Physics Reports, 486*(3–5), 75–174.

Gandomi, A., & Haider, M. (2015). Beyond the hype: Big data concepts, methods, and analytics. *International Journal of Information Management, 35*(2), 137–144.

Girvan, M., & Newman, M. E. (2002). Community structure in social and biological networks. *Proceedings of the National Academy of Sciences, 99*(12), 7821–7826.

Godse, M., & Mulik, S. (2009). An approach for selecting software-as-a-service (SaaS) product. In *IEEE International Conference onCloud Computing, 2009.* (pp. 155–158). Piscataway, NJ: IEEE.

Guillemot, Y. (2017). *2017 Ubisoft Registration Document and Annual Report*. Retrieved from https://ubistatic19-a.akamaihd.net/comsite_common/en-US/images/18ra%20 2017%20final%20en_tcm99-299980_tcm99-196733-32.pdf

Heidemann, J., Klier, M., & Probst, F. (2012). Online social networks: A survey of a global phenomenon. *Computer Networks, 56*(18), 3866–3878.

Hutto, C. J., & Gilbert, E. (2014) VADER: A parsimonious rule-based model for sentiment analysis of social media text. In *Eighth International Conference on Weblogs and Social Media* (pp. 216–225).

Jurman, G. (2016). Metric projection for dynamic multiplex networks. *Heliyon, 2*(2016), e00136.

Kawale, J., Pal, A., & Srivastava, J. (2009). Churn prediction in MMORPGs: A social influence-based approach. In *Computational Science and Engineering, 2009. CSE'09 International Conference on* (Vol. 4, pp. 423–428). Piscataway, NJ: IEEE.

Kitchin, R. (2014). Big data, new epistemologies and paradigm shifts. *Big Data & Society, 1*(1).

Koster, R. (1999). *The laws of online world design*. Retrieved from https://www.raphkoster. com/games/laws-of-online-world-design/the-laws-of-online-world-design/

Laplante, A. (2012). Who influence the music tastes of adolescents?: A study on interpersonal influence in social networks. In *Proceedings of the second International ACM Workshop on Music Information Retrieval with User-Centered and Multimodal Strategies* (pp. 37–42). New York: ACM.

Malliaros, F. D., & Vazirgiannis, M. (2013). Clustering and community detection in directed networks: A survey. *Physics Reports, 533*(4), 95–142.

Massive Entertainment. (2016). *Tom Clancy's The Division* [PC game]. Montreuil, France: Ubisoft.

McAloon, A. (2017). Ubisoft's "Player Recurring Investment" revenues outpace digital game sales. Gamasutra. Retrieved from https://www.gamasutra.com/view/news/309155/Ubisofts_player_recurring_investment_revenues_outpace_digital_game_sales.php.

Morris, C. W. (1946). *Signs, Language, and Behavior.* Oxford: Prentice-Hall.

Mullen, T., & Malouf, R. (2006). A preliminary investigation into sentiment analysis of informal political discourse. In *AAAI Spring Symposium: Computational Approaches to Analyzing Weblogs* (pp. 159–162). Menlo Park, CA: AAAI Press.

Nasukawa, T., & Yi, J. (2003). Sentiment analysis: Capturing favorability using natural language processing. In *Proceedings of the 2nd International Conference on Knowledge Capture* (pp. 70–77). New York: ACM.

Odin, R. (2011). *Les espace de communication.* Grenoble: Presses universitaires de Grenoble.

Olshannikova, E., Olsson, T., Huhtamäki, J., & Kärkkäinen, H. (2017). Conceptualizing big social data. *Journal of Big Data, 4*(1), 3.

Pang, B., & Lee, L. (2008). Opinion mining and sentiment analysis. *Foundations and Trends in Information Retrieval, 2*(1–2), 1–135.

Peirce, C. S. (1931–1958 [1857–1892]). *Collected papers of Charles Sanders Peirce,* (vols. 1–6 ed. by C. Hartshorne & P. Weiss; vols. 7–8 Ed. by A. Burks). Cambridge, UK: Harvard University Press.

Puschmann, C., & Burgess, J. (2014). Big data, big questions, metaphors of big data. *International Journal of Communication,* 8:20.

Quéré, L. (1982). *Des miroirs équivoques: Aux origines de la communication moderne.* Paris: Éditions Aubier-Montaigne.

Rifkin, J. (2005). When markets give way to networks everything is a service. In J. Hartley (Ed.), *Creative Industries* (pp. 361–374). Malden, MA: Blackwell Publishing.

Saint-Charles, J., & Mongeau, P. (2005). *Communication: Horizon de pratiques et de recherche.* Québec: Presses de l'Université du Québec.

Salen, K., & Zimmerman, E. (2003). *Rules of Play: Game Design Fundamentals.* Cambridge: The MIT Press.

Schroeder, R. (2014). Big Data and the brave new world of social media research. *Big Data &Society, 1*(2).

Shen, J., Brdiczka, O., Ducheneaut, N., Yee, N., & Begole, B. (2012). Inferring personality of online gamers by fusing multiple-view predictions. In *International Conference on User Modeling, Adaptation, and Personalization* (pp. 261–273). Springer, Berlin, Heidelberg.

Sotamaa, O. (2010). Introduction. In O. Sotamaa & T. Karppi, *Games as services: Final report* (pp. 3–9). Tampere, Finland: University of Tampere.

Tang, L., & Liu, H. (2010). Community detection and mining in social media. *Synthesis Lectures on Data Mining and Knowledge Discovery, 2*(1), 1–137.

Tashakkori, A., & Teddlie, C. (2009). The fundamentals of mixed methods research. In A. Tashakkori & C. Teddlie, *Foundations of Mixed Methods Research* (pp. 19–39). Thousand Oaks: Sage Publications.

Thurau, C., & Bauckhage, C. (2010). Analyzing the evolution of social groups in world of warcraft. In *IEEE Conference on Computational Intelligence and Games* (pp. 170–177). New York: IEEE.

Tönnies, F. (1887). *Gemeinschaft und Gesellschaft.* Leipzig, Germany: Fues's Verlag.

Toups, Z. O., Hammer, J., Hamilton, W. A., Jarrah, A., Graves, W., & Garretson, O. (2014). A framework for cooperative communication game mechanics from grounded theory. In *Proceedings of the first ACM SIGCHI Annual Symposium on Computer-Human Interaction in Play* (pp. 257–266). New York: ACM.

Ubisoft (2015). *Tom Clancy's Rainbow Six Siege.* [PC game]. Montreuil, France: Ubisoft.

Ubisoft. (2017). *For Honor.* [Online video game]. Montreuil, France: Ubisoft Entertainment SA.

Wang, M., Wang, C., & Chen, J. (2014). CoDEM: An ingenious tool of insight into community detection in social networks. In *Proceedings of the 23rd ACM International Conference on Conference on Information and Knowledge Management* (pp. 2006–2008). New York: ACM.

Warmeling, H., & Siitonen, M. (2013). A decade of research into player communities in online games. *Journal of Gaming & Virtual Worlds, 5*(3), 271–293.

Wasserman, S., & Faust, K. (1994). *Social Network Analysis: Methods and Applications.* Cambridge: Cambridge University Press.

Wellman, B. (1988). Structural analysis: From method and metaphor to theory and substance. In B. Wellman & S. Berkowitz (Eds.), *Social Structures: A Network Approach,* (pp. 19–61). Cambridge: Cambridge University Press.

Whitson, J. R. (2012). *Game design by numbers: Instrumental play and the quantitative shift in the digital game industry* (Doctoral Dissertation). Retrieved from https://curve.carleton.ca/system/files/theses/30273.pdf

Williams, D., Ducheneaut, N., Xiong, L., Zhang, Y., Yee, N., & Nickell, E. (2006). From tree house to barracks: The social life of guilds in World of Warcraft. *Games and Culture, 1*(4), 338–361.

Yee, N., Ducheneaut, N., Nelson, L., & Likarish, P. (2011). Introverted elves & conscientious gnomes: the expression of personality in world of warcraft. In *Proceedings of the SIGCHI Conference on Human Factors in Computing Systems* (pp. 753–762). New York: ACM.

Zelenkauskaite, A., & Bucy, E. P. (2016). A scholarly divide: Social media, big data, and unattainable scholarship. *First Monday, 21*(5). Retrieved from http://firstmonday.org/ojs/index.php/fm/article/view/6358

Zynga (2009). *FarmVille.* [Online video game]. San Francisco, CA: Zynga.

Chapter 10

An Analyst's Guide to Communication

Natalie Selin

Contents

10.1 Introduction

There are so many amazing things that can be achieved with data analytics as the other chapters in this book show. Being able to tap into the potential of the data is now seen as the key for the future growth of gaming companies, and many of the companies will have analysts and scientists as part of the core product development team. It means that analysts no longer work alone and just deliver reports and machine learning prototypes. Instead, analysts are closer than ever to the product and have huge opportunity to affect the direction of the product development. Analysts need to therefore interact with many different people who work on the product, from user interface designers and programmers to product owners and producers, all who have differing levels of understanding to what analysts do and can do at the company. English poet John Donne has said that "No man is an island, entire of itself; every man is a piece of the continent."—an adage that also holds true for modern-day data analysts. Analysts need to be able to communicate with all these different roles if they want to be able to make an impact on business and product development. If findings are never integrated into the product, the value of the research and the work of an analyst is limited.

This chapter will discuss how to communicate with different decision-makers in a company, specifically when it concerns solving the challenges that a game can have. It will outline common pitfalls that analysts tend to fall into when communicating with others than their peers and outline some best practices when it concerns integrating analysis within the company.

Throughout this chapter we will be looking at case examples of communication within a game company. Adam will be the data analyst and Petra the product owner in all these examples. While we focus on a product owner in the examples, the same type of reasoning can also be applied to other people in the company with whom an analyst may need to interact with.

For this chapter, we will look specifically at the process of communication when it concerns analysis in product development. Below are the key stages that will be discussed and delved deeper into:

1. Understand the problem.
2. Prioritize the work.
3. Define the goal.
4. Simplify the results.
5. Teach the learnings.

While the stages are presented linearly, in most cases one will have to jump back and forth through the stages depending on the project in question. Figure 10.1 depicts this process visually.

Communication is very important in the industry, and the subject is widely discussed both among analysts and with other teams. Several people, including

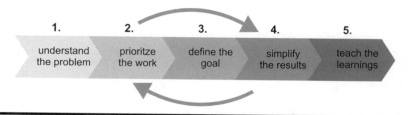

Figure 10.1   Key communication stages concerning analytics in game development. Stages need not necessarily be linear, and it may be required to jump back and forth between them.

data scientists and product managers, were interviewed for this chapter and many of the tips and techniques here are based on these interviews and their experience.

Contrary to other chapters in the book, the tone in this chapter is more casual and there is a reason for it. First of all, there is no presentation of rigorous research in this chapter. The processes and cases presented are based on the experiences of people in the industry and should not be seen as hard facts on how a data analyst has to work in the industry. Second, reading should be both fun and accessible and having a casual tone strengthens this. Finally, the goal of this chapter is to ease the journey for an analyst into the industry. The tone and writing style are tools this author has to help in that journey.

10.2 Stage 1—Understand the Problem

Albert Einstein famously proclaimed that: "Any fool can know. The point is to understand." To understand someone, however, requires more than just understanding their words. It requires putting oneself in their shoes and understand where they are coming from and where they want to go. Words by themselves can easily cause ambiguity as the joke below will hopefully highlight:

Baker to errand boy: Go to the store and buy one liter of milk. If there are fresh eggs buy six.

Errand boy returns with six liters of milk.

Baker: Why did you buy six liters of milk?
Errand boy: Because there were fresh eggs!

It is not always easy to describe matters and formulate requests unambiguously through words, especially when talking to someone not knowing the reasons behind it. People tend to interpret the situation based on their own biases, and analysts are no different. The key to circumventing this is to try to understand, and this means asking questions. This can be quite daunting, especially at work where asking a lot of questions can be seen as disrespectful or that people are not trusting each other. But there are some techniques that can make it easier and which are discussed in the following.

10.2.1 Create a Process

Asking analytical questions is difficult, but it can help to put them in a process. Paradox Interactive has done this, and it is used when defining key metrics for a product. The process helps everyone understand why the questions are important and makes it clear to everyone what to expect when defining an analysis question. This process can be seen in Figure 10.2.

The process involves everyone in the team and thus includes a lot of different perspectives, which, in turn, is a great way to align all team members when thinking about what is important to know about the product.

10.2.2 Play the Game

Becoming a player helps to see the game as a product and understand the basic game mechanics that exists, which results in an intuition of what issues the development team has. It also contributes to a common understanding of the product, which makes it easier to communicate to one another.

10.2.3 Rephrase the Problem

Rephrasing a problem clarifies what has been understood in the problem statement. It can highlight eventual misunderstandings and is a good way of validating if the problem has been understood correctly before working on the issue.

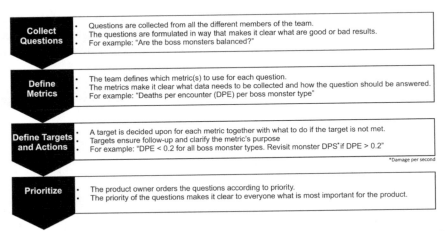

Figure 10.2 Potential process for working with analytical questions during development.

10.2.4 Describe the Next Step

By describing the next action from the analysis, it is easier to align everyone involved and to make it clearer to the involved parties where one is headed. Once the resulting action from the analysis is known, it is more likely that the underlying problem has been understood.

 CASE: UNDERSTAND THE PROBLEM

Petra has come to Adam because she wants to know how many of the new players play multiplayer. Because Adam has some experience as an analyst, instead of rushing off to answer the question, he takes a few moments to talk with Petra about why she is interested in this. Having played the game, he has his own idea to why she might want to know this.

"Interesting question! Are you wondering because you think new players are finding it hard to locate the multiplayer mode in the menu?" he asks.

"Oh, no, but that could be an interesting follow-up! Many on the development team think that playing multiplayer can be a scary thing for new players. We are looking to see if it is worth creating a special marketing event to invite new players to play multiplayer."

"Ok! So what you want to know is, do new players play multiplayer less than older players and if so, why this is the case. You want to know this so that you can decide if it's worth spending part of the marketing budget on a targeted multiplayer introduction event for new players. Have I understood you correctly?"

"Yes, if you can give me the answer to that, it would be great!"

Case Analysis

Adam and Petra have both played the game, which gives them a common understanding of the problems that could exist. Adam starts by rephrasing the problem to try to understand what she wants to know. After getting an explanation, Adam proceeds to describe what the resulting action from the analysis will be so that they are aligned on what needs to be done.

Notice that the question is no longer a simple X number of new players play multiplayer. Instead, there is both a quantitative and a qualitative part to the question, which will require more work. But as Adam now knows this,

(Continued)

CASE: UNDERSTAND THE PROBLEM (Continued)

he can better prepare the work and estimate the workload required. Petra will also get a proper answer to her question instead of only a number with which she can do very little with without context.

Case Solution

For this case, Adam has acted correctly.

■ Adam has played the game so he has a basic understanding of what questions Petra could have.
■ Adam communicates his understanding of the problem by rephrasing it to Petra. This gives Petra the opportunity to make any clarifications.
■ Adam proceeds to identify what the subsequent steps will be in order to align his and Petra's goal with the analysis.

Icon sources: Icon made from www.flaticon.com. Full icon credits listed at the end of the Reference section on p. 221.

10.3 Stage 2—Prioritize the Work

Once upon a time back in the 1990s, there used to be data scarcity. It was expensive to store data, and it was hard to collect it. Companies would have to make do with the data they had and made hard prioritizations about which data should be collected. We have come a long way from those days. Data storage has become much cheaper, and collecting it has become easier thanks to the Internet and software development. Today it is seldom a problem of if the data exists, but more about what to do with it. Time is the constraint in today's world of data, and it is no longer a question if we can get the answer but rather is the answer we are looking for worth the effort? In the spirit of knowledge, all questions are equal, but when it comes to business, some questions are more equal than others.

Prioritization is one of the hardest things in the game industry—which features should be cut, which market should be invested in, should a multiplayer feature be implemented first or a new map mode developed? These types of prioritizations consider two aspects: (1) what the business value is and (2) how complex is it to make.

10.3.1 Value versus Complexity Quadrant

The *value versus complexity quadrant* is one of many methodologies that helps with prioritization. The reason it is included in this chapter is because it is a great communication tool when one person has the knowledge of the business value and

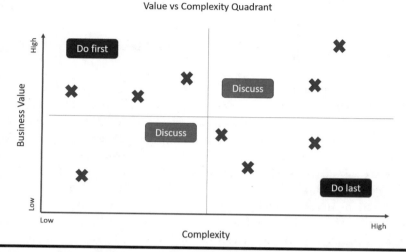

Figure 10.3 The value versus complexity quadrant. Questions are prioritized based on the dimensions of (business) value and (task) complexity.

the other has the knowledge of the complexity. By working together, everyone gets a better understanding of how to prioritize the questions.

The quadrant is straightforward to use. The first step is to give each question a business value score and a complexity score. All the questions can then be plotted out in a way similar to Figure 10.3. The plot can then be divided into four quadrants (cf. Figure 10.3) where high value/low complexity questions should be done first.

By discussing matters with each other, a good balance of important but hard questions (high value/high complexity) and "quick wins" (low value/low complexity) is more likely and easier to achieve.

 TIP: GOOD ENOUGH IS SOMETIMES BETTER THAN PERFECT

Delivering perfect results has usually a high complexity and will end up far to the right in the value versus complexity quadrant. But while it is important to be rigorous in the analysis, analysts need to keep in mind that the results are being used to deliver higher business value, not enter a scientific paper. Be open to discuss when it is OK to deliver good enough results instead of perfect ones, especially when it comes to answering high-value questions.

Icon sources: Icon made from www.flaticon.com. Full icon credits listed at the end of the Reference section on p. 221.

CASE: PRIORITIZE THE WORK

It is the beginning of the year, and Petra is full of ideas for her game. She has lots of questions for Adam and cannot wait to know all the numbers, high and low, about the players, the market, and the game features. Adam is excited too, but as he listens to Petra and starts thinking about all the work, he quickly realizes that there are just not enough hours in the day to answer all the questions. He asks Petra to list her most important questions so that he can focus on them first. At first, Petra seems happy about this, but she soon realizes that the questions that have highest priority are taking really long and she does not have time to wait around without any numbers whatsoever. She starts getting frustrated as her work is blocked by Adam taking such a long time on the analysis.

Case Analysis

Petra and Adam both know that there are more questions than time to answer them and agree that they need to prioritize. But to be able to prioritize, they need to communicate because they each have information that is important for the task. Petra knows the business value of the questions, and Adam knows the complexity involved in answering these questions, but they do not work together to prioritize.

Case Solution

Adam and Petra need to sit down together to discuss the prioritization. Before they have a meeting, Petra should score each question for business value on a relative scale. Adam should score each one based on complexity.

- If there are any high value/low complexity questions, Adam should start working on those.
- The high value/high complexity questions should be discussed and, if possible, broken down into smaller ones.
- Low value/low complexity questions can be done if they are blocking work elsewhere or can be outsourced.

By mapping out both the value and the complexity of the questions, it is easier to understand the work and to obtain insights into what needs to be done.

Icon sources: Icon made from www.flaticon.com. Full icon credits listed at the end of the Reference section on p. 221.

10.4 Stage 3—Define the Goal

Any self-respecting analyst has spent a few too many hours slicing and dicing the data before they start working on what they were supposed to do. There is a magic to just looking at the data in different ways, and it always generates more questions. This is why it is important to define the goal of the analysis before embarking on the journey of exploration. It guides the analyst in which questions to pursue and provides a clear target line for the work. As roman philosopher Seneca once eloquently noted: "When a man does not know what harbor he is making for, no wind is the right wind."

10.4.1 Definition of Done

In agile methodology[1] (Flewelling, 2018) there is a definition of done (DoD) when working on deliverables, and the same methodology can be used by analysts when working on questions. The idea is to clearly define what questions are to be answered so that the people involved do not get sidetracked by the many interesting questions that arise when looking at the data.

It can be hard to define DoD when:

- The analysis is about exploring a topic instead of answering a specific question.
- There is no clear action to be taken based on the results.

When this is the case it is recommended to set the DoD to a time interval. Timeboxing the work makes it clear to everyone involved how much time can be spent on investigating, and when the time has passed it forces an evaluation and prioritization of the questions that came up.

 CASE: DEFINE THE GOAL

Petra goes to Adam and says she wants a heatmap showing players' first city placements and size in the game. Adam asks why she needs this, and Petra responds that she wants to better understand the early game player behavior. Adam finds it challenging but fun and two days later delivers a heatmap to Petra. Petra loves it but asks for a change; she is only interested in players who have less than three hours in-game time. Adam does the change, which requires quite some data cleaning. However, already a day later he delivers a new heatmap. Petra loves the new heatmap and finds a part of it looks especially

(Continued)

---

[1] Agile methodology is a popular aproach to software development that focuses on quick, iterative deliveries.

CASE: DEFINE THE GOAL (Continued)

interesting because she sees it as an unusual behavior for beginners and asks Adam to analyze the specific discrepancy. Adam has now spent three days working on this heatmap and is realizing that he is not really sure where the analysis is headed or when it will be done. He is starting to worry that he is not working on the top-prioritized questions, even if this topic is an important one.

Case Analysis

While there is a reason to why Adam and Petra are looking at the heatmaps (understanding early game player behavior) the reason is not well-defined and does not have a clear focus. There is no way for Adam to know when the work will be done, and Petra has no clear action tied to the findings. There is a high risk that they will spend too much time on this question, and it will not lead to any clear business actions.

Case Solution

Before Adam starts working on the heatmap, he should clarify with Petra what the goal of his work is. Adam can ask some of the following questions to identify the goal and value:

- Is there a clear decision or action that you need to take based on the results?
- Can the question be reformulated so that it is clear what a good or bad result is?
- Is this more important than what he is already working on, and if so why?

If the answers to the above questions are no, Adam should proceed to discuss with Petra what a suitable time allocation would be for the question.

Icon sources: Icon made from www.flaticon.com. Full icon credits listed at the end of the Reference section on p. 221.

10.5 Stage 4—Simplify the Results

A lot of work is put into preparing an analyst report. A common process can include the following:

- Finding a data source and extracting the data
- Cleaning the data

- Designing a data model.
- Designing more models if the others did not capture the data well or if the data has been misunderstood.
- Analyzing anomalies in the data that turned out not to be real anomalies.
- Presentation of the result, including what has been learned from doing this analysis and explanation of the data, models, and the produced graphs.

It is essential that the above process is documented in detail because it contains many indispensable aspects that are important to understand, especially if decisions are made based on the information in the report. But time is of the essence and not everyone has the time to read the full report, and even the most complex analysis is of limited use if the results and findings cannot be communicated properly. When preparing a report, it is thus important to always keep Arthur Schopenhauer's advice in mind: "One should use common words to say uncommon things."

One of the major changes one goes through when leaving the educational institution is that one leaves a place where learning for learning's sake has a value by itself. The industry and workplace have other incentives and structures, which makes it harder to have an environment where learning by itself is promoted. This does not mean that learning is frowned upon in the industry; it just means that it comes at second priority to doing the work and delivering results.

When a product owner is reading a report, they are not interested in the methodology, the model, or learnings. What they want to know is the answer to their question, the recommended action, and a clear summary and presentation so that they feel they have a solid base to take a decision upon and do their work. Some people will want to know the background and the methodology, but that will be second priority.

Every person in a company has his or her own work that he or she is specialized in and hired to do. This leaves little time to learn new areas even if someone would want to. Respecting other people's time is what an analyst has to keep in mind when delivering a report; otherwise, the report will not have the impact on the product and the company that would be possible. Thus, when creating an analysis report or presentation, the recipient has to be always kept in mind. A good report:

- Provides a short summary of the results right at the beginning,
- Offers clear action points for the recipient,
- Includes supporting graphs and data in appendices so that they do not clutter the report, and
- Is written in as layman terms as possible—not everyone is familiar with statistical terms.

TIP: PEER REVIEW SHOULD NOT BE FORGOTTEN

Peer review is something that is easily overlooked when working with analytics in the industry. This is usually because a lot of decisions need to be made quickly. But if the right decisions should be made, then having the right results is essential. A peer review is very good at catching at least basic mistakes. It also helps with knowledge sharing within the analytics department as analysts review each other's work.

Icon sources: Icon made from www.flaticon.com. Full icon credits listed at the end of the Reference section on p. 221.

CASE: SIMPLIFY THE RESULTS

Petra has requested an audience segmentation analysis[2] for her product so she can use it as a basis for the feature priority list. Adam has developed a new model for the segmentation that takes the player behavior, product ownership, and survey data into account. Adam is really excited about the model and wants to explain how it works but realizes that Petra is very busy. After getting the model peer reviewed, he sends over a short summary of the segmentation analysis and a recommended priority for some of the key features. He includes a description of the new model as an attachment and why it is better than what they have used before.

Case Analysis

While Adam has spent a lot of time on his model, he focuses on delivering the result and not the journey to get there. This makes it easier for Petra to do her work, as she only needs to understand the result. As it is a new model, he clarifies this to Petra but makes sure it does not distract from the main result. This helps Petra understand what she is basing her decision on and reassures her in her decision. The model also gets peer reviewed by another analyst so there is a quality check of the work by someone who understands the statistics.

(Continued)

---

[2] Audience segmentation organizes people into homogeneous subgroups based upon pre-defined criteria.

CASE: SIMPLIFY THE RESULTS (Continued)

Case Solution

Adam is acting correctly. He is keeping the recipient in mind and delivers a report that helps Petra.

- He has created a clear summary of the results.
- He has clearly communicated his own recommendation of what Petra should do based on the results.
- He has made the model available for reference but as an attachment so that it does not clutter the result.

Icon sources: Icon made from www.flaticon.com. Full icon credits listed at the end of the Reference section on p. 221.

10.6 Stage 5—Teach the Learnings

Data analysis has a huge potential of changing the product development, the way people work, and decision-making in a company. But it will only make an impact if the recipients understand and act upon the results. Simplifying the results and keeping it specific is key when presenting it to the initial requester, but to truly make an impact it is important to get the knowledge across to others in the company. This is one of the hardest things to do. Not only do data analysts need to become teachers, but they have to become teachers to people who are not always ready to hear what data analysts have to say.

There are many books about how to teach, and it is highly recommended to read or study at least some pedagogy. The techniques listed below are of a more practical nature and are based on what has worked for people in the industry.

10.6.1 Get Them to Ask Questions

A good way to know if the report is being understood is if they start asking questions. This is because asking questions is an active learning technique and helps people remember the presentation and feel more secure in the new knowledge. It also highlights how much has actually been understood and what needs to be clarified in the presentation.

Asking questions is hard and requires an environment that encourages this. Let people know they can ask questions and when they can ask them at the very beginning of the presentation. Validate each question and answer it clearly and shortly.

10.6.2 *Make It Interactive*

A person is more likely to remember what has been presented if the recipients have been involved. If possible, get them to play around with the graphs and data. Have people move around and draw on the board. Anything that involves more than just one sense will help to get the message across and make it stick better. It also makes the presentation more fun than just listening to someone speak.

10.6.3 *Make It Personal*

When presenting, use examples that speak to the audience. If speaking to a product team, use their product in the presentation. If product owners should be convinced to use a new sale estimate, show the estimate on one of their products. By making it clear how the presentation affects them, it is easier to get the knowledge across.

10.6.4 *Repeat—In Different Ways*

One person may get excited by looking at the graph, another person likes to see the numbers, and yet another person wants it to be described in words. By presenting the main point in as many different ways as possible, a greater fraction of the audience can be reached.

 TIP: DO NOT UNDERESTIMATE PEOPLE

While it is important to simplify the results, this does not mean people are stupid. Belittling others understanding or contribution is a common pitfall for people in an "expert" position, which analysts usually are. Each and every person in a company is good at their specific skills, and by acknowledging and respecting their skills, much more can be achieved. A presentation where it is assumed that everyone has something to contribute is usually the best presentation because it involves other people's skills and, if used correctly, can highlight what the presenter is trying to teach.

Icon sources: Icon made from www.flaticon.com. Full icon credits listed at the end of the Reference section on p. 221.

CASE: TEACH THE LEARNINGS

Adam has spent the last week working on a more complicated analysis, requiring some Bayesian probability, and has developed an impressive prediction model for the sales estimates for the coming year that could help the product owners with their forecasts. He has produced a report with several plots showing confidence intervals and regression lines. There are many explanations of the techniques used to generate the reports and detailed descriptions of the underlying data. Adam holds a presentation to all the product owners, explaining that he uses only, what he considers, basic statistical regression models so it should be easy to follow for everyone. When he has finished his talk, he asks:

"Any questions?"

Adam looks out to the group, and it is clear that many people have not really understood the report. But nobody asks any questions, and everyone claps loud and hard and congratulates Adam on the presentation. It is, however, clear that none of the product owners will be using the new model.

Case Analysis

While Adam has done some good work, he has neither thought about the audience of his presentation nor has he gotten them excited about what he was trying to tell them. The product owners need to know how to use the model and why they should use it, not how the model works, the methodology, or the underlying data. He has not involved the product owners in the presentation. Moreover, he made it difficult for them to ask questions by saying that the statistics are basic and easy to follow.

Case Solution

Adam should have thought about what the goal of his presentation is and who the recipients are and how they are motivated. A clear goal could be to get everyone to use the new prediction model for the coming year. To achieve this goal Adam needs to:

■ Make it clear how the model can help the product owners, for example: "By using this model, you will have less deviations from the actual numbers, meaning you will need less time defending your forecast to your boss."

(Continued)

CASE: TEACH THE LEARNINGS (Continued)

- Get the product owners excited about the model, for instance: "This model will use the sale event calendar and Twitter feed to estimate the sales for product *X*."
- Make it clear how the product owners can start using the model, for example: "After this presentation, I will e-mail an Excel template with the new model so that you all can start using it."
- Get the product owners involved in the model, for instance: "Let's look at product *X*. What would you guess the forecast will be if we do not have a sale in June?"

Icon sources: Icon made from www.flaticon.com. Full icon credits listed at the end of the Reference section on p. 221.

10.7 Conclusions

This chapter has been about describing tools and best practices to use when communicating about analytics in the game industry. Specifically, five main stages of communication as summarized briefly below have been covered in this chapter:

1. Understand the problem.
2. Prioritize the work.
3. Define the goal.
4. Simplify the result.
5. Teach the learnings.

The focus of this chapter has been about how analysts can deliver high business value to the company by ensuring they are working on the right problems and by helping others understand how to act upon the conducted analysis.

Acknowledgments

The author would like to express special thanks to the people from Paradox Interactive who participated in the interviews on which this chapter is based: Mathias von Plato (data scientist), Stefan Eld (product manager), Magnus Eriksson (former data scientist), and John Hargelid (chief information officer).

Reference

Flewelling, P. (2018). *The Agile Developer's Handbook: Get More Value from Your Software Development: Get the Best Out of the Agile Methodology.* Birmingham, UK: Packt Publishing.

Icon Sources

lightbulb.png:

Icon made by Good Ware from www.flaticon.com is licensed by CC 3.0 BY
https://www.flaticon.com/free-icon/lightbulb_702814

search.png:

Icon made by Freepik from www.flaticon.com is licensed by CC 3.0 BY
https://www.flaticon.com/free-icon/search_259548

Chapter 11

A Taxonomy of Visualizations for Gameplay Data

Simone Kriglstein

Contents

11.1 Introduction

Data logging has become increasingly popular among game developers and designers to track player-generated data in order to improve the player experience. For example, such data can be used to understand how players move through a game world to identify hot spots, for instance of player deaths (cf. Drachen & Canossa, 2009), or to verify problem areas (cf. Zoeller, 2010). The choice of which kinds of interactions of the players within the game should be logged depends on the aspects on which the subsequent analysis should focus. This is by far not a trivial task. The analysis of data can range from the comparison of values (e.g., the number of collected items for each level) to more exploratory data analysis (e.g., how do players deal with challenges, how do players navigate in the game environment).

Due to the usually large amount of gathered data, analysis of it can be challenging. In this regard, visualizations are helpful or even necessary to capitalize on the collected data and to facilitate the understanding of complex multivariate relationships. In the last decade, many different types of visualizations have been used, adapted for, or specifically created for player behavior analysis (cf. Wallner & Kriglstein, 2013). Since there exist many possibilities to visualize gameplay data, it is often not easy to determine which visualizations are best suited for presenting certain data in the right way. For example, bar charts are better suited for comparisons (e.g., to compare the number of times players completed or failed a level) whereas line charts work better for identifying trends in the data (e.g., to discover patterns of what players are doing over time).

To this end, this chapter introduces a taxonomy of visualizations, which can be used for analyzing various aspects of gameplay data. It aims to show which types of visualizations are suitable for which types of tasks. While it does not claim exhaustiveness, it can be seen as a useful starting point for selecting and making visualizations based on the requirements of the analysis. The proposed taxonomy can support game developers and designers in choosing the right kind of visualizations for a given task. Moreover, as we have seen in Chapter 10, being able to effectively communicate the data and results to other stakeholders is of great importance. In this regard, visualization can be an effective asset for conveying information in an intuitive fashion.

In the following, first a short description of gameplay data is given to highlight the specific characteristics of such data. Afterward, the taxonomy of commonly used gameplay visualizations—or visualizations which can be useful for the analysis of in-game data—is presented. Each category of the taxonomy is described with a list of visualization methods. Furthermore, visualization examples are given in order to show how the methods are already used or can be used for gameplay data.

11.2 Gameplay Data

Although a precise definition is missing (cf. Southey, Holte, Xiao, Trommelen, & Buchanan, 2005), the term gameplay usually refers to players' interactions with the game (cf. Björk & Holopainen, 2004). The goal of the analysis of gameplay data is to understand players' behaviors within the game to get answers to questions such as what items they collected, in which sequence they used these items, where they wandered around, how they interacted with each other, or how they collaborated to overcome challenges together.

There exists two typical ways to collect gameplay data (cf. Bernhaupt, 2015; Drachen, Mirza-Babaei, & Nacke, 2018; Lankoski & Björk, 2015; Wallner & Kriglstein, 2013):

- By observing players while they interact with the game or by asking them (e.g., observation notes or thinking aloud protocols)
- Via instrumentation, that is, logging players' interactions automatically (e.g., triggered by events, such as collected items, or by regular predefined time intervals) within a game

Data collected by observing players or interviewing players has the advantage that it provides context to help understand players' motives for their behaviors and their subjective play experiences. Often, data that comes from interviews, observation notes, or open-ended responses are qualitative. Although qualitative data is not numerical in nature and it is necessary to find ways to quantify this data, it can be visualized in many ways. For example, Kucher and Kerren (2014; 2015) developed a text visualization browser to provide an extensive overview about different text visualization techniques categorized in analytic, visualization, and domain tasks. Shifting the focus to the analysis of gameplay, only a few visualization approaches with focus on qualitative data were published in the last years. One example is the visualization approach presented by Mirza-Babaei, Wallner, McAllister, and Nacke (2014). This approach combines data from players' physiological measures with questionnaire or interview results and in-game movement data. Moreno-Ger, Torrente, Hsieh, and Lester (2012) applied a thinking aloud technique in combination with screen capture software to record the screen and players' voice and face while interacting with a game. Among other things, they categorized the detected events along two dimensions—source of the event and reaction of the player—and visualized the number of identified events and the relative frequencies for each event type.

Automatically collecting instrumentation data is another possibility to obtain information about how players interact with a game. Such data are usually referred to as game metrics. A game metric is defined as "a quantitative measure of one or more attributes of one or more objects that operate in the context of games" (Drachen, El-Nasr, & Canossa, 2013a, p. 18). For example, this can range from the number of daily players to the score players receive when they complete a level. Game metrics can be broken down into subcategories—such as customer metrics, community metrics, gameplay metrics, performance metrics, and process metrics—of which gameplay metrics (cf. El-Nasr, Drachen, & Canossa, 2013) are of main interest in the context of this chapter. Gameplay metrics are measures of players' behaviors whenever they do something inside the game world (e.g., collecting an item, constructing a building, jumping, running, or shooting). For the analysis of gameplay metrics, different visualization techniques were used and developed in the last years (cf. Wallner & Kriglstein, 2015b; Wallner & Kriglstein, 2013). Particularly, different types of charts, heatmaps, movement visualizations, and node-link representations are frequently used.

11.3 Taxonomy

Typically, gameplay data can be categorized into spatial (e.g., position of the player) and non-spatial data (e.g., collected items or the interaction with other characters) (cf. Wallner & Kriglstein, 2013). A further important dimension is time, since analyzing in which order players perform their actions in the game can give interesting insights about their strategies. Over the years, different approaches have been developed for spatial, non-spatial, and temporal data in general and for specific domains. A good overview about visualization of temporal data is, for example, given by Aigner, Miksch, Schumann, and Tominski (2011) while Andrienko, Andrienko, and Gatalsky (2003) review techniques and tools for visualizing spatio-temporal data. Furthermore, different taxonomies and classifications of visualizations have been proposed. The goal of these taxonomies is to give an overview about the different methods in order to identify which are best suited for which type of data or task (e.g., Ahn, Plaisant, & Shneiderman, 2014; Amar, Eagan, & Stasko, 2005; Brehmer & Munzner, 2013; Chi, 2000; Keim, 2001; Kerracher, Kennedy, & Chalmers, 2015; Lee, Plaisant, Parr, Fekete, & Henry, 2006; Schulz, Nocke, Heitzler, & Schumann, 2013; Shneiderman, 1996; Tory & Möller, 2004; Wehrend & Lewis, 1990). These taxonomies and classifications range from low-level tasks (e.g., identifying anomalies within a dataset) to high-level tasks (e.g., using visualizations to communicate information or to verify hypotheses) (cf. Brehmer & Munzner, 2013). Many of these taxonomies are very general classifications and hence independent of a specific visualization application domain (e.g., Chi, 2000; Kerracher et al., 2015; Shneiderman, 1996; Wehrend & Lewis, 1990). However, in recent years, taxonomies (e.g., Ahn et al., 2014; Kerracher et al., 2015; Lee et al., 2006) that focus on a specific domain or type of data to deal with the associated needs and tasks have gained in popularity.

In the context of games, Bowman, Elmqvist, and Jankun-Kelly (2012), Medler and Magerko (2011), Wallner and Kriglstein (2015b; 2013), and Zammitto (2008) give an overview about different visualization approaches and techniques. However, to the best of the author's knowledge, a taxonomy of visualizations for gameplay data is still missing. Since games are very complex systems and the tracked gameplay data depends on the questions that game developers and designers want to answer, such a taxonomy is a useful starting point to help an analyst determine which methods might work best depending on the analysis tasks. According to Drachen et al. (2013a, p.23), the following types of questions that can be answered with gameplay data exist: What is happening? Where is it happening? At what time is it happening? And when multiple objects (e.g., players) interact: to whom is it happening? The present taxonomy is influenced by these four types of questions. For this purpose, visualization methods, which are already applied in game analytics or can be useful for answering these types of questions, were reviewed. A literature review was conducted by means of the search engines Google including Google Scholar and the publisher databases ACM Digital Library, SpringerLink, and IEEE Xplore. The visualization methods found in the literature were then classified into the following frequently occurring categories covering common tasks and types of data: *Comparison, Distribution, Relationships, Time, Space,* and *Flow*. However, it should be mentioned that although each category is useful for different kinds of analysis tasks, in many cases the analysis tasks are complex, and hence the analysis of data from different perspectives is necessary. Therefore, it is likely that different visualization methods from different categories are required to help with a certain analysis task.

Figure 11.1 gives an overview of the identified visualization methods with respect to the different categories. It has to be noted that the focus lies on the most commonly used visualization methods, so this should not be seen as an exhaustive list. Furthermore, several visualization methods can be useful for more than one type of task, and hence methods can be assigned to more than one category. In the following, the categories and visualization methods are described in detail.

Comparison

Distribution

Relationships

Time

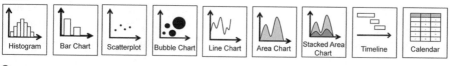

Space

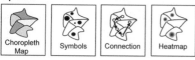

Flow

Figure 11.1 **Taxonomy of visualizations that are already applied or may be useful for the analysis of gameplay data.**

11.3.1 Comparison

Comparing data values or groups of data is one of the most relevant visualization tasks as pointed out by Tominski (2015). Comparisons are helpful to rank values and to see differences or similarities within the data, for example, to spot groups or outliners. Depending on what an analyst is looking for this can range from comparing a single variable to comparing multiple variables. Good candidates for comparing variables are the following visualization methods:

Bar Chart (or *Column Chart*): Bar charts use horizontal bars or vertical bars to facilitate the comparison of categories. On one axis, either the *x*-axis for horizontal bars or the *y*-axis for vertical bars, the categories are listed and on the other axis the corresponding values are shown. The length of the bars represents the values: the larger the value, the longer the bar. Bar charts are among the most popular chart types. They work well for comparing values and for assessing the values of different categories. For example, the visual game analytics tool *Data Cracker* (Medler, John & Lane, 2011) for the game *Dead Space 2* compares the number of rounds that human and necromorph[1] teams won with the help of bar charts. As part of the analysis of the game *Pixel Legions*—to name a further example—Gagné, El-Nasr, and Shaw (2012) used bar charts for comparing the number of sessions played depending on the levels of the game.

Stacked Bar Chart (or *Stacked Column Chart*): This type of chart is similar to the bar chart and is helpful for comparing categories that consist of subcategories. Each subcategory is represented with a bar, which is then stacked on top of each other (which distinguishes it from the bar chart). For example, Gagné et al. (2012) used stacked bar charts to compare how many players successfully completed or failed at each level of the aforementioned real-time strategy game *Pixel Legions*. The visualization system presented by Moura, El-Nasr, and Shaw (2011) compared how long players spent in a specific room of a game with how many times they visited the room via stacked bar charts. To facilitate the analysis of gameplay data from the game *Gears of War 2*, Schoenblum (2010) used as set of different visualization methods, for instance, stacked bar charts to compare the use of default weapons depending on the experience levels of the players.

Pie Chart: This chart type is also very frequently used, especially for presentation tasks. Pie charts are very helpful for showing proportions and percentage distributions amongst categories. A category or quantity is presented as a section (slice), with all sections forming a circle. However, pie charts only work well if the number of categories is small. If the number of categories grows, more slices are necessary, causing them to become smaller and smaller, which,

---

[1] The necromorphs are the main antagonists of the *Dead Space* series.

in turn, makes them more difficult to compare. In addition, accurate comparisons may be harder if the differences between the size of the areas are similar. In such cases, bar charts might be more appropriate (cf. Kriglstein 2015).

In the context of gameplay, Li et al. (2017a) developed a visual analytics system for exploring the evolution of egocentric player intimacy with a focus on massively multiplayer online role-playing games. Among other visualization methods, pie charts are used to compare the different types of interactions within the game. Drachen, Canossa, and Sørensen (2013c) utilized pie charts for different purposes. One pie chart shows the help requests for the different challenges and puzzles in *Tomb Raider: Underworld*, while another pie chart gives an overview about the percentage of the roles of players who kill another player or AI-bot in the game *Fragile Alliance 2*.

Donut Chart: In comparison to a pie chart, a donut chart has an empty area in the center of the circle. This area is often used for a label or further information about the data. For example, when comparing the usage of weapons of different player classes, a donut chart can show the percentage of used weapons for a player class, and the free area can give information about the corresponding player class.

Heatmap (*grid-based*): For comparing the values of two categories, heatmaps based on grids form are a very useful visualization method. Each row and column represents a variable of the corresponding category. The cells are color-coded according to their value. For example, Qu and Song (2017) compared races and classes in *World of Warcraft* with the help of a grid-based heatmap to find out which combinations of races and classes were preferred by the players. Sifa et al. (2018) introduced a multi-profile recommendation framework for massively multiplayer online games such as *Destiny*. In this context, they analyzed different archetypes of playstyles, and a heatmap was used for showing the archetypes corresponding to players with specific weapon preferences.

Parallel Coordinates: This is a further visualization method for comparing multiple variables. Each variable has its own axis with its own scale, and all axes are arranged parallel to each other. Each data element is a collection of points placed on each axis, which are then connected by a line from the left to the right. However, it is important to arrange the variables (i.e., the parallel axes) in a meaningful way, which makes sense to the viewers. For example, Soancatl et al. (2017) used parallel coordinates to compare measures of balance data recorded via force plates while players interacted with a custom-made ice-skating exergame.[2] The axes showed the measures of balance, and the lines corresponded to the different age groups.

---

[2] Exergames are games that promote some form of physical exercise.

Figure 11.2   Star plots showing game metrics of four different players.

Star Plot: This chart is similar to the parallel coordinates plot but instead of arranging the axes parallel to each other, all axes are arranged radially from the center at an equiangular distance. Each star represents one observation. However, showing too many observations in a single plot can make this type of chart hard to read and too cluttered. Therefore, often a separate star plot for each observation is used that are then displayed side by side. For example, Wallner and Kriglstein (2015a) represented game metrics of individual players of the game *Internet Hero* as star plots. In order to compare different players, small multiples were used to show the star plots for multiple players side by side. Figure 11.2 shows an example for four players. Each axis shows one measured variable of the tower defense mini-game part of *Internet Hero*.

11.3.2 Distribution

Inspecting data values to determine how often they occur or how spread out they are is a further important visualization task, as it facilitates the detection of outliners or patterns. These can be an interesting starting point for further analysis, for example, to find out why or in which context they appear. The following visualization methods are commonly used for showing the distribution of data:

Histogram: One easy and quick way to represent the distribution of a continuous numeric variable are histograms. Although the visual representation of a histogram is similar to a bar chart, they are essentially different. A bar chart displays categorical variables while a histogram represents a frequency distribution of one variable. The *x*-axis splits the values of the variable in question into a series of intervals (called bins), which are of usually equal size. The height of a bar represents how many values are within the respective interval. For example, Drachen, Gagné, and El-Nasr (2013b) used a histogram to show the distribution of the game completion times of players. Minar (2014) combined a histogram with a scatterplot (see Section 11.3.3) for analyzing *Battlefield 4* statistics, in particular the distribution of different variables such as kill/death ratio or rounds won. Figure 11.3 shows an example of a histogram that represents the distribution of casualties during a *StarCraft: Brood War* match based on 30-second intervals.

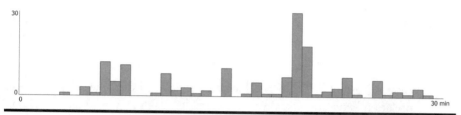

Figure 11.3 **Histogram showing the distribution of casualties during a *StarCraft: Brood War* match by using bins of 30-second intervals.**

Box Plot: Box plots can either be arranged vertically or horizontally and summarize the distribution of a data using several descriptive measures: minimum, maximum, lower and upper quartile, the median, as well as outliers. To represent the lower and upper quartile, a rectangle is used and a line inside the rectangle shows the median. Lines extending above and below the rectangle (called whiskers) show the minimum and maximum. Outliers are displayed by using individual points (or a similar symbol). This type of chart has the advantage of giving a good summary of data while at the same time requiring less space in case more groups or datasets have to be analyzed. In the context of games, Lewis and Wardrip-Fruin (2010), for example, used box plots to display the times players of different classes (e.g., Warrior, Priest, Mage) in *World of Warcraft* needed to level up from 10 to 80. Qu and Song (2017)—also focusing on *World of Warcraft*—analyzed, with the help of box plots, the time that the players spent in each character level.

Violin Plot: Similar to the box plot, this type of chart shows the median, the interquartile range as a rectangle centered around the median, and the 95% confidence interval as lines extended above and below the rectangle (although sometimes some of these statistics are omitted). The main difference to a box plot is that a violin plot also represents the shape of a probability distribution. This is useful for assessing how the values are distributed. For example, Soancatl, van de Gronde, Lamoth, Maurits, and Roerdink (2016) analyzed the balance control during gameplay of an exergame and used violin plots to depict the distribution of the center of pressure coordinates for each participant.

11.3.3 Relationships

Relationships are a further aspect of data that one may wish to explore through visualization. The purpose of analyzing relationships within a dataset can range from describing the degree of relationship between two variables to interpreting the structures and dependencies within a dataset. The following visualization techniques are well-known methods that are used to show relationships between entities or the correlations between two or more variables together with their properties:

Scatterplot: Scatterplots are a good starting point to assess the relationship or correlation between—usually two—variables. Each axis of a Cartesian coordinate system shows one variable. Dots represent the values of the two variables, with the position along the axes being determined by the values of the variables. With the help of scatterplots, different types of correlations can be visually identified. For example, a positive correlation is indicated if the data points are clustered along a trend line going from the lower-left to the upper-right. Contrarily, if the collection of dots produces an upper-left to lower-right pattern, then this indicates a negative correlation. Colors or different symbols for the points can be used to show different categories. In Chapter 3, we have seen a scatterplot being used for comparing actual and predicted win rates for the purpose of tweaking matchmaking systems. Other examples include the work of Minar (2014) who analyzed *Battlefield 4* statistics by using a scatterplot to see the relationship and correlation between two variables, including win/loss ratio, skill, rounds lost, rounds played, or time played. Soancatl et al. (2017) analyzed various measures of balance recorded during playing an exergame in consideration of two age groups via a scatterplot matrix to investigate the pairwise correlation between them. Drescher et al. (2018) proposed an interactive web-based tool providing different visualization methods for the analysis of *Twitter* activities of players. In order to analyze the relation between the players' in-game behaviors and their number of tweets, the tool offers a scatterplot that compares *Twitter* activity with different in-game data.

Bubble Chart: This type of chart is similar to a scatterplot and can also be helpful for displaying multiple variables at once. The difference to a scatterplot is that the size of the points—called bubbles—is used to represent the value of a further variable. For, example, Smith, Hickmott, Southgate, Bille, and Stephens (2016) visualized the time players spent in levels or trainings for the serious game *Apostrophe Power* using a bubble chart. Accordingly, the time spent was mapped to the size of the bubbles.

Node-Link Diagram: In order to show the relationships between entities in a dataset, node-link diagrams are one of the most popular visualization methods. Objects are represented as nodes, and links, which are drawn as lines, connect the nodes to indicate the relationships between them. Generally, two types of connections are distinguished: directed and undirected connections. Undirected node-link diagrams show only the connection between nodes, whereas directed node-link diagrams also consider the direction of the relationships with the direction commonly visualized as an arrow. Further variables can be considered by using, for example, colors for nodes and links or changing node size or thickness of the lines proportional to particular values.

For example, Qu and Song (2017) represented each zone in *World of Warcraft* as a node and directed edges between the nodes to show if the players moved from one zone to another zone. The size of a node represents the number of players in the zone, and the thickness of the edges shows how many players moved between the corresponding zones. A further example is *PLATO* (Play-Graph Analysis Tool) (cf. Wallner & Kriglstein, 2012, 2014), which uses a node-link approach to show an aggregated overview of player behavior. Nodes represent different in-game states, and the size of the nodes is proportional to the number of players reaching that state at some point. Edges describe the actions that are performed by the players and indicate state transitions. In order to reduce visual clutter, edges between the same states are merged into a single meta-edge. The thickness of this meta-edge is proportional to the number of bundled edges. *Playtracer*—introduced by Andersen, Liu, Apter, Boucher-Genesse, and Popović (2010)—is a further example that shows player paths through a game using a node-link representation. Similar to *PLATO*, nodes depict game states with the size of the node being proportional to how many players arrived at that state. Edges show how the players moved between the states.

A major drawback of node-link diagrams is that with increasing size and complexity they start to become harder to read due to becoming increasingly cluttered. In such cases, matrix representations may be a useful alternative. Another option is to use edge-bundling techniques that visually bundle adjacent edges together (Holten, 2006; Holten & Van Wijk, 2009).

Chord Diagram: A further visualization method to convey relationships between entities in a dataset is the chord diagram. The data is arranged radially around a circle, and the relationships between data items are visualized as arcs. The thickness of arcs can be used to represent, for example, the strength of the relationship. Colors can be used to depict a certain property of the data items. Chord diagrams are helpful in conveying similarities within a dataset and between groups of data. Figure 11.4 shows an example of a chord diagram, which visualizes the structure of a clan of players from a fictive game. Each sector represents a player, and the lines show who played with whom. The colors indicate the different roles the players have in the clan (e.g., green for veterans or orange for a leader who can invite and accept players to the clan).

However, similar to node-link diagrams, the inner part of a chord diagram can easily become cluttered with an increasing number of displayed connections. As with node-link diagrams, edge bundling can also be beneficial for increasing visual clarity.

Arc Diagram: In contrast to node-link diagrams or chord diagrams, the characteristic of this visualization method is that all nodes are placed along a single line. Additionally, the nodes are connected with arcs to show

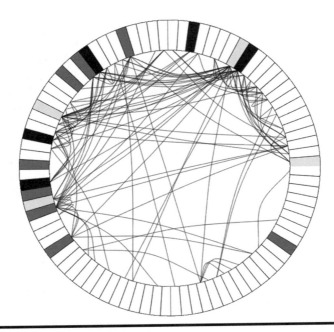

Figure 11.4 (See color insert.)   A chord diagram showing the internal structure of a clan. Sectors represent the individual members, and arcs show which players have played together. (Courtesy of Günter Wallner.)

the relationship between them. Possible multiple connections between the same two nodes can be summarized by a single arc with the thickness of this arc reflecting the number of aggregated arcs. Although the overall structure of the connections between the nodes is usually better visible with a two-dimensional layout, this visualization method allows the analyst to easily find groups, given that the ordering of the nodes is appropriate. A proper ordering is also important for minimizing the number of edge crossings. For example, players may be visualized as nodes located along the horizontal axis, and the arcs could show who selected whom to build a team. Similar to node-link diagrams and chord diagrams, the arc diagram can become hard to read if too many arcs have to be visualized.

Matrix: Matrix representations are often used as an alternative to node-link diagrams because they are always free of occlusions and overlappings. The rows and columns of the matrix show the data elements. If two elements have a connection, the corresponding cell is marked or shows an associated value of the connection. Furthermore, colors can be used to encode the values in the cells. In that case, the matrix resembles a grid-based heatmap. For example, the visual game analytics tool *PLATO* (cf. Wallner & Kriglstein, 2014) offers several visualizations to support the analysis of gameplay data from different perspectives. In addition to the node-link approach mentioned before, a matrix representation is provided where the rows and columns of the matrix show the game states, and the transitions between them are indicated by colored cells.

However, the order of the rows and columns plays a very important role to be able to identify meaningful patterns or clusters. Matrix reordering algorithms can be beneficial in such cases (see, e.g., Behrisch, Bach, Henry Riche, Schreck, & Fekete [2016] for an overview).

11.3.4 Time

Time is one of the most important data dimensions. Especially for recorded data, time-relevant information plays an important role and helps to identify trends, temporal patterns (e.g., seasonal cycles), and changes over time. Temporal data can be either continuous or discrete. Depending on if the data is continuous or discrete, the following visualization methods are viable options:

Histogram/Bar Chart: For visualizing discrete temporal data, histograms and bar charts can be useful. These types of charts can be used for various data types. Bar charts, as pointed out earlier, are useful for comparison tasks (see Section 11.3.1) whereas histograms are often used for analyzing distribution patterns (see Section 11.3.2). For temporal data, the *x*-axis usually represents the time (e.g., days, months, years). In order to analyze the time players spent in the game *World of Warcraft*, Tarng, Chen, and Huang (2008) used bar charts, for instance, to show the average daily playtime for the different days of a week and the average number of gamers logged into the game over a 24-hour period.

Scatterplot/Bubble Chart: Another way for visualizing discrete temporal data are the afore discussed scatterplots and bubble charts (cf. Section 11.3.3). Both cannot only be used for non-temporal data but also for visualizing the relationships and correlations between temporal variables. Similar to the bar chart, usually the *x*-axis represents the time. For example, Tarng, Chen, and Huang (2008) used scatterplots to display relationships between different time-related factors (e.g., daily playtime versus season length) in *World of Warcraft*.

Line Chart: For visualizing continuous time series in order to show trends and to see how the data has changed over time, line charts are one of the most used visualization methods. Usually, the *x*-axis is the time scale or divided into time intervals, and the *y*-axis represents the values. The individual data points are connected with a line. The inclination of the line shows if the values increase (upward line) or decrease (downward line), which can be helpful for identifying changes over time. For example, *Data Cracker* (Medler et al., 2011) uses line charts to show the number of total rounds played in the game *Dead Space 2* over a given time period. For the analysis of gameplay

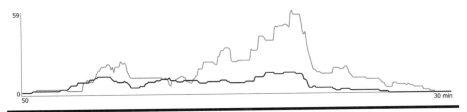

Figure 11.5 A line chart showing how the army strength of two teams changed over time during a *StarCraft: Brood War* match.

data of *Gears of War 2*, Schoenblum (2010) also used line charts, for instance, to visualize weapon kill and game-type trends. To give another example, Qu and Song (2017) investigated player retention over time by analyzing how many months the players played *World of Warcraft* after their first login with the help of a line chart. Figure 11.5 shows an example of a line chart using data from the real-time strategy game *StarCraft: Brood War*. The two lines represent the two opposing teams and how their army strength (depicted in units) changed over the course of the match.

Area Chart: This type of chart works in the same way as the line chart with the advantage that this chart type can also visually represent volume since the area below the line is filled with a color or texture. For example, the formerly mentioned visual game analytics tool *Data Cracker* (cf. Medler et al., 2011) for *Dead Space 2* depicts the number of matches played for each map as a function of time using area charts. However, if many data series need to be visualized, a line chart is usually more suitable.

Stacked Area Chart: For visualizing multiple data series, areas can also be stacked upon each other, resulting in a stacked area chart. Although trends are generally harder to see, stacked area charts show the total of all the data series and how much each part contributes to the whole amount (cf. Yau, 2011). A special type of the stacked area chart is the stream graph. In contrast to a stacked area chart, the values are displaced around a central baseline. For example, Li et al. (2017a)—concerned with massively multiplayer online role-playing games—used a stream graph in their visual analytics system to visualize the overall change ratio of an ego-network over a certain time period.

Timeline: If it is not only from interest when an event has happened but also for how long, a timeline can be helpful for (1) analyzing patterns appearing over time periods and (2) for quickly understanding temporal relationships. For this purpose, start time and durations of events are presented in a chronological order using a, usually, linear timescale. Simultaneous events are stacked on top of one other. Often a line or a bar is used to depict an event's starting point and duration. For example, Mirza-Babaei et al. (2012) presented a player evaluation approach called *Biometric Storyboards*, which uses a timeline to analyze the relationships between a player's physiological changes and game events. Milam and El-Nasr (2010), on the other hand, used a timeline to show players' playstyles and to identify level design problems for the games *BioShock* and *Lost*. Li et al. (2017a) visualized, among others, logon/logout activities with the help of timelines to enable the analysis of temporal dynamics of players' activities.

Calendar: Calendars are yet another way to visualize temporal patterns. Calendar charts are a good way to show how quantity varies depending on specific days (e.g., difference between weekend or work day) or weeks (e.g., weeks before or after Christmas). The typical units of a calendar (days, weeks, months, and years) facilitate the analysis of chronological sequences of events. For assigning values, visual properties, such as size, color, or brightness, can be used to support viewers to see trends at a glance. For example, *Scelight* (cf. Belicza, 2014a)—a visual analytics tool for replay analysis of *StarCraft II* matches—offers different visualization methods, including a calendar visualization to give an overview about how often the game is played and the total duration of play for each day.

11.3.5 Space

Space is a further important data dimension since recorded data cannot only contain information about when it was recorded but also where. Spatial data describes all types of data objects or elements with a specific location in the physical (or virtual) world. In the context of gameplay data, the analysis of spatial data helps to understand how players behave and navigate in the game world. It can provide valuable insights for optimizing the spatial layout in order to improve the player experience (cf. Drachen & Schubert, 2013d) or level design. Showing the collected data in relation to the game environment also offers additional context for interpreting the data. The following visualization methods are good options for analyzing geographical patterns in the data:

Choropleth Map: One of the most common ways to overlay data on a map is the choropleth map. Regions are colored, shaded, or patterned depending on the assigned values in order to show patterns across areas and locations. For instance, Figure 11.6 shows a choropleth map for a *StarCraft: Brood War* match depicting the amount of destroyed units within different areas of the game map using a color gradient from yellow (low number of kills) to red (large number of kills).

However, care has to be taken when reading these maps, since, for example, the size of the regions can lead to misinterpretations (e.g., larger regions may appear more important than smaller regions).

Map with Symbols: For analyzing spatial patterns or observing the distribution of data, symbols (e.g., dots) can be superimposed over geographic regions. A symbol can represent a single value or a specific entity. The size of the

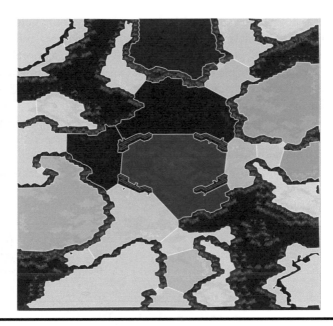

Figure 11.6 (See color insert.) A choropleth map showing the number of destroyed units in different regions during a *StarCraft: Brood War* match using a yellow (low number of kills) to red (large number of kills) gradient.

symbol can be proportional to its value in the dataset. On the downside, small differences or the exact values might be difficult to infer and to compare. Furthermore, if the size of the symbols is getting too large, it can happen that the symbols overlap each other or occlude important parts of the map. In case more than one category needs to be displayed, different chart types (e.g., pie charts or bar charts) are often placed on the map instead of symbols. Drachen et al. (2013c) used such a visualization for the analysis of gameplay data from the game *Kane & Lynch: Dog Days*. The locations of the players were visualized as dots and various events as different symbols (e.g., weapon pickups as red triangles) on the map. *Sc2gears* (Belicza, 2014b) is a visual analytics tool for the analysis of individual replays and mass replays of *StarCraft II*. The tool offers different visualization methods, including a visualization that shows the units of players as dots on the map in order to convey their distribution. On the other hand, the interactive visualization system presented by Moura, El-Nasr, and Shaw (2011) offers the possibility to analyze the total amount of time the players spent in different areas by using circles. The size of a circle reflects how long the players stayed in a particular area (the larger the circle, the longer the players stay). Kriglstein, Wallner, and Pohl (2014) conducted a user study comparing heatmaps and two graphical representations that make use of clustering algorithms to group spatial gameplay data (e.g., death locations). One graphical representation displays clusters as circles on the game map. The size of the circles is proportional to the number of objects within the cluster. The second graphical representation encloses the area of the cluster using a polygon. By using color coding for the circle or polygon, additional data can be displayed (e.g., weapons that were used in a particular area).

Connection Map: If the order of the points placed on a map bears important information (e.g., which locations were visited in which order), it is useful to connect these points using straight or curved lines. For example, Li et al. (2017b) developed a visual analytics system for the analysis of multiplayer online battle arena games. Among other visualization methods, connection maps are used to see how a player moved around in a game environment. The visual analytics system *PLATO* (cf. Wallner & Kriglstein, 2014; Wallner et al., 2014) uses connection maps, which show the individual paths of the players within a game world by using connected line segments.

Heatmap: Heatmaps are an effective method to depict the frequency of occurrence of a variable, for example, to identify patterns or hot spots. A color gradient with two or more colors is used to represent the different values on the map. For example, darker colors are often used to indicate low activity and brighter colors to indicate high activity on a map. Heatmaps are well-established in the game industry for analyzing the frequency of occurrence of an event (e.g., position of player deaths or where weapons are fired) in relation to the game environment (see, e.g., Ashton & Verbrugge, 2011; Drachen et al. 2013c; Drachen & Schubert, 2013d; Drachen & Canossa, 2009; Kriglstein et al., 2014; Li et al. 2017b; Wallner & Kriglstein, 2014; Schoenblum, 2010; Zoeller, 2010).

11.3.6 Flow

Analyzing movements or sequences between two or more locations, states, or conditions is useful for understanding what is going on (e.g., for identifying when and where a problem occurred) and for understanding relationships between different steps of a process. The following two visualization methods are good candidates for showing the flow of quantities or of aggregated movement data:

Flow map: Flow maps are typically used for displaying movements of objects or information from one location to another (e.g., movement of goods, traffic volume, stream flow, or the number of people in a migration and its geographic distribution). The movements of the people and goods between various locations are usually depicted as lines, and arrows show the direction of movement. The thickness of the lines represents the quantity of flow.

Flow maps can be considered to be a type of connection map that shows the individual trajectories as aggregated data.

For example, Wallner and Kriglstein (2016) evaluated three different types of visualizations intended for retrospective analysis of battles fought in the massively multiplayer online game *World of Tanks*. One approach—so-called battle maps (cf. Wallner, 2017)—are a kind of flow map that shows troop movements, major sites of combat, and long-distance attacks between these combat sites. Figure 11.7 shows an example of such a battle map. Each team has an individual color and arrows show the troop movements (colored textured arrows) and long-range attacks (colored semitransparent arrows) between combat sites (white areas on the map). The width of the arrows reflects the number of involved units in case of troop movements and the amount of shots fired for long-range attacks. Icons show the bases of the teams and spawn points.

Sankey Diagram: This diagram is a specific type of a flow diagram and can be used, for example, for visualizing multidimensional categorical data. It shows different quantities in proportion to each other. Nodes are depicted using boxes and the links between them, represented as lines or arrows, visualize the flow. The width of the line or arrow is proportional to the quantity of the flow: the thicker the line or arrow between two nodes, the larger the quantity of flow. This visualization method helps to identify changes in

Figure 11.7 (See color insert.)   Example of a battle map showing troop movements, combat regions, and long-distance attacks. (Courtesy of Günter Wallner.)

the flows from one node to another. To distinguish between different categories, different colors can be used. For example, Drachen, Riley, Baskin, and Klabjan (2014) showed how Sankey diagrams can be used to observe variations in player behavior over time, for example, to identify differences between player types.

11.4 Conclusions

The analysis of player behavior can be a challenging endeavor due to the usually large amounts of gameplay data that can be logged while players interact with a game. Visualizations are necessary to extract insights from and to effectively communicate the data and, in turn, to derive actionable insights from it. Over the years, a large amount of different visualization approaches was developed for various domains and applications. Choosing a suitable visualization for a given analysis task from the many available methods is often not an easy and straightforward task.

In this chapter, a taxonomy of visualizations was presented, which can be used for analyzing various aspects of gameplay data. This taxonomy gives an overview about many visualization methods commonly used for the analysis of gameplay data. However, due to the many different variations and combinations of visualization methods, this overview should not be seen as exhaustive. Rather it should be seen as a useful starting point for selecting and creating visualizations. The visualization methods were categorized into the groups: *comparison*, *distribution*, *relationships*, *time*, *space*, and *flow*. It should be mentioned that in many cases it is necessary, or at least helpful, to analyze the data from different perspectives; hence, a combination of various visualization methods from different categories is recommendable. A further limitation of the taxonomy is that it is not possible to clearly assign one visualization method to only one category since several visualization methods can be useful for more than one type of task. Having said that, the review and discussion of visualization methods together with examples from games analytics can help to form a starting point and can give an overview of which visualization might work best for which kinds of tasks.

References

Ahn, J. W., Plaisant, C., & Shneiderman, B. (2014). A task taxonomy for network evolution analysis. *IEEE Transactions on Visualization and Computer Graphics, 20*(3), 365–376.

Aigner, W., Miksch, S., Schumann, H., & Tominski, C. (2011). *Visualization of time-oriented data*. Heidelberg, Germany: Springer.

Amar, R., Eagan, J., & Stasko, J. (2005). Low-level components of analytic activity in information visualization. In *Proceedings of the IEEE Symposium on Information Visualization* (pp. 111–117). IEEE.

Andersen, E., Liu, Y. E., Apter, E., Boucher-Genesse, F., & Popović, Z. (2010). Gameplay analysis through state projection. In *Proceedings of the 5th International Conference on the Foundations of Digital Games* (pp. 1–8). ACM Press.

Andrienko, N., Andrienko, G., & Gatalsky, P. (2003). Exploratory spatio-temporal visualization: an analytical review. *Journal of Visual Languages & Computing, 14*(6), 503–541.

Ashton, M., & Verbrugge, C. (2011). Measuring cooperative gameplay pacing in World of Warcraft. In *Proceedings of the 6th International Conference on Foundations of Digital Games* (pp. 77–83). ACM Press.

Behrisch, M., Bach, B., Henry Riche, N., Schreck, T., & Fekete, J. D. (2016). Matrix reordering methods for table and network visualization. In *Computer Graphics Forum, 35*(3), 693–716.

Belicza, A. (2014a). *Scelight.* Retrieved from https://sites.google.com/site/scelight/.

Belicza, A. (2014b). *Sc2gears.* Retrieved from https://sites.google.com/site/sc2gears/.

Bernhaupt, R. (Ed.). (2015). *Game user experience evaluation.* Cham, Switzerland: Springer.

Björk, S., & Holopainen, J. (2004). *Patterns in game design (Game development series).* Boston, MA: Charles River Media Group.

Bowman, B., Elmqvist, N., & Jankun-Kelly, T. J. (2012). Toward visualization for games: Theory, design space, and patterns. *IEEE Transactions on Visualization and Computer Graphics, 18*(11), 1956–1968.

Brehmer, M., & Munzner, T. (2013). A multi-level typology of abstract visualization tasks. *IEEE Transactions on Visualization and Computer Graphics, 19*(12), 2376–2385.

Chi, E. H. (2000). A taxonomy of visualization techniques using the data state reference model. In *Proceedings of the IEEE Symposium on Information Visualization* (pp. 69–75). IEEE.

Drachen, A., & Canossa, A. (2009). Analyzing spatial user behavior in computer games using geographic information systems. In *Proceedings of the 13th International MindTrek Conference: Everyday Life in the Ubiquitous Era* (pp. 182–189). ACM.

Drachen, A., Canossa, A., & Sørensen, J. R. M. (2013c). Gameplay metrics in game user research: Examples from the trenches. In M. S. El-Nasr, A. Drachen, & A. Canossa (Eds.), *Game analytics: Maximizing the value of player data* (pp. 285–319). London, UK: Springer.

Drachen, A., El-Nasr, M. S., & Canossa, A. (2013a). Game analytics—The basics. In M. S. El-Nasr, A. Drachen, & A. Canossa (Eds.), *Game analytics: Maximizing the value of player data* (pp. 13–40). London, UK: Springer.

Drachen, A., Gagné, A., & El-Nasr, M. S. (2013b). Sampling for game user research. In M. S. El-Nasr, A. Drachen, & A. Canossa (Eds.), *Game analytics: Maximizing the value of player data* (pp. 143–167). London, UK: Springer.

Drachen, A., Mirza-Babaei, P., & Nacke, L. (Eds.). (2018). *Games user research.* Oxford, UK: Oxford University Press.

Drachen, A., Riley, J., Baskin, S., & Klabjan, D. (2014). Going out of business: Auction house behavior in the massively multi-player online game Glitch. *Entertainment Computing, 5*(4), 219–232.

Drachen, A., & Schubert, M. (2013d). Spatial game analytics. In M. S. El-Nasr, A. Drachen, & A. Canossa (Eds.), *Game analytics: Maximizing the value of player data* (pp. 365–402). London, UK: Springer.

Drescher, C., Wallner, G., Kriglstein, S., Sifa, S., Drachen, S., & Pohl, M. (2018). What moves players? Visual data exploration of Twitter and gameplay data. In *Proceedings of the SIGCHI Conference on Human Factors in Computing Systems*. ACM Press.

El-Nasr, M. S., Drachen, A., & Canossa, A. (Eds.). (2013). *Game analytics: Maximizing the value of player data*. New York: Springer.

Gagné, A. R., El-Nasr, M. S., & Shaw, C. D. (2012). Analysis of telemetry data from a real-time strategy game: A case study. *Computers in Entertainment (CIE), 10*(1), 2.

Holten, D. (2006). Hierarchical edge bundles: Visualization of adjacency relations in hierarchical data. *IEEE Transactions on Visualization and Computer Graphics, 12*(5), 741–748.

Holten, D., & Van Wijk, J. J. (2009). Force-directed edge bundling for graph visualization. *Computer Graphics Forum, 28*(3), 983–990.

Keim, D. A. (2001). Visual exploration of large data sets. *Communications of the ACM, 44*(8), 38–44.

Kerracher, N., Kennedy, J., & Chalmers, K. (2015). A task taxonomy for temporal graph visualisation. *IEEE Transactions on Visualization and Computer Graphics, 21*(10), 1160–1172.

Kriglstein, S. (2015). A bird's eye view: Comparison of visualization types for high level analysis of changes. In *Proceedings of the EdMedia: World Conference on Educational Media and Technology* (pp. 69–78). Association for the Advancement of Computing in Education (AACE).

Kriglstein, S., Wallner, G., & Pohl, M. (2014). A user study of different gameplay visualizations. In *Proceedings of the SIGCHI Conference on Human Factors in Computing Systems* (pp. 361–370). ACM.

Kucher, K., & Kerren, A. (2014). Text visualization browser. Retrieved from http://textvis. lnu.se/.

Kucher, K., & Kerren, A. (2015). Text visualization techniques: Taxonomy, visual survey, and community insights. In *Proceedings of the IEEE Pacific Visualization Symposium* (pp. 117–121). IEEE.

Lankoski, P., & Björk, S. (Eds.). (2015). *Game research methods: An overview*. Pittsburgh, PA: ETC Press.

Lee, B., Plaisant, C., Parr, C. S., Fekete, J. D., & Henry, N. (2006). Task taxonomy for graph visualization. In *Proceedings of the AVI Workshop on Beyond Time and Errors: Novel Evaluation Methods for Information Visualization* (pp. 1–5). ACM Press.

Lewis, C., & Wardrip-Fruin, N. (2010). Mining game statistics from web services: A World of Warcraft armory case study. In *Proceedings of the 5th International Conference on the Foundations of Digital Games* (pp. 100–107). ACM.

Li, Q., Shen, Q., Ming, Y., Xu, P., Wang, Y., Ma, X., & Qu, H. (2017a). A visual analytics approach for understanding egocentric intimacy network evolution and impact propagation in MMORPGs. In *Proceedings of the IEEE Pacific Visualization Symposium* (pp. 31–40). IEEE.

Li, Q., Xu, P., Chan, Y. Y., Wang, Y., Wang, Z., Qu, H., & Ma, X. (2017b). A visual analytics approach for understanding reasons behind snowballing and comeback in MOBA games. *IEEE Transactions on Visualization and Computer Graphics, 23*(1), 211–220.

Medler, B., John, M., & Lane, J. (2011). Data Cracker: Developing a visual game analytic tool for analyzing online gameplay. In *Proceedings of the SIGCHI Conference on Human Factors in Computing Systems* (pp. 2365–2374). ACM Press.

Medler, B., & Magerko, B. (2011). Analytics of play: Using information visualization and gameplay practices for visualizing video game data. *Parsons Journal for Information Mapping*, *3*(1), 1–12.

Milam, D., & El-Nasr, M. S. (2010). Design patterns to guide player movement in 3D games. In *Proceedings of the 5th ACM SIGGRAPH Symposium on Video Games* (pp. 37–42). ACM.

Minar, N. (2014). *Battlefield 4 player plots*. Retrieved from http://www.somebits.com/bf4plots/.

Mirza-Babaei, P., Nacke, L., Fitzpatrick, G., White, G., McAllister, G., & Collins, N. (2012). Biometric storyboards: Visualising game user research data. In *CHI'12 Extended Abstracts on Human Factors in Computing Systems* (pp. 2315–2320). ACM.

Mirza-Babaei, P., Wallner, G., McAllister, G., & Nacke, L. E. (2014). Unified visualization of quantitative and qualitative playtesting data. In *CHI'14 Extended Abstracts on Human Factors in Computing Systems* (pp. 1363–1368). ACM Press.

Moreno-Ger, P., Torrente, J., Hsieh, Y. G., & Lester, W. T. (2012). Usability testing for serious games: Making informed design decisions with user data. *Advances in Human-Computer Interaction*, *2012*, 4.

Moura, D., El-Nasr, M. S., & Shaw, C. D. (2011). Visualizing and understanding players' behavior in video games: Discovering patterns and supporting aggregation and comparison. In *Proceedings of the ACM SIGGRAPH Symposium on Video Games* (pp. 11–15). ACM Press.

Qu, J., & Song, Y (2017). Visual analysis of players' activities in World of Warcraft game. In *Proceedings of the International Conference on Advances in Big Data Analytics* (pp. 3–8). CSREA Press.

Schoenblum, D. (2010). Zero to millions: Building an XLSP for Gears of War 2. Presentation at the 2010 *Game Developer Conference*. Retrieved from https://www.gdcvault.com/play/1012329/Zero-to-Millions-Building-an.

Schulz, H. J., Nocke, T., Heitzler, M., & Schumann, H. (2013). A design space of visualization tasks. *IEEE Transactions on Visualization and Computer Graphics*, *19*(12), 2366–2375.

Shneiderman, B. (1996). The eyes have it: A task by data type taxonomy for information visualizations. In *Proceedings of the IEEE Symposium on Visual Languages (VL)*. IEEE.

Sifa, R., Pawlakos, E., Zhai, K., Haran, S., Jha, R., Klabjan, D., & Drachen, A. (2018). Controlling the crucible: A novel PvP recommender systems framework for Destiny. In *Proceedings of the Australasian Computer Science Week (ASCW)*.

Smith, S. P., Hickmott, D., Southgate, E., Bille, R., & Stephens, L. (2016). Exploring play-learners' analytics in a serious game for literacy improvement. In *Joint International Conference on Serious Games* (pp. 13–24). Cham, Switzerland: Springer.

Soancatl, V., van de Gronde, J. J., Lamoth, C. J. C., Maurits, N. M., & Roerdink, J. B. (2016,). Visual data exploration for balance quantification during exergaming. In *Proceedings of the Eurographics/IEEE VGTC Conference on Visualization: Posters* (pp. 25–27). Eurographics Association.

Soancatl, V., van de Gronde, J. J., Lamoth, C. J., van Diest, M., Maurits, N. M., & Roerdink, J. B. (2017). Visual data exploration for balance quantification in real-time during exergaming. *PLoS One*, *12*(1), e0170906.

Southey, F., Holte, R. C., Xiao, G., Trommelen, M., & Buchanan, J. (2005). *Machine learning for semi-automated gameplay analysis*. Presentation at the 2005 Game Developer Conference. Retrieved from http://webdocs.cs.ualberta.ca/~holte/Publications/GDC-05.pdf

Tarng, P. Y., Chen, K. T., & Huang, P. (2008). An analysis of WoW players' game hours. In *Proceedings of the 7th ACM SIGCOMM Workshop on Network and System Support for Games* (pp. 47–52). ACM.

Tominski, C. (2015). Interaction for visualization. *Synthesis Lectures on Visualization*, *3*(1), 1–107.

Tory, M., & Möller, T. (2004). Rethinking visualization: A high-level taxonomy. In *Proceedings of the IEEE Symposium on Information Visualization* (pp. 151–158). IEEE.

Wallner, G. (2017). Automatic generation of battle maps from replay data. *Information Visualization*, *17*(3), 239–256.

Wallner, G., & Kriglstein, S. (2012). A spatiotemporal visualization approach for the analysis of gameplay data. In *Proceedings of the SIGCHI Conference on Human Factors in Computing Systems* (pp. 1115–1124). ACM.

Wallner, G., & Kriglstein, S. (2013). Visualization-based analysis of gameplay data–A review of literature. *Entertainment Computing*, *4*(3), 143–155.

Wallner, G., & Kriglstein, S. (2014). PLATO: A visual analytics system for gameplay data. *Computers & Graphics*, *38*, 341–356.

Wallner, G., & Kriglstein, S. (2015a). Comparative visualization of player behavior for serious game analytics. In C. S. Loh, Y. Sheng, & D. Ifenthaler (Eds.), *Serious games analytics* (pp. 159–179). Heidelberg, Germany: Springer.

Wallner, G., & Kriglstein, S. (2015b). An introduction to gameplay data visualization. In P. Lankoski & S. Björk (Eds.), *Game research methods* (pp. 231–250). Pittsburgh, PA: ETC Press.

Wallner, G., & Kriglstein, S. (2016). Visualizations for retrospective analysis of battles in team-based combat games: A user study. In *Proceedings of the 2016 Annual Symposium on Computer-Human Interaction in Play* (pp. 22–32). ACM.

Wallner, G., Kriglstein, S., Gnadlinger, F., Heiml, M., & Kranzer, J. (2014). Game user telemetry in practice: A case study. In *Proceedings of the 11th Conference on Advances in Computer Entertainment Technology*. ACM.

Wehrend, S., & Lewis, C. (1990). A problem-oriented classification of visualization techniques. In *Proceedings of the 1st IEEE Conference on Visualization* (pp. 139–143). IEEE.

Yau, N. (2011). *Visualize this: The flowingdata guide to design, visualization, and statistics*. Hoboken, NJ: John Wiley & Sons.

Zammitto, V. (2008). Visualization techniques in video games. In *Proceedings of the Electronic Visualisation and the Arts Conference (EVA)* (pp. 267–276). BCS: The Chartered Institute for IT.

Zoeller, G. (2010). *Development telemetry in video games projects*. Presentation at the 2010 Game Developer Conference. Retrieved from https://www.gdcvault.com/play/1012227/Development-Telemetry-in-Video-Games.

Chapter 12

Co-Design of an Interactive Analytics System for Multiplayer Online Battle Arena Game Occurrences

Quan Li, Ziming Wu, Huamin Qu, and Xiaojuan Ma

Contents

12.1 Introduction

Multiplayer online battle arena (MOBA) games create immersive virtual gaming worlds in which two teams of players compete with each other to win a battle. Players controlling different game characters in a team coordinate to take down the opponent's base. Existing MOBA games such as *Dota 2, League of Legends (LoL),* and *SMITE* have attracted millions of players to invest their time and money, making MOBA games, in turn, one of the most profitable genres in the digital games industry. To succeed in fierce business competitions, MOBA games designers therefore strive to attract and retain players over long periods of time. One effective way to promote players' long-term engagement with a games is to ensure its playability (Febretti & Garzotto, 2009), which, in a multiplayer setting, particularly relates to teamwork satisfaction, a sense of fair competition, and mastery of complex gameplay interactions (Huber, 2009). In other words, a MOBA game should be reasonably challenging at both the individual and the team level while at the same time maintaining fairness and the right amount of prospective success throughout gameplay. This motivates game designers to identify critical factors that may influence game dynamics by closely inspecting individual and team gameplay behaviors.

While game outcomes (win or lose) primarily indicate the level of players' gaming skills and the effectiveness of gaming strategies, game occurrences—as defined in this chapter—capture the match development in terms of changes in a team's advantage (or disadvantage) over its opponent. Apparently, three major categories of game occurrences in MOBAs—*snowballing, comeback*, and *back and forth*—can be identified and experienced by game players.

- **Snowballing** occurs when a team achieves and maintains dominating advantages over its adversary without much effort and takes the lead throughout the match.
- **Comeback** occurs when a team overcomes substantial disadvantages and eventually wins the battle.
- **Back and forth**, in comparison, defines the situations in which both teams are very close and there is no clear winner until the end.

To some extent, the distribution of the different occurrences reflects the playability of a game. Having a considerably larger number of *snowballing* (or *comeback*) occurrences than occurrences of the other two categories may inevitably raise questions about the fairness of the game. By contrast, if the majority of the matches are *back and forth*, players may feel that there is no adequate differentiation in the game. Either way, the game engagement is at stake. Therefore, it is critical for game designers to identify common patterns of key gaming behaviors that contribute to each type of game occurrence and pinpoint the underlying reasons. They can consequently modify game design settings based on the findings to optimize playability and engagement.

However, analyzing patterns that are indicative of occurrences in MOBA games can be challenging due to the following reasons:

1. **Loose Definition of Patterns**: There are no fixed rules of what constitutes a "pattern" in gameplay, and thus any dimension (e.g., time, position, events) or a combination of multiple dimensions can contain the factor(s) that define(s) a pattern of behaviors.
2. **High Spatio-Temporal Variance**: Typically, a MOBA match takes about half an hour, during which in-game avatars manipulated by different players take different paths and perform various types of actions at different points in time. Therefore, it is difficult to locate a pattern in space and time, especially when it involves a sequence of actions spanning across multiple players.
3. **Complex/Ambiguous Collaborative Activities**: Similar to many other multiplayer sports and games, MOBAs involve two opposing teams. Sometimes,

members within a team act on their own, and at other times, they coordinate with one another to perform attacks on or defend against the opponents. Just by looking at the spatio-temporal traces, it can be difficult to tell whether a set of player actions in a team is independently executed or planned collectively.

In this chapter, we utilize the power of deep learning and human domain knowledge to address the aforementioned issues. That is to say, we exploit the computing capability of machines while keeping humans in the loop. Our approach consists of two steps. First, to alleviate the effort of the manual search for player behavior patterns among a big volume of game data, we leverage a machine learning framework to automatically identify critical time and space segments that, with high probability, contain determinant patterns shared across many matches in a high-level feature space constructed by a deep neural model. Since no labeled data with information on the contribution of each segment of game data to an occurrence is available for training, we employ an unsupervised technique. That is, by introducing a noise-based feature perturbation[1] (Chen, Goldgof, Hall, and Eschrich, 2007) using a sliding window into the network, we can locate data segments where adding the disturbance significantly alters the projected game occurrence. Second, we design an interactive visualization system to assist users with summarizing possible patterns behind the candidate segments, and further explore the reasons why they lead to the associated occurrences. As opposed to existing work, our method relieves users from scanning through an entire match by automatically (efficiency) recommending and ranking all possible data segments of interest derived from a large set of gameplay data (sufficiency). Moreover, our system can compile a list of matches that contain a user-specified pattern in a selected segment for further investigation (generality). Overall, the major contributions of this chapter are as follows:

1. We apply a deep learning model on a large set of MOBA data to automatically identify interesting gameplay segments (i.e., time periods and geographical positions) that may contain determinant behaviors of the aforementioned occurrences. This greatly reduces the efforts required on behalf of domain experts.
2. We develop a suite of interactive visualization techniques enhanced with new features to support game occurrence analysis on MOBA gameplay data, ensuring the sufficiency, generality, and efficiency of the findings.
3. We showcase the iterative design, evaluation, and deployment of a deep model-based visual analytics system for exploring the reasons behind different MOBA game occurrences with game analysts and designers.

---

[1] The method assumes that irrelevant features will only have a small influence on the classification performance when perturbed by noise. Such features will thus be removed from the set of features used in the classification.

12.2 Related Work

Game analysis plays a crucial role in identifying and reasoning about gameplay patterns for the purpose of aiding game designers in understanding gaming behaviors and optimizing the game design. Previous research (Ang & Zaphiris, 2010; Chen, Sun, & Hsieh, 2008; Cole & Griffiths, 2007) was heavily focused on the social interactions (e.g., teamwork, chatting, and trading) among players of massively multiplayer online games. Chen, Duh, and Renyi (2008) showed that various features of a game affect in-game social interaction, including interpersonal relationships, community size, and social alienation. Core players rely massively on in-game social interactions and even make offline friends through socialized game activities (Cole & Griffiths, 2007). Johnson, Nacke, and Wyeth (2015) found that MOBA games can produce a sense of satisfaction for players, which is derived from teamwork, competition, and mastery of complex gameplay interactions. This, in turn, can give insights on player engagement. Nevertheless, these kinds of works merely focus on the interaction between and perception of MOBA players, without considering gaming behaviors as well as the patterns behind them. The latter, however, can also be insightful for game designers to promote player engagement and optimize the game design. Additionally, questionnaires from online communities, interviews with computer players, or trial play are useful methods for user studies and evaluations of MOBA games (El-Nasr, Desurvire, Aghabeigi, & Drachen, 2013; Lapaš & Orehovački, 2015).

12.2.1 *Visual Analysis of Gameplay Behavior*

Many visualization techniques have been exploited to aid in gameplay behavior analysis and show their advantages in intensive data analysis, especially for spatio-temporal games. Visualization techniques for game data are discussed in detail in Chapter 11 of the present book. Wallner and Kriglstein (2013) provide an extensive literature review of work dealing with the visualization of game metric data. In addition, Wallner and Kriglstein (2014) proposed PLATO, which takes advantage of subgraph matching, pathfinding, data comparison, clustering, and several visualization techniques to analyze game data. Bowman, Elmqvist, and Jankun-Kelly (2012) categorized five visualization elements in their framework for Wallner and Kriglstein (2013) also provide an extensive literature review of work dealing with the visualization of game metric data game analysis: primary purpose, target audience, temporal usage, visual complexity, and immersion integration. Furthermore, Hoobler, Humphreys, and Agrawala (2004) presented a system to visualize large-scale combat behavior data of players in virtual environments. The system allows users to view and summarize game data interactively and, moreover, to reduce information overload. Besides, some game data analysis systems were developed to assist game designers in analyzing game data, but these focus on technical issues such as game frame rate data analysis (Li et al. 2015) only. Li et al. (2017) proposed an interactive visualization system that enables the analysis of occurrences in a single MOBA game match data. The system consolidates the multivariate gameplay data into insights regarding trends, game replay, and players' tactics in multiple views, which requires an active exploration and inspection of specific match periods and locations on behalf of the users and highly relies on users' domain knowledge. However, all of these visualization techniques fail to support the analysis of hundreds or even thousands of game matches at the same time. To identify gameplay patterns it is, normally, important to compare game behaviors in different matches and summarize their commonalities and differences. However, most of the previous work is focused on single matches, which means that the extraction of generalized gameplay patterns still remains a challenge for domain experts.

12.2.2 Data-Driven Approaches to Gameplay Data

Game pattern mining has been partially studied by research communities. Véron, Marin, and Monnet (2014) built a database of *League of Legends* matches to analyze the matchmaking service of the game. Drachen et al. (2014) modeled spatio-temporal gaming behaviors by using three data-driven measures: zone changes, distribution of team members, and fuzzy clustering of time series. Miller and Crowcroft (2010) examined character movement in *World of Warcraft* by mining data from the server–client stream. Pobiedina, Neidhardt, Calatrava Moreno, and Werthner (2013) investigated in-game collaboration based on large-scale game logs of *Dota 2*, revealing that the existence of friendships within a team has a positive impact on the game result. To distinguish different players, Shim, Kim, and Kim (2014) took advantage of a domain-knowledge approach to develop an efficient and automatic abnormal player decision support method based on PageRank to find and judge players with bad performance. However, these methods are mainly focused on mining team-based and social interactions within the game rather than the gameplay patterns that lead to the final game outcome. Our work is more centered on discovering gaming behaviors that dominate certain game occurrences. As for match outcome prediction, Yang, Harrison, and Roberts (2014) proposed a graph metric to model the patterns that are predictive of match success. Low-level topological clues to characterize the spatial structure of a MOBA were introduced by Rioult, Métivier, Helleu, Scelles, and Durand (2014). Bosc, Kaytoue, Raïssi, and Boulicaut (2013) identified a method of encoding a player's actions into sequences. Using this method, they mined sequential patterns and introduced a balanced measure that describes to what extent different strategies lead to success. Although the authors demonstrated good results and predictions, the dynamics of intermediate results cannot be revealed using this approach, since there are no clear labels of such results for supervised learning. Traditional supervised machine learning frameworks have also been utilized to classify player behaviors (Eggert, Herrlich, Smeddinck, & Malaka, 2015). However, these approaches require external efforts from data experts to manually extract features, which is complicated and inefficient owing to the complex and highly dynamic nature of team-based combats. In our case, we need to automatically identify the key time periods of a game match, which involves important game events and players' behaviors that dominate the game occurrences, without any external manual effort. To be specific, we utilize both the power of deep learning and the cognitive abilities of humans, maximizing the usability of machine-computing capabilities while keeping humans involved in the analysis process.

12.3 Background and Requirement Analysis

12.3.1 About MOBA Games

MOBA games involve two opposing teams of a maximum of five players competing against each other with the objective of destroying the base of the opponent's team to score a win. Typically, a game map is divided in half, with each side containing defense towers and the main base of a team. Two or three main pathways connect the two parts together. Each player controls a hero with specified skills, who will become more and more powerful throughout the game by gaining experience and earning money by standing near or killing enemies or by destroying the opponent's buildings. The accumulated experience and money can be used to level up the hero and to buy items that can strengthen their ability and power. In the MOBA game *Wildfire* (NetEase, 2016) analyzed in this chapter, two special units are available. The first one is the "light tower", which can heal its own team's avatars. However, if they are occupied by the opposite team, the opposite team can see everything within the tower's field of view, helping them to detect the tactical actions of the other team. The second special unit is the "trooper". This unit is a neutral unit, which, once hit by a hero of a team, will belong to this team.

12.3.2 Requirements from Domain Experts

To deploy our framework in real scenarios, we worked with a team of experts from NetEase Games,[2] comprised of one game user experience analyst (E.1), one data analyst (E.2), and two game designers (E.3, E.4). Before the official launch, the game *Wildfire* had gone through three small scaled trial runs from February 9, 2017 to June 26, 2017. The purpose was to collect feedback from players, helping designers develop some initial assessment of their designs and predict the distribution of the game occurrences. During the trial period, we shadowed (with their consent) the team's daily working process, videotaping how they observed players experiencing the game and conducted on-site interviews with the players, etc. In general, the experts conduct a two-stage analysis to understand the reasons behind MOBA game occurrences. First, they classify the game occurrences. Subsequently, they select and analyze a single match to understand the potential reasons that lead to

---

[2] https://www.neteasegames.com/(Accessed: April 2019).

this occurrence. However, this approach still encounters the previously mentioned problems of "sufficiency" and "generality." To resolve these issues, our main target users, E.1 and E.2, require the following features:

1. **Visualization of the features learned by the deep learning model.** Our system should display a summary of the learned feature map throughout the observed time period. For example, E.2 expressed the desire to observe the overall distribution of the significance of the effect on the confidence for occurrence classification throughout the unified observation period.
2. **Grouping of similar game matches to confirm patterns.** To confirm the "generality" of a pattern, a case-by-case analysis is evidently insufficient. The system should also be able to automatically summarize several game matches that share similar patterns.
3. **Simulating replay of a selected game match.** For a selected match and a specified time period, our system must provide a simplified view of the match replay to observe the changes in the players' movement and tactic behaviors in order to understand how each player plans to launch an attack, a retreat, or other actions in one screen.
4. **Clustering of gameplay events to facilitate analysis.** Given various events that may strongly determine game occurrences, our system should display a clear record of time, location, and other details for these important events.

12.4 Workflow and System Overview

This section presents a deep model-based visual analytics workflow (cf. Figure 12.1) that facilitates the analysis of the reasons behind game occurrences based on discussions with domain experts. It helps to translate the output of the deep model and domain knowledge into visualized patterns. The proposed workflow comprises four components: (1) a game occurrence extraction module, (2) a data processing module, (3) a deep model module, and (4) a visual analytics module. We focus on three major game occurrences: *snowballing, comeback,* and *back and forth* (cf. Section 12.1) among extensive game match data and extract them by using a deep convolutional neural network (CNN) model.[3] Thereafter, the detailed resource raw data of the two teams and the position raw data of the involved players in a match are extracted and further normalized to a fixed length of gameplay time (3,000 seconds in this study) to make the matches comparable. A deep model-based analysis is conducted to obtain the feature weight maps. Then, an automatic detection of segments of interest is conducted to guide users through the process of exploring the detailed in-game activities. To further confirm the assumptions

---

[3] CNNs are introduced in Chapter 6.

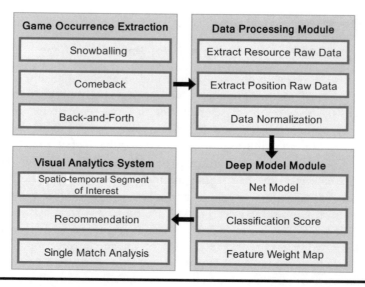

Figure 12.1   Workflow for exploring and identifying patterns for game occurrences.

that may potentially lead to a certain type of game occurrence, a detailed analysis of several recommended game matches is performed to facilitate the verification of the hypothesis and to explore the reasons behind such an occurrence.

12.4.1 Data Preprocessing

In general, timestamps play a major role in aligning different groups of information. Although different MOBA games may differ in terms of some specific behaviors and have their own rules, the events and states for most of them fall into several high-level categories. Data preprocessing consists of two main steps. The first step is to align the log data based on the timestamps, which provides spatio-temporal information of different game units and their corresponding actions. Then, for the deep CNN models, we extract three major resources (i.e., *cash*, *experience*, and *kill/death* values) and player position information for each timestamp as the original input for our deep neural network. For detailed occurrence analysis, we extract critical events, such as *combats* and *destroying towers*, from the activity logs by calculating the individual hits over time. Furthermore, to differentiate activities conducted by heroes from those performed by computer-controlled units and to extract players' involvement in the game status, we need to classify players and AI activities and sum up their contribution to the corresponding team.

12.5 Deep Model-Based Analysis

12.5.1 Motivations for Deep Model-Based Analysis

Our goal here is to specify the key periods and locations of a game match that dominate the final result. Specifically, we need to identify which segments of data—that is, spatio-temporal segments of interest—contribute significantly to the final occurrence. However, lacking some sort of label information that indicates the contribution of different segments of a match makes it challenging to attain that information directly by means of supervised learning models. At the same time, leveraging the insight that a large-scale data-based training enables networks to ignore non-discriminative information in their input (Yosinski, Clune, Nguyen, Fuchs, & Lipson, 2015), sensitivity analysis can be applied to extract the regions of a given input that are largely contributive to the classification result. In the context of image classification, Simonyan, Vedaldi, and Zisserman (2013) proposed a partial derivative-based heatmap analysis to measure how much small changes locally in the pixel value affect the network output. Layer-wise relevance propagation (Bach et al., 2015), on the other hand, uses pixel-wise relevance to indicate the contributions of a pixel to the overall classification score. However, all of these methods fail to take temporal information into account, which is critical for game data. Moreover, it is important to note that as suggested by Samek, Binder, Montavon, Lapuschkin, and Müller (2017), this problem should not be formulated as a feature selection problem where features salient for an ensemble are selected. Borrowing the idea from Samek et al. (2017) and Chen, Goldgof, Hall, and Eschrich (2007), we apply a patch-based noise perturbation to address this problem, in which a certain amount of noise is added iteratively to the raw data within a predefined temporal range. Next, we identify which perturbed patches lead to severe performance decay in the classification task. Those patches with an active response would be taken as the spatio-temporal segments of interest. Therefore, the pipeline of the deep model-based analysis consists of two main steps. First, a discriminative model is trained to classify the game occurrence of a match based on a large MOBA dataset. Then, we identify which parts of the data contribute the most to the classification outcome and take them as the spatio-temporal segments of interest for analysis (cf. Figure 12.2).

12.5.2 Occurrence Classification

To apply sensitivity analysis, we first need to describe MOBA raw data in a representative feature space. Existing data-driven game analysis methods require data experts to manually construct such a feature space with external knowledge. Driven by the remarkable capability of neural networks to generate high-level representative features, we build a discriminative CNN—following a similar structure as

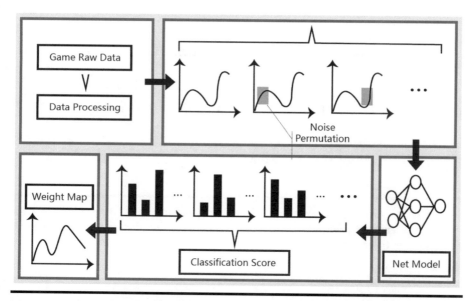

Figure 12.2 **Workflow for identifying spatio-temporal segments of interest: First, data processing acquires structured raw data. Second, the processed data is iteratively permuted by a certain amount of noise and then fed into a pre-trained CNN model. Using the classification score output of the model, we obtain a weight map by measuring the discriminant contribution of each part of the input using a class-based estimator.**

AlexNet[4]—for the purpose of constructing a high-level feature space without the need for manual effort and external knowledge. The model is focused on the occurrence classification task in which a match is assigned the corresponding occurrence.

12.5.3 Deep Neural Network Architecture

AlexNet has shown its remarkably discriminative performance on image classification tasks. We follow a similar structure as AlexNet but simplify the network by deleting some of the layers and compressing the filters due to the lower complexity of occurrence classification compared to image classification (cf. Figure 12.3). Basically, our model consists of five layers with four stages: convolution, rectification, pooling, and fully connected mapping, formulated as

$$f(x) = Fc(Pool(Ref(Conv(x)))),$$

where $f(x)$ denotes the classification function of a trained neural model, and x is the input of the network (see Section 12.5.4). The convolution stage scans the input

---

[4] AlexNet is a CNN for image classification (see Krizhevsky, Sutskever, & Hinton, 2012).

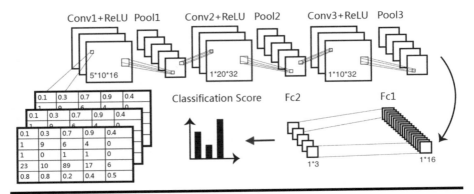

Figure 12.3 An illustration of our CNN architecture, consisting of three convolution layers and two fully connected layers. Between two consecutive layers, there are rectification and pooling operations.

by applying a rectangle filter to the raw data. The rectification stage then serves as a non-linear mapping, making deep neural networks more meaningful and simulating more complex models. The max pooling stage down-samples the rectified response by taking the maximum value over a grid and filtering those elements with a smaller response so that the subset of an input with less discriminative information can be ignored. Finally, the output from the previous layer is fed into two consecutive, fully connected layers, which map it onto classification scores indicating to which category the input belongs to.

12.5.4 Model Training

Our dataset consists of data from 3,000 game matches collected from *Wildfire*. In our experiments, 2,500 matches are used for training and the remaining 500 for testing. The raw data for each match has 16 dimensions, of which cash, experience, and the kills of both teams contribute 6 dimensions and the remaining 10 are the positions of the players (5 players per team). The gaming period for each match is normalized to 3,000 seconds, as suggested by the experts. Therefore, each match data is transformed into a $16 \times 3,000$ matrix, serving as the input for our network. All the matches were labeled according to our three categories (*snowballing, comeback,* and *back and forth*) by game designers. We trained the neural network using stochastic gradient descent and set the momentum as 0.9. The initial learning rate was 0.01 and decreased after every 1,000 iterations. The training was stopped when the loss converged as well as when it achieved highest test accuracy. Finally, the trained model achieved around 96% accuracy over the test data.

12.5.5 *Spatio-Temporal Segments of Interest Identification*

To identify the spatio-temporal segments of interest in a match, we propose a patch-based noise permutation strategy to infer which part of the input data significantly affects the classification result. To put it formally, we first define a spatio-temporal segment as the continuous entries in patches of the input data with the predefined size of $W*H$, where W and H denote the width and the height of a segment, respectively. Concretely, H corresponds to the length of a temporal period, while W is the dimension of the involved features. In our experiment, H is 30 s (as suggested by the experts) to cover the average duration of a game event, and W is 16 to cover the input dimensions. The permuted area that results in significant performance decay is taken as the spatio-temporal segment of interest. To obtain the estimation, a patch-based noise perturbation process is conducted iteratively by generating additive noise on a $W*H$ patch with a certain stride. The noise follows a uniform distribution given by $noise \sim uniform(-C*\sigma, C*\sigma)$, where σ denotes the standard variance of the input x, and C is a constant. We use a perturbation process that follows the ordered sequence of input data. More specifically, the patch perturbation process can be considered as performed consecutively along timestamps. It can be modeled as:

$$x'_{ij} = x_{ij} + noise\left(x_{ij} \in p_k, \forall p_k \subset x\right),$$

where p_k is the kth patch in x with the size of $W*H$, and x_{ij} is the ijth data point of p_k. Then, the weight of p_k can be attained by:

$$W_k = \frac{1}{N}\sum H\left(f\left(p'_k\right), f\left(p_k\right)\right),$$

where W_k corresponds to the weight indicating to what extent the performance decay resulted from a permuted patch p_k'. The larger W_k is, the more important p_k is. $f(x)$ is a vector of which the ith dimension is the confidence that the model believes that input x belongs to the ith class. $H(A, A')$ is an estimator that measures the difference between the classification results of the original data A and the permuted data A'. The most intuitive way to measure the difference is using a metric distance—for example, Euclidean distance. However, it would lead to bias since the sum of the score difference of the outer classes would dominate the overall distance, while the score of ith dimension is actually more crucial if x belongs to the ith class. To eliminate the bias, we propose a class-based estimator $H(A, A')$, where

$$H\left(A, A'\right) = \left|\left(a_i - a'_i\right) - \max\left(a_j - a'_j \middle| \forall a_j \in A, a'_j \in A' \text{ and } j \neq i\right)\right|.$$

Here, i denotes the index of the category that A belongs to.

12.6 Visualization Design

Our visual analytics system contains three interactive views to enable the free exploration of the output produced by the deep model and of the details of the MOBA gameplay data. These three views are discussed in detail in the following.

12.6.1 Feature Map View

The Feature Map View (cf. Figure 12.4) provides an overview of the feature weight output by the aforementioned deep model. The higher the feature weight is, the more the data segment contributes to the final occurrence. We focus on the three aforementioned game occurrences and conduct a "pairwise comparison" between any two of them. However, if additional occurrences are added, this mechanism can be easily extended by using a drop-down list. To determine the contribution of each timestamp, as well as the similarities and differences between the selected two occurrences, we conduct three main processing methods to automatically recommend these significant timestamps for further analysis:

1. **Peak Detection.** Although timestamps with considerably high feature weights affect the confidence of the final classification, we also consider which concrete reasons may affect the trend of feature weights. Therefore, we develop a peak detection algorithm to extract such "peak" timestamps. Prior to this process, the least squares method (Miller, 2006) is used to smooth the feature weight curve.

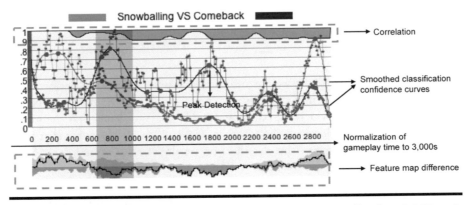

Figure 12.4 The *x*-axis represents the gameplay time (normalized to 3,000 sec); the *y*-axis represents the feature map weight; the non-smooth curve represents the feature weights associated with timestamps; two solid lines represent the smoothed classification confidence curves of the corresponding occurrences: *snowballing* and *comeback* in this example. The area at the top indicates the correlation between the feature maps of the two occurrences, and the bottom curve area indicates the feature map variances and their differences between the two feature maps.

2. **Correlation Analysis.** To quantify the association between two continuous feature maps, we conduct a correlation analysis to detect the time periods with different correlations. When the trends of feature maps are the same, the correlation between them is higher; otherwise, it is lower.

3. **Difference Analysis.** If the difference between the values of the feature maps at a certain timestamp is higher, then a significant discrepancy exists between the two game occurrences, thereby necessitating further observation.

The use of the outlined methods allows us to easily determine the data segments of interest. However, we also added an interactive time slider in the feature map view to allow users to observe different periods of time, thereby enabling them to change the size of the time window of the spatio-temporal segments for further detailed analysis of what happens in such areas.

12.6.2 Statistical View

Viewing the distribution of data in the feature space can be insightful for game analysis, particularly for identifying outliers (i.e., matches that are significantly different from others) and evaluating the data correlation. However, we need to abstract each match into a feature description. Similar to the work of Krizhevsky, Sutskever, and Hinton (2012), the output of the second-to-last fully connected layer is taken as the feature representation of a match because it is more representative, high-level, and time-efficient than hand-drafted features. Furthermore, the feature vectors are projected onto a two-dimensional plane using principal component analysis (PCA) for visualization purposes. After obtaining a general idea of the distribution of different occurrences through the PCA view, along with the automatic recommendation of important time periods that contribute significantly to the final occurrence—as depicted by the Feature Map View—users can select a certain type of occurrence and obtain details of it. The most important aspect that may affect the game occurrence outcome is in what behaviors the players engage in and whether they efficiently grasp opportunities for defending themselves against the opponents. Upon discussion with the domain experts, we use the tactical behaviors of the players as the basis for extracting several high-level critical events for detailed analysis regarding a specific game occurrence. However, only a few events have concrete timestamps, whereas others, such as *team combat* and *occupying light towers*, vary in timing, thereby necessitating special handling. A few others have accompanied geographical positions, which may be meaningful when considering the geographical factors. By contrast, others, including *team combat, occupying light towers*, and *equipment upgrade* can happen anywhere and anytime. Therefore, we need to separate them for visualization (cf. Figure 12.5).

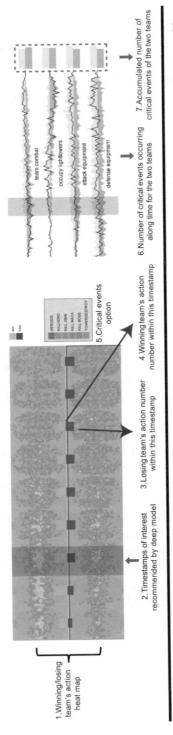

Figure 12.5 Statistical view for analyzing a certain type of game occurrence: (1) heatmap of behaviors of both winning and losing team. (2) The highlighted area corresponds to the area of interest recommended by the deep model. (3, 4) Comparison of the number of actions—encoded by the length of bars—performed by the two teams. (5) Users can select different critical events for analysis. (6) Events irrelevant to the geographical distribution are visualized by curves, with their accumulated number displayed by the length of horizontal bars (7).

12.6.3 Detailed Match View

The Feature Map View and the Statistical View provide cues about critical timestamps that may need further observation and analysis. Accordingly, the observer may form several hypotheses and assumptions. However, confirming them entails a detailed match analysis based on the recommendation match list. That is, we use *k*-means to cluster the instances of a specified occurrence into *k* clusters (set empirically to *k* = 5) to further assist users to verify, understand, and interact with the data for a specified occurrence. Hence, users can specifically look into a subset of instances of high similarity. To provide a detailed analysis of the game progress and of the status of players during a match, we categorize the related information into three components: trajectory, rhythm, and resources/equipment in terms of teams and players throughout the match.

12.6.3.1 Trajectory Simulation

Following the requirement of the experts, we need to display the gameplay dynamics in a game map to simulate real matches (cf. Figure 12.6, Trajectory View). The players' movement positions are recorded only every 5 seconds due to the large data transferring cost. However, when players launch certain behaviors, the accompanied positions where these behaviors occur are also recorded. Therefore, before we can derive a relatively comprehensive trajectory with the temporal dimension for a single player, we need to combine the simple movement position data with the behavioral data to offer a more comprehensive picture of the flow of gameplay. We adopt the algorithm proposed by Li et al. (2017) to simulate how a hero moves between two discrete positions on the game map: accelerating from a standstill until they reach full speed halfway and then decelerating until the endpoint. This enables the reconstruction of a continuous trajectory from discrete trajectory points. Such a continuous path is more noticeable and traceable than, for instance, blinking dots indicating the movements of each player. In this view, we use some special visual cues to better simulate a real gameplay scenario. Players from the same team form a bubble if they are close to each other to simulate the cooperation relations, while the bubble border intensifies when the opponents meet. Trajectories are shown in advance to indicate the future movements of players, their transparency increasing with the elapsed time.

12.6.3.2 Critical Events Timeline

Certain critical events happening within specified timestamps can be directly displayed on the Position Dynamics/Critical Events View, where they can be interactively selected by the user. By contrast, other events (e.g., *combat, hitting towers,* and *occupying towers*) involve a different number of players and vary in timing, thereby necessitating special handling. Bars on the critical events timeline encode the results of *team combat,* that is, which team wins more often than the other. Rectangles on the top indicate the periods of *hitting towers.* Glyphs—aligned

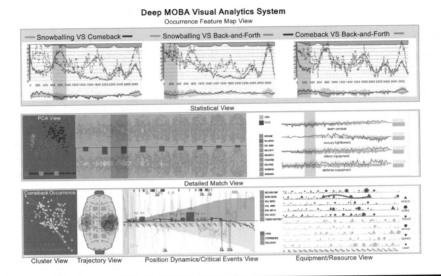

Figure 12.6 (See color insert.) Deep MOBA Visual Analytics System. The Occurrence Feature Map View offers a pairwise comparison of the features obtained by the deep model by game occurrence. The PCA View shows the distribution of the three occurrences. Key regions and critical events are detected to give visual clues on both important timestamps and geographical areas (Statistical View). A number of recommended matches of a certain occurrence are displayed in the Cluster View. Users can select one node (a representative match) to view details, including simulating the movements of all players in the Trajectory View, comparing the performance of both teams in the Position Dynamics View, and observe critical events and equipment/resource changes in the Equipment/Resource View.

along the timeline—show the timestamps when *occupying light tower* events happen. Users can also freely select other critical events by clicking the legend button.

12.6.3.3 Equipment Upgrade Timeline

By upgrading the equipment of avatars, the abilities of each avatar can be leveled up. To determine such an evolution, we designed an equipment upgrade timeline, with different types of equipment encoded by different glyphs and the levels of equipment visualized by the size of the glyphs. The evolution hierarchy is illustrated with a curve. The equipment involved in the evolution process is highlighted by hovering over the corresponding glyph.

12.6.3.4 Resource Distribution

Players' behaviors are largely associated with the distribution of resources, particularly in terms of *cash*, *experience*, and *kill counts*. We provide the changes in the accumulated resources of both teams (cf. Figure 12.7, labels 9 and 10). The black

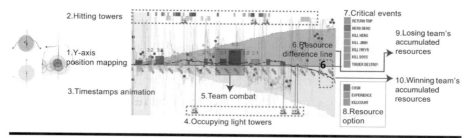

Figure 12.7 **(1)** *Y-positions of the units in the game map over time.* **(2)** *Hitting towers* events from both teams are encoded by rectangles along the top axis. **(3)** A time slider (timestamps animation) allows users to select the interesting time period for trajectory analysis. **(4)** Glyphs indicate when *occupying light towers* events happen. **(5)** *Team combats* are encoded by two vertical bars with scores indicating the results of them. **(7)** The critical events option allows users to display selected events on the Position Dynamics View (cf. Figure 12.6). **(8)** Resource options consist of *cash, experience,* and *kill count.* **(9-10)** Accumulated resource values are visualized by two areas with a **(6)** black curve indicating the difference between them.

line (cf. Figure 12.7, label 6) in the middle shows the value difference. As equipment evolution costs a certain amount of cash and experience, we further divide the resource changes by player level to facilitate the analysis of how players decide to upgrade their equipment. Users can discover any sudden increase in these resources through an accumulation of the peaks in the timeline (cf. Figure 12.6, Equipment/Resource View).

12.7 Use Cases

To illustrate how the tool can be leveraged for gameplay analysis, we present two use cases which repeatedly occurred when E.1 and E.2 were working with the proposed visualization system.

12.7.1 Case One: Inter-Occurrence Comparison

The first case focuses on the comparison of the similarity and the discrepancy between game occurrences by leveraging the observations from the Feature Map View and the detailed Statistical View of a certain type of occurrence.

12.7.1.1 Observing Differences/Similarities among Occurrences

The experts first noticed that in the early stage, the feature map weights are higher for *snowballing*, followed by a gradual decrease as time passes. Another peak in the feature weight occurs at the end of the gaming period as a whole (3,000 s), indicating that for *snowballing*, the most important periods closely associated with this game occurrence are the first 1/6 and the last 1/10 parts of the whole duration. As opposed to *snowballing*, *comeback* experiences some twists and turns. The experts located several existences of "comeback time-points" (around 800 s, 1,800 s, 2,400 s, and 2,800 s; remember that the gameplay periods of all matches are normalized to 3,000 s). When comparing *comeback* with *back and forth* occurrences, the analysts found that *back and forth* is quite similar, as such "comeback time-points" also appear, except in the initial and final parts of a match. These time-points indicate that both teams are struggling and waiting for opportunities to succeed over the opponent.

12.7.1.2 Reasoning About Potential Activities Behind an Occurrence

Suggested by experts, those observations make sense to them, and to some extent verify the effectiveness of our framework on extracting segments of interest. They also give some further potential explanations:

- **Snowballing:** In the beginning, a large difference in the accumulated resources between the two teams may easily cause this occurrence. Contrariwise, in the final moments of a match, several team combats may be of importance to snowballing.
- **Comeback:** The observed four "comeback time-points" may be a result of the early disadvantaged team taking a certain opportunity to achieve superiority over the early advantaged team and then moving toward the opponent's base or by the two teams fighting for neutral resources (e.g., troopers, see Section 12.3.1), during which opportunities for a "comeback" may arise.
- **Back and forth:** is quite similar to *comeback*, except for the initial and the final parts of the whole match. The experts guess that in the initial stage, the resource discrepancy between the teams is much smaller than it would be in case of a *comeback*. They speculate that there may exist a "back and forth" in terms of resources, while in *comeback*, the gap of resources between the teams is much larger. In *back and forth*, the well-balanced competition between the two teams lasts for a longer time than that in *comeback* until the final stage of the match, in which the very last combats between the two teams determine the final *back and forth* occurrence, while in *comeback*, the early advantaged team is unable to reverse the already established occurrence and loses the game.

12.7.1.3 Statistical Analysis of an Occurrence

After the experts' early assumptions, they refer to the statistical view to find evidence that supports their initial speculation. They find that in *snowballing*, the *snowballing* team has more *destroying towers* and *team combat* events, which, in turn, leads to more *killing hero* events compared to the disadvantaged team (cf. Figure 12.8, label 1). This may cause an incremental gap of accumulated resources between the two teams.

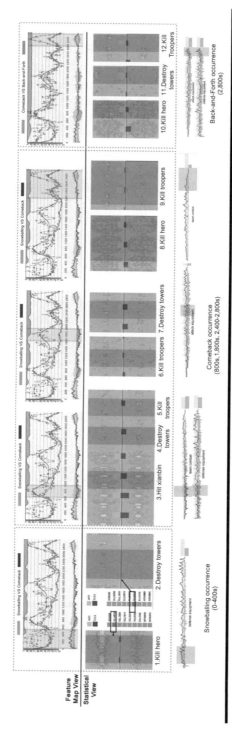

Figure 12.8 In case of *snowballing*, the first 1/6 and the last 1/10 parts of the entire gameplay time contribute most to the final occurrence. For *comeback*, four "comeback time-points" are witnessed. *Back and forth* is quite similar to *comeback* at these "comeback time-points," except for the last stage.

In *comeback*, the four "comeback time-points" correspond to the following witnessed phenomena:

■ At around 800 s, the *comeback* team mainly focuses on *killing troopers*, which can generate large amounts of cash for the team. Notice that the number of defense equipment upgrades of the *comeback* team is larger than those of the opponents. The trend in the number of *team combats* indicates that a *comeback* is about to occur.

■ At around 1,800 s, the *comeback* team starts to perform overwhelmingly well on *killing troopers* and *destroying towers* compared to the other team. At the same time, the experts witness more *attack equipment* upgrades.

■ At the last two "comeback time-points" (2,400 s, 2,800 s), the gap of the number of *kill hero* events increases considerably, and furthermore, more *killing trooper* events on behalf of the *comeback* team are witnessed.

In general, the experts think that the role of troopers is very important for a general *comeback* occurrence. The important features for a *comeback*—as the experts note—are a large gap in terms of the number of *killing heroes*, *destroying towers*, and *killing trooper* events. At the same time, more upgrades of equipment are performed by the *comeback* team. Therefore, the feature weight within this period (around 2,800 s) is more significant than during others.

12.7.2 Case Two: Intra-Occurrence Pattern Verification

This case shows how the experts leverage the detailed match view to further verify the assumptions concerning reasons for a certain game occurrence. Moreover, they are curious about questions, such as: "If the gap of resources between the two teams grows, what exactly makes this happen?" or "What are the four important 'comeback time-points' that contribute substantially to the occurrences of the comeback and what happens in the final stage of back and forth?"

12.7.2.1 Verification of Snowballing

Before analyzing a specific game match, the experts noticed five clusters with different ratios of the *snowballing* occurrence. The nodes within a cluster share similar features (this fact was learned by our deep model). From the previous observation, the initial and the final stage are more important than others for a *snowballing* occurrence. The experts focused their attention on these two stages, and by clicking on one of the nodes, they could retrieve more details for a specified match. From the overview in Figure 12.9 (label 1), they witnessed that in the initial phase, the *snowballing* team accumulates advantages mainly by winning the first few combats, which allows them to upgrade the equipment (cf. Figure 12.9, label 2), while the opponents' skill remains

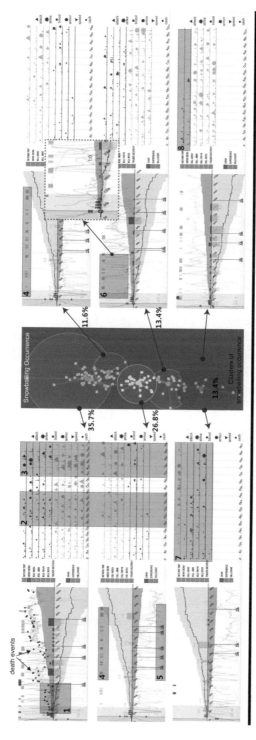

Figure 12.9 (See color insert.)   *Snowballing occurrences pattern set.* (1) In the initial stage, the team in advantage overwhelms the opponent in several combats (note that the dark nodes indicate death events of the disadvantaged teams, resulting in a significant upgrade of equipment). (2) In the final stage, another upgrade of equipment leads to the final occurrence (3). (4) The sequence of *hitting towers* is mainly conducted by the *snowballing* teams, indicating a passive resistance of the disadvantaged teams. (5) All the light towers of the disadvantaged teams are occupied in all representative matches. (6) The irregular trajectories show that some particular behaviors such as "away from keyboard" may contribute to losing the initial combats. (7, 8) Overwhelming performance by some individual players may also result in *snowballing*.

at the same level. This gives them an advantage in subsequent combats, allowing them to keep upgrading their defense equipment (cf. Figure 12.9, label 3) before confronting the powers of the opponents' base towers in the final stage. Another obvious phenomenon to explain why the disadvantaged teams cannot accumulate resources in other ways, for example, by killing creeps,[5] is because as noted by an expert "nearly all the light towers of the inferior team are occupied," by which the *snowballing* teams can easily get to know the tactical actions of their opponents (cf. Figure 12.9, label 5). Therefore, the advantages are sustained until the end of the match. Some relatively large clusters are a result of *passive resistance* behaviors of the disadvantaged teams, which may further consist of *idling behaviors* (i.e., being away from the keyboard) or *abandoning defending efforts*, which can be demonstrated by the irregular trajectories of some players in disadvantaged teams (cf. Figure 12.9, label 6). Furthermore, the experts noticed that all the *hitting towers* events are conducted by the *snowballing* teams, while the disadvantaged teams show fewer efforts to destroy the opponents' towers (cf. Figure 12.9, label 4). Other patterns frequently occurring in *snowballing* are the huge gap between the *performance of the teams* or the *unbalanced number of players* at the beginning of the match, as some players may leave the game early. In Figure 12.9 (label 7), usually certain players from one side contribute the most and thus *snowballing* mostly occurs due to the overwhelming performance of these players. In Figure 12.9 (label 8), the unbalanced number of players immediately results in *snowballing*. Since *snowballing* occurrences stem partly from the unbalanced performance/number of players, they can be reduced by modifying the matchmaking rating mechanism[6] to provide greater fairness and to offer more equal chances of winning. Besides, offering weaker rewards at the early stage could be another possible way to avoid overwhelming *snowballing*. The experts find the design of *light towers* to be too favorable for the *snowballing* teams, making it difficult for the disadvantaged teams to compete for resources for future development. Actually, one expert remarked: "We are thinking about removing the design of these light towers, or at least narrowing down the field of view of light towers."

12.7.2.2 Verification of Comeback Time-Points

All *comeback* matches can be grouped into five clusters with three of them covering 80% of the *comeback* occurrences. In the largest cluster, the experts observed that this occurrence is mainly due to some unwise actions of certain players in the early-advantaged team. As shown in Figure 12.10 (labels 1–4), the unwise action that the purple player (labeled the "unwise player") conducts gives the opposite green team an opportunity to destroy towers and upgrade equipment and finally win the game.

---

[5] Creeps, also sometimes called "minions" in MOBA terminology, are units that are spawned periodically and which players can kill to gain gold or experience.

[6] The design of matchmaking systems is discussed in Chapter 3.

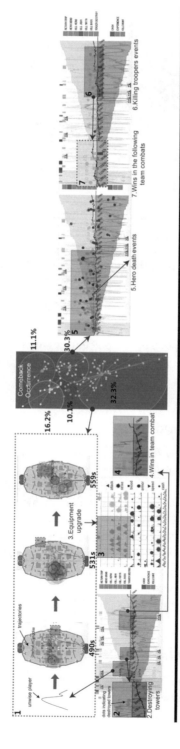

Figure 12.10 (See color insert.) (1) Two players return home to their base (indicated by the arrow labeled trajectories), but an opponent (the unwise player) advances deep into the eventually victorious team's camp (the purple trajectory), chases them alone, and is killed. (2) The two players then destroy two towers (indicated by two dots), followed by (3) an equipment upgrade—represented by the icons—before winning the subsequent team combats and finally making the *comeback* happen (4). (5) In the early stage, the *comeback* team is defeated in most of the *team combats*. However, they kill many troopers (6) that help them to win the following *team combats* (7).

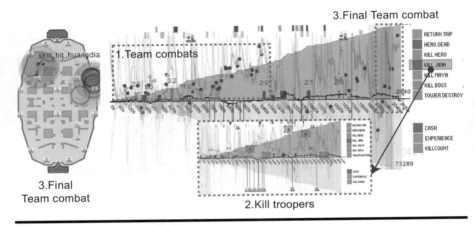

Figure 12.11 (See color insert.) **In the earlier stages, both teams achieve some success on (1)** *team combat, kill heroes,* **and (2)** *kill troopers.* **However, (3) in the final combats, the victorious team wins through a series of** *killing hero* **events.**

The second largest cluster focuses on seizing the precious resources (e.g., troopers, as in this case) to help them remedy the early disadvantaged position (cf. Figure 12.10, labels 5 and 6).

12.7.2.3 Final Push in Back and Forth

As shown in the Feature Map View (cf. Figure 12.4), most of the stages of the entire match make a similar contribution except for two major periods: the initial stage and the final one. It is easy to understand that in the initial stage of a *back and forth* game, the strength of the two teams is better balanced compared to *comeback*. As shown in Figure 12.11, in the early stage, the matches show ups and downs in terms of *team combat, hitting towers,* and *killing troopers* on both sides, (labels 1 and 2). However, the experts are more curious about what happens in the final stage. In this stage, there are the final *team combats,* in which the eventually victorious team uses the opportunity to win (cf. Figure 12.11, label 3). In this case, the experts stipulated that "both teams have a good chance of winning the game."

12.7.3 Experts' Feedback and Discussion

We conducted semi-structured interviews with E.1–E.4, who have all worked in the game industry for more than four years.

12.7.3.1 System Usability

The experts were excited by our system to visually and interactively explore and compare three major game occurrences. E.1 prefers the effectiveness of using the system to reduce his workload for evaluating MOBA game design. Previously, he needed to go through every week's new release of the game, gather all the modified features and compare them with the previous version, familiarize himself with any new content added to the game, and take notes. Before releasing a new version into the market, he also had to organize playtesting sessions and invite players to come and experience the game. After that, he had to consult with them to gather feedback. The whole process was thus quite labor intensive and time-consuming. With our system, he said that "I can easily select and explore different game occurrences and matches." E.2 is satisfied with our framework, which combines a deep model with an interactive visualization system, and thus, the analysis can be extended to a larger set of data. He commented that "It is very useful because it provides a novel and highly interactive way to explore what the deep model discovers." After being introduced to the basic components of the system and the function each view serves, they started to develop a workflow for using the system. However, E.3 and E.4 remarked that although the system is valuable for expert users, it may be a bit complicated to use for users who may not have sufficient background about MOBA games. However, they further stated that they believe that with a brief training, the system could be well leveraged.

12.7.3.2 Visualization Design and Interactions

All the experts in the interview were impressed by the detailed match analysis since it is intuitive and animation-based with a real gameplay map. The simple but efficient way to simulate the movements of players by visually representing the trajectories and the corresponding behaviors removes the efforts for labor-intensive lab observations. As an expert noted: "Showing the game process in a timeline, movement, and actions of each player through the y-axis mapping helps us to better compare the teams' performances."

12.7.3.3 Suggestions

All the experts inquired about the scalability of our system. They care about how to quickly adapt our system to other similar but different MOBAs. After our explanation that we extract the high-level patterns of players' behaviors, rather than focusing on specific behaviors that may differ from game to game, they all agreed that only small changes would be sufficient. They also noticed that the system lists all the critical events, which may not be suitable if the number of events increases. This can be resolved by using a drop-down list. In other words, our framework could be easily extended by making minor modifications. With regard to possible improvements, the experts suggested that in the Statistical View, the information could be further divided into subsets according to the clustering result of a certain type of game occurrence. Besides, the data segments extracted by the deep model are currently analyzed in an independent manner. This, however, does not account for situations where some data segments are correlated.

12.8 Conclusions

In this chapter, we proposed an efficient framework for analyzing MOBA matches. We used a deep model-based strategy to automatically identify segments of game data that significantly contribute to the final game occurrence and developed an interactive visual analytics system to support the detailed analysis of game occurrences, visually assisting domain experts to efficiently and effectively reason about players' behaviors without the need for intensive manual effort.

During the whole collaboration with the game team, we found that game designers often have misconceptions about what automated methods, such as machine learning and deep learning, can actually do and produce. Many of them consider it to be like "magic" or requiring collaborative expertise (Dove, Halskov, Forlizzi, & Zimmerman, 2017). We need to realize that game designers treat data quite differently than these automated methods. Therefore, an interactive visualization system that imitates the conventional practices taken by the experts may be a good start. It also improves game designers' understanding of and interaction with low-level input features and the outputs produced by automated methods by depicting them visually.

References

Ang, C. S., & Zaphiris, P. (2010). Social roles of players in MMORPG guilds: A social network analytic perspective. *Information, Communication & Society, 13*(4), 592–614.

Bach, S., Binder, A., Montavon, G., Klauschen, F., Müller, K. R., & Samek, W. (2015). On pixel-wise explanations for non-linear classifier decisions by layer-wise relevance propagation. *PLoS One, 10*(7), e0130140.

Bosc, G., Kaytoue, M., Raïssi, C., & Boulicaut, J. F. (2013). Strategic patterns discovery in RTS-games for e-sport with sequential pattern mining. In *MLSA@ PKDD/ ECML* (pp. 11–20).

Bowman, B., Elmqvist, N., & Jankun-Kelly, T. J. (2012). Toward visualization for games: Theory, design space, and patterns. *IEEE Transactions on Visualization and Computer Graphics, 18*(11), 1956–1968.

Chen, C. H., Sun, C. T., & Hsieh, J. (2008). Player guild dynamics and evolution in massively multiplayer online games. *CyberPsychology & Behavior, 11*(3), 293–301.

Chen, L., Goldgof, D. B., Hall, L. O., & Eschrich, S. A. (2007). Noise-based feature perturbation as a selection method for microarray data. In *International Symposium on Bioinformatics Research and Applications* (pp. 237–247). Berlin, Germany: Springer.

Chen, V. H. H., Duh, H. B. L., & Renyi, H. (2008). The changing dynamic of social interaction in World of Warcraft: The impacts of game feature change. In *Proceedings of the 2008 International Conference on Advances in Computer Entertainment Technology* (pp. 356–359). ACM.

Cole, H., & Griffiths, M. D. (2007). Social interactions in massively multiplayer online role-playing gamers. *CyberPsychology & Behavior, 10*(4), 575–583.

Dove, G., Halskov, K., Forlizzi, J., & Zimmerman, J. (2017) UX Design Innovation: Challenges for Working with Machine Learning as a Design Material. In *Proceedings of the 2017 CHI Conference on Human Factors in Computing Systems* (pp. 278–288). ACM.

Drachen, A., Yancey, M., Maguire, J., Chu, D., Wang, I. Y., Mahlmann, T.,... & Klabajan, D. (2014). Skill-based differences in spatio-temporal team behaviour in *Defence of the Ancients* 2 (DotA 2). In IEEE *Games Media Entertainment* (pp. 1–8). IEEE.

Eggert, C., Herrlich, M., Smeddinck, J., & Malaka, R. (2015). Classification of player roles in the team-based multi-player game *DotA 2*. In *International Conference on Entertainment Computing* (pp. 112–125). Cham, Switzerland: Springer.

El-Nasr, M. S., Desurvire, H., Aghabeigi, B., & Drachen, A. (2013). Game analytics for game user research, Part 1: A workshop review and case study. *IEEE Computer Graphics and Applications, 33*(2), 6–11.

Febretti, A., & Garzotto, F. (2009). Usability, playability, and long-term engagement in computer games. In *CHI'09 Extended Abstracts on Human Factors in Computing Systems* (pp. 4063–4068). ACM.

Hoobler, N., Humphreys, G., & Agrawala, M. (2004). Visualizing competitive behaviors in multi-user virtual environments. In *Proceedings of the Conference on Visualization'04* (pp. 163–170). IEEE.

Huber, W. H. (2009). Epic spatialities: The production of space in Final Fantasy games. In P. Harrigan & N. Wardrip-Fruin (Eds.), *Third Person: Authoring and Exploring Vast Narratives* (pp. 373–384). Cambridge, MA: MIT Press.

Johnson, D., Nacke, L. E., & Wyeth, P. (2015). All about that base: Differing player experiences in video game genres and the unique case of MOBA games. In *Proceedings of the 33rd Annual ACM Conference on Human Factors in Computing Systems* (pp. 2265–2274). ACM.

Krizhevsky, A., Sutskever, I., & Hinton, G. E. (2012). ImageNet classification with deep convolutional neural networks. In *Advances in Neural Information Processing Systems* (pp. 1097–1105).

Lapaš, T., & Orehovački, T. (2015). Evaluation of user experience in interaction with computer games. In *International Conference of Design, User Experience, and Usability* (pp. 271–282). Berlin, Germany: Springer.

Li, Q., Xu, P., Chan, Y. Y., Wang, Y., Wang, Z., Qu, H., & Ma, X. (2017). A visual analytics approach for understanding reasons behind snowballing and comeback in MOBA games. *IEEE Transactions on Visualization and Computer Graphics, 23*(1), 211–220.

Li, Q., Xu, P., & Qu, H. (2015). Fpsseer: Visual analysis of game frame rate data. In *IEEE Conference on Visual Analytics Science and Technology* (pp. 73–80). IEEE.

Miller, J. L., & Crowcroft, J. (2010). Group movement in *World of Warcraft* battlegrounds. *International Journal of Advanced Media and Communication, 4*(4), 387–404.

Miller, S. J. (2006). The method of least squares. *Mathematics Department Brown University*, 1–7. Retrieved from http://web.williams.edu/Mathematics/sjmiller/public_html/105Sp10/handouts/MethodLeastSquares.pdf.

NetEase (2016). *Wildfire* [PC game]. Guangzhou, China: NetEase.

Pobiedina, N., Neidhardt, J., Calatrava Moreno, M. D. C., & Werthner, H. (2013). Ranking factors of team success. In *Proceedings of the 22nd International Conference on World Wide Web* (pp. 1185–1194). ACM.

Rioult, F., Métivier, J. P., Helleu, B., Scelles, N., & Durand, C. (2014). Mining tracks of competitive video games. *AASRI Procedia, 8*, 82–87.

Samek, W., Binder, A., Montavon, G., Lapuschkin, S., & Müller, K. R. (2017). Evaluating the visualization of what a deep neural network has learned. *IEEE Transactions on Neural Networks and Learning Systems, 28*(11), 2660–2673.

Shim, J. Y., Kim, T. H., & Kim, S. W. (2014). Decision support of bad player identification in MOBA games using pagerank-based evidence accumulation and normal distribution-based confidence interval. *International Journal of Multimedia & Ubiquitous Engineering, 9*(8), 13–16.

Simonyan, K., Vedaldi, A., & Zisserman, A. (2013). Deep inside convolutional networks: Visualising image classification models and saliency maps. Retrieved from https://arxiv.org/abs/1312.6034.

Véron, M., Marin, O., & Monnet, S. (2014). Matchmaking in multi-player on-line games: studying user traces to improve the user experience. In *Proceedings of Network and Operating System Support on Digital Audio and Video Workshop* (pp. 7–12). ACM.

Wallner, G., & Kriglstein, S. (2013). Visualization-based analysis of gameplay data—A review of literature. *Entertainment Computing, 4*(3), 143–155.

Wallner, G., & Kriglstein, S. (2014). PLATO: A visual analytics system for gameplay data. *Computers & Graphics, 38*, 341–356.

Yang, P., Harrison, B. E., & Roberts, D. L. (2014). Identifying patterns in combat that are predictive of success in MOBA games. In *Proceedings of the 2014 Foundations of Digital Games Conference*. Society for the Advancement of the Science of Digital Games.

Yosinski, J., Clune, J., Nguyen, A., Fuchs, T., & Lipson, H. (2015). Understanding neural networks through deep visualization. Retrieved from https://arxiv.org/abs/1506.06579.

Index

Note: Page numbers in italic and bold refer to figures and tables, respectively.
Page numbers followed by n refer to footnotes.